PRAI [barcode: T0030973]
Mothership: A Memo

"A brave, beautiful testament to love both past and present, a meticulously researched account of our relationship to ourselves and the world.... *Mothership* does for coral what Richard Powers's *The Overstory* does for trees. I can't wait to assign this to my students."

—GARRARD CONLEY, *New York Times* bestselling author of *Boy Erased*

"A powerful testimonial and call to action to save the equal opportunity healer that is Mother Nature."

—CARINE MCCANDLESS, author of *The Wild Truth*, the *New York Times* bestselling follow-up to *Into the Wild*

"As humanity stands at the crossroads of catastrophe and consciousness, Wrenn's wonder-filled, carefully researched memoir makes a strong case for not only the sacramental value and healing power of psychedelics but also for safe, legal access to psychedelic-assisted therapy for PTSD. *Mothership* is a deeply moving roadmap through the intertwined destinies of individual well-being and the urgent need to heal our planet."

—RICK DOBLIN, PhD, Founder and President of the Multidisciplinary Association for Psychedelic Studies (MAPS)

"A deeply felt, clear-eyed memoir examining what it means to grieve nature's losses and yet still manage to find healing and love in what remains."

—FLORENCE WILLIAMS, author of *The Nature Fix* and *Heartbreak: A Personal and Scientific Journey*

"*Mothership* is a story of personal and, hopefully, global healing. With rare insight, Wrenn captures a mystical reciprocity with the natural world that leads to a love affair with all life he encounters under the sea. At the same time, he is learning, painfully and little by little, to love himself and to be loved. The turning point in his memoir is his encounter with the spirit of ayahuasca, Madre Ayahuasca. Wrenn elegantly describes his own emotional journey as well as the psychological process of working with this powerful psychedelic medicine. *Mothership*, a story of how healing happens after a traumatic childhood, is an important contribution to the growing field of psychedelic study.

—RACHEL HARRIS, PhD, author of *Listening to Ayahuasca* and
Swimming in the Sacred

"Greg's life story and spiritual journey are one of the greatest examples of the power that ayahuasca and plant medicines have to bring about personal transformation. The first time I met Greg, he had a crippling fear of life. Through a deep commitment to self-healing, he has transmuted this fear into a full embrace with life itself. A raw, real, and riveting personal story, *Mothership* brings the reader on a journey through the darkness of deep traumas, woundings, and addictions into the light of divine consciousness. Page by page, we witness a transformation from being broken to becoming whole once again."

—ALANNA COLLINS, RN, co-founder of Truth is One Interfaith
Church, kambô & plant medicine facilitator

MOTHERSHIP

A MEMOIR
OF WONDER AND CRISIS

GREG WRENN

New York • Nashville
regalopress.com

Published in the United States of America
1 2 3 4 5 6 7 8 9 10

This book is dedicated to Tony.
With you, it's morning.

Contents

Part Three

"Do we need forests? Do we need trees? Do we need reefs?
Or can we sort of just live in the ashes of all of that?"

—PHIL DUSTAN, *Chasing Coral*

"Nothing on earth is more gladdening than knowing
we must roll up our sleeves and move back the boundaries
of the humanly possible once more."

—ANNIE DILLARD, *The Writing Life*

Wonder and Crisis

It was fall 2019, the first day of classes. The windowless auditorium was like a spaceship filled with 160 students in suspended animation. As their English professor, I felt rather extraterrestrial—instead of khakis and a herringbone blazer, I was wearing my wet suit, my dive mask hanging from my neck. If I have to look ridiculous to get my students' attention during lecture, so be it. Of all the courses I teach, this is my favorite.

"Let's begin Environmental Literature of Wonder and Crisis," I said, "by going into the ocean."

I clicked to the first slide. "This is a sea snake. A yellow-lipped krait, to be exact." The ropey reptile, striped like the Hamburglar, looked like it was sipping the water's surface. "It's taking a breath—they don't have gills. There's an urban legend that their mouths are too small to bite you, but they can actually swallow a moray eel whole. The venom? Well, it could kill you." I told them about the time I followed a baby sea snake into the mangroves of Gam, past thick schools of snapper with saucer plate eyes, until I felt a crocodile watching me and got the hell out.

I explained the underwater photos were from my research site, a reef-sheltered haven: a group of islands in the Pacific called Raja Ampat, a smidge south of the equator in Indonesia. About fifty thousand people live there in tiny villages in an area about the size of Switzerland. Much of it is a steamy wilderness of rainforests and worn limestone peaks. Rare birds-of-paradise call out in the morning. The bays shimmer with phosphorescent plankton at night. There's little pollution except for swarms of floating plastic. And the most biodiverse coral reefs in the world are there and still thriving. They lie at the edge of the Coral Triangle, an area encompassing Indonesia, the Philippines, and Papua New Guinea that is so ecologically important, it's been called the "Amazon of the Seas."

Then I skipped ahead to a video of a five-foot-wide manta ray flying toward me off the beach at Birie: "From my hut I saw it splashing its wingtips like floppy dorsal fins, so I swam out. There he is feasting on a raft of plankton, jellies, and plastic—now he's barrel-rolling to show us his belly markings. Wait for it, wait for it...yes! He was coming right at me but turned at the last minute!"

Without any chitchat, I shared a few more photos. A thorny seahorse floating alone at Ayai, its tail curled tightly like an ammonite, like a stargate closed to traffic because the world on the other side has too many people. The grand staircases of table coral at Wai. A dome of coral near Tamaku that was so big I could live inside it.

One last one: spiral coral in Beser Bay that looked like an attempt to map the multiverse, dark matter and dark energy translated into tiers of whorls begetting whorls. As a student might joke, *pics or it didn't happen.*

"Coral is pitted," I said. "In each little pit lives a polyp, a tiny jellyfish-thingy that uses minerals from the water to grow itself a limestone home. At night its tentacles reach out to grab zooplankton, but it gets most of its calories from the plants within it, helpful algae called zooxanthellae. The chlorophyll, using sunlight and CO_2, makes sugars for the polyp. Imagine eating only one potato a day and getting the rest of your sustenance from the sun: an easy, low-cost life of sunbathing and abundant vitamin D.

"Raja Ampat was so beautiful," I continued, deepening my voice to sound more manly, "that sometimes I'd cry underwater with my mask on. Would it be the last time I'd see a healthy reef? So little time remains, folks. Over 90 percent of coral has died in Florida since I was born there. And you've probably heard what's happened to the Great Barrier Reef."

Then I showed them the graph plotting carbon dioxide and global temperatures for the past eight hundred thousand years. With my laser pointer, I circled the recent unprecedented surge of heat-trapping carbon, that darker line shooting straight up. "410 parts per million of CO_2 is about what we have now in 2019. Our university's namesake James Madison breathed in 280 ppm as he helped draft the Constitution. Temperatures right now are playing catch up with carbon levels," I said, pointing to the gap between the end of the two curves. "And coral is one of the most sensitive creatures we have to temperature."

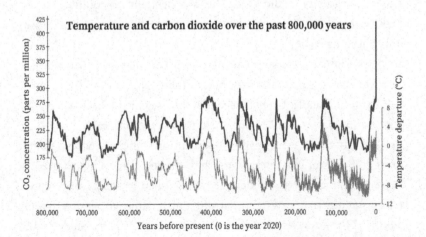

Temperature and carbon dioxide over the past 800,000 years

Years before present (0 is the year 2020)

With the ominous graph still on the screen, I read the quote at the top of our syllabus from Rachel Carson's slim book *The Sense of Wonder*, which was inspired by her time in nature with her grandnephew: "One way to open your eyes to unnoticed beauty is to ask yourself, 'What if I had never seen this before? What if I knew I would never see it again?'"

Remembering that much of the Amazon was on fire when I was there two weeks ago, I read them Carson's words again but more softly, as if her trustworthy ghost filled my lungs.

"We'll talk more about the crisis next class," I told my students. "So—what is wonder?"

No hands went up.

"We've all at least seen wonder caricatured in the movies. Disney's Pocahontas running the hidden pine trails of the forest, yada yada yada. The spacecraft captain in *Wall-E* holding the last plant from Earth. Jake and Neytiri plugging their brains into the purple tendrils of the Tree of Voices in *Avatar*—'I am with you now,' she tells him on that bomb-diggity, forested moon called Pandora, 'we are mated for life.'"

In the front row, Danielle raised her hand. "Isn't it kind of like the intermingling of happiness and preciousness?" One of the few engaged students in the class, she was brilliant but didn't want to make a show of it. Sometimes to boost my morale, I pretended I was only speaking to her.

"Yes, that's a great start—it involves a mix of emotions. A sense of impermanence. Anyone want to add to that?"

Again, no hands. Later I learned a frat boy in the back said to his friends that day, "Coral? I don't fucking care about coral."

Though there were inspiring exceptions, most students didn't want to be here, but to graduate they needed three English credits. To reduce Snapchatting under the tables, I had to stay at once entertaining and strict. Few of them did the reading; a handful openly admitted they'd never read an entire book in their lives. Subjected to standardized "No-Child-Left-Behind" tests from an early age, they wanted me to pour my exam answers into them like grain into a silo and be done with it. My office hours were often spent alone.

AS THEY READ THOREAU and Octavia Butler, Wendell Berry and Robin Wall Kimmerer, they put climate change science in conversation with the literature. What is it like to appreciate an ecosystem that will collapse in our lifetimes? To be moved by beauty that we're pushing toward extinction? Thoreau didn't ask those questions as he bathed in Walden Pond, but we asked them in my class. We covered a lot—lobsters and weasels, cow farts and Easter Island's cannibalism, AI, photosynthesis, ecofeminism, reindeers with anthrax, shrooming, Afrofuturism, the theology of evil, time travel. For their final paper, applying all they learned about wonder and crisis, they wrote about a treasured moment they've had outside.

If I could get my undergrads re-enchanted with nature and educated about the crisis, understanding that we're proverbial frogs in a pot of heating water, maybe they'd work to fight climate change, expanding their circle of compassion. Ask the endangered Shenandoah salamander found on only three nearby peaks: we're in a biodiversity hotspot that's getting hotter.

I was too concerned about my students' future to just teach seventeenth-century metaphysical poetry and call it a day. Unlike me, my students were born into a digital world, in diapers on 9/11, many of them forbidden to roam freely outside and play. When they were in second grade, the *Oxford Junior Dictionary* removed words like *acorn*, *moss*, and *fern* and added *database*, *MP3 player*, and *broadband*. Most of them know they were born into a world whose long-term habitability is uncertain. They're anxious and depressed. Addicted to the digital cocaine of screens. Craving views of their Instagram stories as if their survival depended on it. If they haven't attempted suicide, they know friends who have.

MOTHERSHIP

Have they ever sat under a tree and read a book with paper pages? Have they gazed up at the clouds without their phones for a while and in all the puffiness seen acorns and moss and ferns? Or is nature too boring, best appreciated as a backdrop for selfies?

Do they feel wonder?

Those are not hysterical questions. As time rushes by, I too have felt my attention and imagination—my very dignity—dying back like seagrape after a hard winter freeze. In this numb blur of a cyborg life, what would it take to be happy? It might take going outside and cultivating wonder, even when we don't feel like it.

In teaching this course, I wanted my students to taste what I felt snorkeling once with my mother as we looked at the underside of the ocean's surface. It was a quicksilvery mirror of sorts for the coral below, psychedelically colored as Fairyland Caverns at Rock City, Tennessee, where my great-aunt dressed as Mother Goose and taught kids to give more than you take. It was a living abstraction— one utterly responsive, like a mood ring, like octopus skin. If we had looked at it long enough, our egos might have fizzled out, our bodies might have been traded for those of melon-headed whales or Picasso triggerfish. My arm was linked with my mother's in eighty-two-degree water. I thought I'd forgiven her and she'd live forever.

I CLICKED AHEAD TO the dictionary definition of wonder—"a feeling of surprise mingled with admiration, caused by something beautiful, unexpected, unfamiliar, or inexplicable"—and read it more robotically than I meant to. "Who wants to add to that?"

A couple of students left. Danielle glanced at me sympathetically.

I cooed "Wonderrrrrr...?" into the mic like a gnome, which was supposed to be funny since I'm nearly six and a half feet tall and wear size-thirteen shoes.

Prologue

"We're going to be reading a lot about wonder this semester," I said, looking right at the kid vaping in the back. "Thoreau fishing in the moonlight in Walden Pond. Annie Dillard learning to see insect egg cases. Amy Leach contemplating a stressed sea cucumber expelling its insides on the ocean floor. Wonder is WOW, quiet or loud."

Dramatic infomercial pause. I needed to give it another try, this time less conceptual.

"When have you experienced wonder?"

That was when the hands started going up.

"Once on the way to my 8:00 a.m. accounting class, I saw a praying mantis," Kyle said. "I thought it was dead but really it was just cold."

Peter told us about the first time he saw the night sky away from a city. He was sitting on a boulder in the middle of New Mexico. Later in an essay he'll say more: "I have friends on either side of me, but they are not who I am having a conversation with; I can feel God and the universe looking down upon me in the form of shooting stars and the wind rustling through the trees around us."

Edwin recalled fly-fishing for brown trout not far from campus in Mossy Creek. Danielle lost herself in the cliffs of Big Sur, Ryan in a sunrise at Virginia Beach. Yolanda marveled at squirrel monkeys in Costa Rica, a mother and baby. A few others mentioned their pets.

I wanted to tell them about the sassy, saucy giant clam I saw underwater in Raja Ampat, but I didn't. A frilly Glamazon of neon adductors, she and I were real to one another. Fabulous. *Remember, this isn't a TED Talk or group therapy. You're not Oprah or Brené Brown. You're an English professor in Lycra and rubber booties. Keep it together.*

So I shared a parable.

"Sometimes toward the end of a dive," I said with my unpredictable Southern twang, "a story comes back to me, one I heard at a noisy monastery. The Buddha asked his monks to imagine the earth entirely covered in water. An ox yoke with a single hole is thrown in—it's

7

tossed on the waves, the wind pushing it every which way. Somewhere far below is a blind sea turtle that comes up to breathe only once a century. How likely is the turtle to stick its neck through the floating yoke? It's the same chance, the Buddha said, as being born human. This life as a person, it's that extraordinarily rare."

I showed them one more photo. "That's a green sea turtle. A species that has changed little in 210 million years. He didn't seem scared when I dove down, which was weird because they're still hunted for their meat. When I swam back up, so did he." What I didn't say: the breath he took at the surface sounded like a gasp, as if he were taking it for all of us.

As THE LECTURE WENT ON, anxiety was hardening around my ankles. I was talking too fast, as if I were speaking to my father.

"Who do you think you are?" he asked when I voiced too many opinions. "Someday someone's going to pop you in the mouth." On the way to T-ball practice or the donut shop, he filled our Pontiac with conservative radio host Rush Limbaugh, who said things like, "Despite the hysterics of a few pseudo-scientists, there is no reason to believe in global warming," and "The most beautiful thing about a tree is what you do with it after you cut it down."

After I finished grad school, my father wanted to know what I was writing about, why I was spending all my money on diving. I tried explaining the ecological crisis to him, thinking that his nearly dying a decade earlier might have woken him up.

"Well, even if all of that's true, I'll be gone before it would affect me," he said.

"But what about your children?" I asked. "What about your grand-kids?" He coughed in his dismissive way.

Trying to convince my students that the world deserves our care, I felt like one of those transparent dolls used in anatomy classes.

Instead of my internal organs, I feared my students could see my insecurity. I overcompensated by becoming a preacher-teacher, channeling the Double Rainbow Guy from YouTube ("Whoa!!! My God!!! Oh my God! Oh my God! Woooo! Oh Wow! Woooo!") and Robin Williams in *Dead Poets Society* ("Carpe diem! Seize the day, boys! Make your lives extraordinary!"). Projecting authority and cosmic connectedness when often I felt more like an open wound than a person.

Could they see what happened to me, that I was too weak to stop it? Could they see my family's secrets?

Of course not. I was more confident in the classroom than I'd ever been. As I would walk back home from campus, though, the void would come back. *I'm not real, none of this is,* I would think to myself. *I'm doomed, everything is shit.*

That's my childhood talking. In her landmark text *Trauma and Recovery,* Harvard psychiatrist Judith Herman defines complex post-traumatic stress disorder (C-PTSD) as the result of "prolonged, repeated trauma" from which the victim can't escape. "In most homes, even the most oppressive, there are no bars on the windows, no barbed wire fences," she writes. "Children are rendered captive by their condition of dependency."

C-PTSD, also known as relational, developmental, or complex trauma, is the label closest to what I struggle with. Ever since I visited the Amazon for the first time earlier that year and Raja Ampat in 2018 for the fifth time, my symptoms had improved.

Fading was the panic I couldn't distinguish from nihilism and deranged loneliness. The flashbacks, sometimes in pictures, sometimes in pure feeling. The nightmares. The writhing of my cells from feeling dirty, impossible to clean. The hypervigilance, scanning frantically for a rescuer to save me from my abyss and then leave me more devastated than before. Neuroplasticity, the ability of the brain to rewire itself, had been my lived experience. I was getting better even as the planet's fever was growing. The reefs and rainforests had been lifting me up into a new identity. I was beyond excited to return to the Peruvian Amazon during my semester-long sabbatical that spring.

Cut off by choice from my family, I've never wanted children of my own—being a teacher is the closest I'll get to being a parent. Distrustful of authority, worried I'll mess up big time because my parents did, I haven't felt equipped to mentor anyone. And yet more than ever, I want to be the teacher—the father *and* mother figure—I never had but needed.

Behind my judgment and cynicism is deep love for my students. I express that love not only through setting high standards but also by framing everything we read in an uncomfortable paradox—there's absolutely no time to waste in appreciating nature and in saving it; and at the same time, we can relax and exult: we are eternal. As my teacher in Brazil says, "Souls come to earth to learn. It's the best school there is."

"You have the syllabus," I said, closing my laptop. "Let me know if you have any questions." I smoothed out the wrinkles in my wetsuit and, just this once, let them out early to read under a tree.

Part One

CHAPTER 1

What Would E.T. Do?

"Maybe what we can do when we feel overwhelmed
is to start small. Start with what we have loved as kids
and see where that leads us."

—AIMEE NEZHUKUMATATHIL, *World of Wonders*

In the woods behind my Christian kindergarten, I once found a *Miami Vice* ball cap and proudly wore it home. Rushing me to the tub, my mother said I'd infest the whole house with bugs.

"Miami Lice," she shuddered.

I also learned not to play rowdy with the pale girl whose mother baked cookies at Publix. Not to pretend with the dentist's son that we were T. rexes settling a score before the killer asteroid arrived. I should stay sensible and clean. Smell honeysuckle on the chain-link fence. Coach banana orb weavers in web repair.

When my mother picked me up from school, I was at the curb holding my Care Bears lunchbox, my T-shirt tucked into my matching shorts, and she might ask when I opened the car door, "Did you roll around in the dirt again?" My answer was always no, that I played like everyone else on the playground.

"Don't you sit down yet, Greg, you're filthy," she said, even though I wasn't. "Now shake out your shorts and shirt! Kick your shoes! Black earth gets tracked into the house and you ground it up into the carpet and there's no getting it out. I've been vacuuming in ninety-degree heat, and this is what you do to me? How do I get you to stop that?" Before becoming a full-time mom, she'd been an award-winning elementary school teacher but couldn't grasp that her sons got dirt in their nails. Her breaking point was unpredictable, and it was my job to keep her from getting there. My first name, after all, comes from the Greek word for "vigilant." Her name was Priscilla, but everyone called her Pris.

One morning at recess I couldn't help myself. I was drawn to the dirt, maybe because soil contains bacteria called *M. vaccae* that's like instant Prozac when you sniff it. Settling into a spot away from everyone, I crouched down. Like the paleontologist I saw on *Reading Rainbow*, I sifted through the mulch with the paintbrush of my hand to find roly-polies. If I was careful in the far corner of the playground, I could stay clean.

I suddenly froze, steam rising from the baseball diamond and the cemetery behind it. Time slowed down; my pulse raced.

Did my mother hit me the night before? Or did she goad my father into doing it, questioning his manhood until he spanked me too hard on my bed? "Turn over, you brat, you spoiled rotten brat!" he'd roar. "Obey your mother!"

Staring out at the maypole our school never used, I imagined it was a rocket I could ride to Chuck E. Cheese's for a whack-a-mole afternoon. That's when an ebony jewelwing, which is like a dragonfly, landed beside my shoe. I gently pinched its folded-back wings like my father taught me, the toothpick body shimmering and squirming.

What Would E.T. Do?

As I brought the writhing insect to my face, the mean voices in my head quieted. Entering a numb vastness, I became a new crayon, the Weeki Wachee rhinestone blue of the jewelwing, darker than the aquamarine watch my mother always wore to the beach. "The capacity for induced trance or dissociative states," Judith Herman writes, "is developed to a fine art in children who have been severely punished or abused." In other words, my stillness wasn't necessarily contentment. I wasn't a Buddha then, and I'm not one now, even after spending close to a year of my life meditating on silent retreat.

Then I noticed froggy babies the size of my thumbprint. Neato! No ribbits. They were Southern toads. *Bufo terrestris*. Dark-green like the pimento-stuffed olives that tasted like pee. Their eyes were black and full of possibility as the screen of our big Zenith television.

"You're it!"

I whipped around—some dweeb had tapped my head and run off. The jungle gym in the distance looked like a cage. The swing set creaked like a haunted house.

I turned back to the toads. They were beginning to hop around. Scared, I bet, as I was. Recess was revving up, and I was worried for them.

The only question left to ask: what would E.T. do?

SOME MONTHS BEFORE at a second-run theater, I had seen Steven Spielberg's *E.T. The Extraterrestrial* with my mother. E.T.'s eyes were as blue as hers, his skin as wrinkled as my grandmother's. At the time, I looked like a younger version of Elliot, especially when I wore my red hoodie. Along with *Star Trek*, *E.T.* is still one of my sustaining mythologies. It's a fable about mutual rescuing and grace—about trying to understand someone different from you and realizing you're basically the same. A coming-of-age story for a boy, family, and civilization. A parable of wonder and crisis that taught me things my parents couldn't.

15

Its ecological message is underappreciated. To my adult mind, E.T. and his shipmates, knowing the earth is in trouble, are here saving specimens in their interstellar ark. Early on in Melissa Mathison's screenplay, E.T. collects "a sapling—a miniature redwood, a perfect bonsai, growing at the feet of its elders." Much of the film was shot in Redwood National Park in 1981, when the logging of old-growth forests made the headlines. Now climate change in the form of more wildfires and less fog is an existential threat to the trees. Our planetary crisis finds a haunting symbol in E.T., white as a powdered donut, dying in a ditch. It's a scene that's still burned into my conscience. Our civilized, single-use world—the Reese's Pieces, potato salad in plastic, and suburban sprawl—sickened him. As Elliot tells a NASA scientist, "He needs to go home."

LETTING THE JEWELWING GO, I tucked a couple toads between my gray sock and ankle. That compartment was a spaceship, warm and steamy as E.T.'s womb-shaped craft. My homeworld, I thought, would be safer than the toads' mulch. Just as Elliot, mind-melded to a drunk E.T., liberates the frogs about to be dissected in his biology class, I'd save the toads from trampling sneakers.

Earlier that year, a couple days after bringing it home from the school carnival, I found my goldfish floating on its side like an orange detergent pod. The fishbowl had turned into a dead zone—no one had told me the water needed to be changed. That fish was the first animal ever in my care. And I killed it.

Toads don't need an ocean, though. I'd make sure they had happy childhoods in our house. This time I was going to be better. My sock and I were on a rescue mission.

WHEN MY MOTHER PICKED me up from school that day, she didn't say I was dirty. At home she cheerfully made me lunch, microwaving a slice of Kraft cheese between two pieces of bread. Grilled cheese, she called it.

"Crank it up, Gregory Pegory!" my mother called out before we ate, meaning I was to turn on the TV as loud as it would go. The soap opera *All My Children* was about to come on. Around this time in the series, her favorite character, kidnapped by Adam Chandler, is roaming the Canadian wilderness alone after their plane crashes. "You may not come near me! I am Erica Kane and you are a filthy beast!" is all she has to yell at a grizzly bear to scare it away. She soon finds a priest, who carries her in his arms to a glass home shaped like a boxcar.

"How was Mrs. Kilgore today?" my mother asked me.

"She taught us planets. My Very Educated Mother Just...Served Us Nine Pizzas. Mercury, Venus—"

"Okay, where are this week's worksheets?"

"Earth, Mars—"

"We need to go over them. How many are there?"

"Jupiter! Saturn! Mommy! I have a surprise."

"Sweetie baby Pegory, what, what?"

"Close your eyes..."

"Now don't be silly," she said, keeping her eyes open. Recently I scared her to bits with a rubber roach on the bathroom floor. When she wasn't scrutinizing or scolding me, we were laughing. Sometimes she stuck out her teeth like Bucky the Beaver and pretended to brush and floss.

The microwave beep-beeped.

I pulled down my socks a few inches. She glanced down. "Why did you put Tootsie rolls in your socks?" she sighed. "Look, they've melted. That'll attract ants, you know."

One blob was stuck to my ankle. The other fell to the dinosaur-bumpy floor.

"That's not it," I said, pulling my sock down to my shoe.

As she stooped down to look, I saw the tissues stored in her bra. Her romper bristled all on its own, like the Haddon's carpet anemones that I'll see diving decades later in the Pacific.

"One for you, one for me. A boy and girl."

"Oh, no, no, no!" she cried. Each "no" was spanking the popcorn ceiling, our backyard oaks, and the thinning ozone layer. It all seemed to shatter and fall.

"What's wrong?"

"They're dead! In your sock!"

Her howls momentarily quieted to whimpers. "How could you?" With several paper towels she threw the two lifeless toads into the trash can that was Oscar-the-Grouch green. "Gross!" With wet wipes, she cleaned the spot on my ankle where the toads had been, all the while making high-pitched sputters, as if having surgery without enough anesthesia. "I spent the morning mopping this floor, and now you've ruined it and I have to wash your clothes. This isn't fair."

"I, I didn't mean to," I said. "I promise I didn't, I didn't."

She washed her hands again and stripped everything off me but my shirt. In twenty seconds, I was Porky Pig. Silent. Frozen.

"This isn't fair to me," she kept saying. "It's just not fair!"

On the TV blaring in the family room—was that Erica Kane's other lover, Jeremy Hunter, radioing for help in a French accent? Or was it Adam plotting to kidnap her again and never let her go?

My mother turned on the faucet. Then came the hot center of the flashbulb memory: her suddenly lifting me up, her yelling, the grody weightlessness between ground and running water. Up in the air I was sick and lost, closer to the windowsill than ever before.

I bawled, finally. She made sure, as always, her crying was louder than mine. I was petrified, since my parents rarely held me, let alone roughhoused with me. Their touch wasn't safe anyway. Now that I'd killed the toads, mine wasn't either.

For entirely too long, she washed my ankle with a rough bar of soap, the kind with pumice. She didn't reach for the Brillo pad, thank goodness, steel wool impregnated with soap.

The memories end there but live on.

MAMMALS ARE EASILY TRAUMATIZED. And by traumatized, I mean so overwhelmed by an upsetting event that part of us is diminished, seemingly forever. The threat from the past remains, priming us to be on high alert. All it takes, researcher Jaak Panksepp found in a famous experiment, is putting a bit of cat hair into an enclosure of newborn rats: their playing stops immediately. The fur is soon removed, but they never return to the same level of play. We aren't rats, most of us anyway, and yet the study's findings ring true when I think about broken trust.

It's cat fur, though, not the rats' mother, that's freaking them out, and their traumatic experience happens only once. When it's your main caregiver who's repeatedly traumatizing you and you can't escape—unlike, say, the trauma of a single car crash—that can lead to C-PTSD. Bonding with others is the foundation of a livable life, but for me it's been painful and scary, sometimes pure panic—connection and rejection fired together for so long, they wired together. This is why I've feared I had to be perfect or else I'd be harmed again. Why I've assumed people who adore me hate me, resent me, think I'm gross. My catnip? Out-to-lunch people who are deeply ambivalent about me.

Unlike a gazelle after a thwarted cheetah attack, I couldn't simply shake off the trauma right after it happened in the kitchen. My brain kept believing I was in danger. Like the rat pups, I was never the same after the toad incident, the likes of which were all too common growing up.

That day I learned many things I'm still unlearning with the help of nature: that I'm dirty and unlovable; what we love we will destroy;

what we try to save we will ruin; what surrounds us isn't the Divine Mother's love but the cold, annihilating vacuum of outer space. Love will squash you until you're suffocated or your internal organs burst, whichever comes first, and you'll be wiped away, thrown out.

Alongside the clarity of E.T.'s caring example and the goldfish's earlier preventable death, the toad incident also taught me how easy it was to injure other creatures, that their needs were important.

It's as if I'm still making amends for killing the toads, for horrifying the only mortal stand-in for Gaia I had: my mother. For so long, I've felt outside nature—unnatural and extraterrestrial. I believed I was polluted but, I reasoned, the natural world shouldn't have to be also. My boyhood home couldn't be saved, so as an environmental educator and citizen scientist, I've tried to help save our planetary home. It's given me a reason to not end it all even in the moments I hate myself.

Some days, if E.T. were to ask me to come with him, I'd walk right up that gangplank into the mothership. Ask him to genetically reengineer me so that I didn't have to be human any longer, maybe more like coral, which is a partnership of animal and plant, or like a redwood with a family of trusted elders. Some creature that can't be traumatized.

For years I've sent out homing beacons—not from a Speak & Spell toy, buzzsaw blade, and umbrella like E.T. does to call his mothership, but through tortured poems, flashbacks and broken resolutions, screams upon waking from nightmares, eczema outbreaks, recurring ear infections, prayers to gods I knew little about, Craigslist ads, desperate Grindr and Tinder messages sent in the middle of the night. *Get me out of here*: my compulsions were an understandable response to my family and yet almost destroyed me long after the threat had passed.

CHAPTER 2

Row

*R*OW! My first word. When my mother sang me the nursery rhyme, she pretended to paddle a boat with her arms.

I said it in our brick house with blue shutters, which was on a wide point where the St. Johns River turns and flows ten miles to the sea. Mornings often smelled of coffee from the Maxwell House factory, but if the breeze was right, we could smell the brackish tannins of the river, its saltier mouth, conjuring a place much safer than that house. A place of cordgrass and clams and whiskered manatees. Mermen who only rescue children who believe.

I couldn't quite pronounce the R in *row*, so did it sound more like *oh*, a faint grunt of delight or pain? In any case, it was my *Om*. It created my universe, bizarre galaxies of hard water, declaring me a strange child. A disloyal Muppet destined to conspire with the singing tides.

Not *Dada* or *Mama* but *row*—life is but a dream, an echo of a dream, as when you put a conch to your ear.

If *row* was my essential seed syllable, *clean* was my mother's. Her hands were so red and cracked from washing that in winter she wore rubber gloves filled with ointment to bed. After she showered, she wouldn't touch me. When wet wipes were on sale at Publix, she would buy so many the cashier would ask if she owned a daycare. She used them to wipe off the groceries before putting them away, my dresser drawers at summer camp, every toy that left the house and tried to come back inside. But my favorite toys, like my Inspector Gadget doll and my teddy bear Farrell, she wouldn't clean for months at a time. Instead, she kept them in a heap in her mildewy bedroom. I could look, but I couldn't touch.

I used to blame myself. Because I was so big, she needed many stitches after I was born. "It was the worst pain of my life," she said of my birth, "and you definitely should've been a C-section," teaching me the word *episiotomy* from an early age, reminding me how gross it was for her postpartum in the bathroom. She called me her Bouncing Baby Boy, her Gregory Pegory, but I was also Pigpen from *Peanuts* in a poopy cloud of dirt. Gregory the Terrible Eater, the renegade goat from the children's book.

Hitting me with her wooden spoon, she called me other names and said, "I'm going to spank the living daylights out of you." Couldn't my soul have been cleaned instead of driven away?

As a child, I found it hard to sleep at night. My door's lock had been disabled. A man, I thought, was watching me.

From my bed, there was so much I couldn't perceive, such as marsh oysters beating algae into the mucus of their gills. Fiddler crabs blowing bubbles in order to breathe on land. Our power plant burning coal, nuggets of Paleozoic trees. And my mother, with her talking stuffed animal, who must have been asking God to help us.

If I listened hard enough, though, I could make out the barges blowing their horns as if they were Poseidon's sons, messengers of upcurrents, undertow, and ceaseless change. I could hear drips in the drain of our bathtub. The next day it would be refilled with water from the ancient aquifer below.

Row

As I WOULD WAIT in the tub for my mother, my fingers wrinkled. I scratched the soles of my feet until bits of skin floated like larvae during coral spawning. I counted specks of mildew in the grouting, lost count, and started over. Every pockmark in the tiles was another excuse for punishment. Every drip down the drain. I raked the soap holder's teeth across the folds of my brain. Counted the tiles. Divided that number into pi; the answer was infinite, so I gave up.

That was how I dissociated in water. How I deserted my body when the truth of my home life was too upsetting to contemplate, to even nod toward. I needed to forget that she did this to me once a week, usually on the day she changed my sheets and made me get down to just my underwear in her bedroom. She made me play dolly dress-up with what she had bought me on sale at JCPenney. When we were done, she told me to take off my underwear and run—run!—to the tub and not touch anything, because fabric chemicals and mall germs were all over me.

I would wait and wait in the tub. My father didn't care. E.T. and Captain Picard didn't either. "You think you have the upper hand," she said when I'd call out for her after half an hour of sitting there, "but the more you bug me, the longer I'll take."

By that time, I didn't feel the water any longer. It was the color of greenish milk—if I could have smelled that color in some burst of synesthesia, it would have smelled like Martha Stewart and new My Little Ponies and blind patriotism. If I could've heard it, I would've heard the cries and slams of my childhood, and hers and my father's, of the ancestors.

When she walked in like Cleopatra in a terrycloth romper, her hair was curly and TV-ready. She stood above me, my pubes and happy trail swaying. I was so tall my knees were bent, my feet flat against the tub.

Before she even had to ask, I handed her the soap. She started at my nape, getting between the bones. Taking two soapy fingers to wipe behind my ears, swiping around to my throat, she swirled in the hollow below my voice box. She soaped up my nipples, chest, and stomach. Between my shoulder blades. Down to the small of my back and into the top of my crack. Into the webbing of my fingers, up and down my arms, past the tan line from my Casio calculator wristwatch.

"Give me those chicken legs!" She scrubbed my thighs and calves, and got Mother Goosey with my toes: "Wee, wee, wee, all the way home!"

"Oink," I said half-heartedly.

"Here," she said, putting the Zest in my hand, "do your crotch." As I washed it, she compared my genitals to my father's. While she dug in my navel for lint, the tip of my dick zapped like a tooth root.

It was time: I pulled the lever to get the showerhead going. Over and over she sprayed me. So my crush on the zany cross-country runner might be rinsed away. My love for Orion and the star that changes color like a radioactive Skittle. The dander and pheromones of my father. She massaged in the Motel 6 shampoo, and I closed my eyes. After she doused me again, she cut off the water. The drain guzzled down my pollution—it would find its way into the river and the sea. Evaporate and fall as hail and acid rain.

She was gone. Using the tiny Smurfette towel, I dried myself.

MY MOTHER DID THIS to me until I was seventeen. She did it when I came home from Space Camp, where I was the inept shuttle commander and a boy named Buddy Mayo told me he loved me. She did it after the Florida State Science Fair, where I represented Jacksonville with a project on water pollution. She did it after I left prom early in my sophomore year: "Take off that nasty rented tux," she said when I walked in, the perfume of my twelfth-grade date still on me, "and hurry to the tub! I've already run it for us." Exactly when she stopped washing my groin, I don't know, but I know I was way too old. Trying to remember, I twitch and recoil. It's hard to breathe. By the time the feckless, warm body called my father put an end to the weekly nightmare, I believed I was shameful and weak. In the years to come, though, I refined ways to compensate—too many one-night stands, nonstop crushes, academic workaholism, a boisterous, overconfident personality that could charm you then knock you over. I needed the dopamine to keep going. I'm past forty now, exhausted from self-medicating.

When I tried to say no, my mother's face turned as red as her obsessively washed hands, and she breathed like a wounded boar. She clenched her fists and made her eyes huge and yelled through her wet teeth, "Let me do this!" She spit on my face. She said she had to wash me, because if I did it myself, I'd get water "everywhere"—she said there couldn't be a shower curtain because it would get mildewy. When I later saw *The Exorcist*, it felt more like a documentary than a horror film: my family was my long apprenticeship to darkness, whose lies I mistook for truth. Evil, I learned, is fundamental to us, throbbing at our core, and can't be made right. Not by prayer, therapy, or the law. Squash it down but that only strengthens it. It will rise up and possess you, and you will do harm.

We are animals, I learned. Delusional, ultimately suicidal monkeys convinced of our rationality. The woman who forcibly showered me once a week until I was in eleventh grade was the same woman who had me reading at age three. She sent the Birthday Man flying to us to leave presents on the stoop and had a baker make us gourmet cakes. She nearly turned the house into the North Pole at Christmas, showering us with incredible gifts, our stockings handmade and monogrammed in red felt. She raised me to tell the truth and be polite, and if I disobeyed her, I felt my life might be in danger. She might go get her spoon, which she used to stir macaroni and cheddar in the pot, and agitate peas thawing on the stovetop. She might hit me with it, and not lightly.

Here me out, Mother Earth and Father Sky: whatever it takes, I want my life to answer the question, *What's the opposite of trauma?*

CHAPTER 3

The Lantern

I was eight. I can't recall how we ended up there, but one cloudy day in the 1980s when I was in third grade, my family stopped to relax at tide pools on some island off Florida, a good chance for me to wander off by myself and play naturalist. Instead of palm trees, along the beach were invasive ironwood trees, whose roots keep sea turtles from nesting. The green needles blew like my father's thinning hair; the waters of the cove rippled like my soccer shorts.

Once a month we went out into nature like this, usually by the water. We left the house to shed suburbia and psychosis, to find the horizon and salt. To take what wasn't ours. It was something we could do together that didn't involve Mickey Mouse or all-you-can-eat Mongolian BBQ buffets. At the end of such days, as we roasted marshmallows over the grill, people sometimes waved and smiled in that evangelical way and told us what a nice family we were.

That day as we tiptoed like rookie firewalkers around the tide pools, spiny brittle stars waved us off. Stuck to the rocks were snails called bleeding teeth. Along their inner lip were two nubby incisors that looked infected.

I warned everyone about the urchins. If you step on one, I'll remind my injured father a few years later at a Panama City jetty, you pee on the puncture wound to dissolve the spine, then iodine it. At the time, I was convinced I'd grow up to be a marine biologist living on a sailboat with Ben Affleck on the PBS show *Voyage of the Mimi*. He and I would be bunkmates and wear each other's turtlenecks. As we sailed the world taking a census of humpback whales thousands of miles away from home, he'd teach me how to be a cool, manly nerd.

Already in elementary school, in case I needed to run away to the ship, I could navigate crudely with the stars and read tide charts. I memorized field guides for the night sky, seashells, minerals, insects, hummingbirds, flowers, and tropical fish.

In second grade I wrote to a Smithsonian shell expert for career advice, but by the time he replied several years later, I wanted to be a writer like the one sixth-grader Leigh Botts obsessively writes to in Beverly Cleary's *Dear Mr. Henshaw*, still my favorite book. Cone shells with harpoons that can kill you, eels with slimy teeth covered in gnarly bacteria: I thought I knew all the dangerous creatures out there.

My mother, squinting down at a large tide pool filled with turtle grass, called out to my father: "Come quick!"

He would touch anything. When I was four, he called me over during yard work gripping a chameleon and let it bite my finger. I was positively transfixed, as if an alien scout were trying to communicate with me beside our pittosporum bushes. He loved it when I volunteered at Silver Springs to have a boa constrictor draped around my neck. He clapped and hollered the loudest as I fed Sassy the Seal at the Florida Keys Aquarium in my purple shorts and purple shirt.

"What on earth is it?" my mother asked over the sound of the surf, pointing to a brownish blob the size of a heart.

"Can't say," my father called out, stepping down to pick it up with both hands, "but it's got tiny little hairs." The same brown bristles as his Pringles-man mustache. "They don't appear to sting."

Leaving some colorful minnows, I rushed over just as boy detective Encyclopedia Brown would have. "It looks like a fat sand dollar," I said, panting, "but it's not a sand dollar. It's, it's an invertebrate for sure. It doesn't have bones in its back." Elsewhere recently, we had used our feet to find live sand dollars in the shallows, bagging a half dozen at a time. After they died and dried out on the porch, we scoured them of quills and Cloroxed them overnight to make them better than the ones on the beach.

Actually, it's a gayfer, the bully in my mind said, *just like you.*

I held out my hand to my father, begging him to let me hold this pin cushion of a sea creature, but he was taking his time.

"Ooh!" my mother said, filled with the possibilities that her shell craft class taught her. "An aquatic yeast roll! Adorable. Let's take it back and bleach it. It could be a nightlight!"

We didn't understand that kidnapping and asphyxiating living creatures wasn't right. As a child, I chloroformed damselflies and pinned them to a board; I burned red-legged locusts alive with sunlight and a Fisher Price magnifying glass. But these insects weren't just bugs. They had rainbowed hindwings and forewings. They had sensitive nerves and stunning compound eyes. Every family, without even trying to, offers its kids an ecological education, which is to say a moral one.

"But what in blazes is it?" I asked, trying to sound British.

My father finally plopped it in my hand. I remember it now as very alive, awake even, slowly moving its dull, short spines, agitated by an unknowable consciousness, burning with mitochondrial fires lit by the same primeval torch as ours, scratching onto my hand the Grand Unified Theory of Everything and Nothing with dozens of inkless quill pens. It sucked on me with its tube feet, desperate for water.

"Wowsers!" I said, looking at the underside. It was like a diagram straight from Stephen Hawking: the food grooves were lines of space-time plunging into a wormhole.

"Why don't we look for more?" my mother exclaimed as I gave the animal back to my father. "Hold my hand so I don't fall," she told me. Like me, on land she was distrustful of her body.

Soon enough she half-stumbled at a slick place between pools. Still holding on to me, she landed on her butt.

She started shouting. "I always knew you wanted to kill me!" she said to me. The switch had been flipped.

"If I really needed you, you'd let me die," she said more softly, not making much sense.

My father and I pretended not to hear what she was saying. It was one way we coped with her sudden breaks with reality. Before puberty and the internet, my go-to's for denial as a boy included making sandwiches and coolers talk, wiggling my ears one at a time to the beat of "Jingle Bells," putting a shrimp tail on each finger at seafood restaurants, and having an invisible baby on the floor every Labor Day. To survive, I had to be a zany Ken doll with khakis and boat shoes, a flat stomach, and straight As.

"What are you *talking* about?" I asked after losing my patience.

"Help me up," she told me. "It's time for you to apologize." The tide, milky green and cool, was coming in. During even minor disagreements, my mother could announce she was getting on a Greyhound bus and never coming back. "Do you want some *candy*? Candy, candy, candy! You can have all the candy you want because I'm getting the hell out of here."

"I didn't do anything," I said, "but all right I'm sorry, Mother—all right?" We weren't allowed to call her "Mom."

"Get over here. Now."

Meanwhile the animal in my hand couldn't breathe.

WHY DID MY MOTHER DO THINGS like accuse us of wanting to kill her? Why did she hurt me over and over, even as she strove to take care of my every basic need? Those are questions I've asked my whole life.

One big clue came in college when we were visiting Mamo, my grandmother who lived three hours south of us. It was probably 2001 or 2002, when I was about twenty-one. Emboldened by my well-meaning therapist, I blurted out to Mamo what my mother, her only child, had done to me against my will. I made it clear these hundreds and hundreds of traumatic incidents were not bonding experiences.

"Abuse?" Mamo said when I told her. "That isn't abuse. It's just a bath! You mustn't ever say things like that!" She had never yelled at me before. With scorn, almost hatred.

Mamo was the only family member who didn't try to own me. As I listened to her stories late into the night, I held her hand as long as I wanted to, which wasn't insect-like and rejecting like my mother's. She told me about the rinsed gleam of the Tetons in the 1920s, the bobcats in her backyard jungle, and the time at Cedar Key she stepped on a stingray, by far the worst pain of her life. Our love for one another, which made my mother jealous, felt cosmic and sustaining, like that of companion stars. Mamo was my long-distance surrogate mother, the first of many, and I was her do-over, her second-chance wormhole back to motherhood. All my childhood she sought to have the uncomplicated relationship with me that she couldn't with her daughter. Her non-possessive love, absorbed over many years, is one reason I've never taken my life. "I love you galaxies and galaxies" is what we said to one another as we fell asleep.

A few hours later she told my mother what I confided in her. In the ensuing fight in Mamo's living room, I asked my mother point-blank, with all the kindness I could muster, "Why did you do that to me? What happened to you? Who hurt you? This stuff doesn't come out of nowhere."

"You don't know anything about anything!" she said, her delivery perfected from years of watching soap operas. "My father didn't have sex with me on the floor if that's what you mean!" That was the big clue that continues to haunt me. It upset my traditional, eighty-nine-year-old grandmother to no end, and they both turned on me: "Are you happy now? Are you happy?"

WALKING IN SHOCK to the ocean nearby, I thought about my mother. I saw her as a toddler splashing in the waves in Puerto Rico, saying her first word in Spanish. I saw her eating a piece of fresh coconut after Mamo dried her off in the shade. I saw her saying goodbye to her newest batch of friends because her Army colonel father had been reassigned to yet another base. In negating the possibility that she'd been violated, she affirmed it, it seemed to me.

I looked down as I walked: the world seemed to consist only of foam, broken glass, and halves of sunrise tellins. That's another way to survive a wackadoodle upbringing: get lost in the details, don't take in your life's sweep of sky, keep searching for the best scraps.

Eventually I stopped and sat just up from the tide line, holding my knees to my chest. Looking out at the waves breaking on the eroded reef, I called out to the sky for help. No answer. I looked at my feet. I began scraping the tar off with a shell, but no matter how hard I tried, there were bits that stayed. I didn't want to face the fact that human love, even a grandmother's, is always conditional. But already I knew that saying you love someone is infinitely easier than living it out.

I picked up what looked like a melted shard of black plastic: it was a mermaid's purse, the egg case of a cartilaginous fish called a clearnose skate. As I pulled on the dark tendrils that once anchored it to the seafloor and felt the slit where the baby fish escaped, I remembered in a home movie my overdue mother standing in profile, pointing excitedly to her enormous stomach because I'm floating inside—a clearnose boy, kicking and somersaulting, who in a couple of weeks will take his first breath. Then my cousin hands her Kermit the Frog, and she laughs and rocks it in her arms as if she were Miss Piggy, hamming it up for my father behind the camera.

Skip ahead two minutes: home from the hospital with me and looking refreshed, she's bathing me for the first time. On the kitchen island, she wipes me down as if I were a holy statue about to be put back into its niche. She looks gorgeous in her fitted blue blouse and gray wool slacks. Her hair is on the short side and permed like Joan Lunden's on *Good Morning America*. Self-conscious and stiff as she's filmed, she doesn't want to make a mistake and have it recorded for her relentlessly nitpicky parents and in-laws. Joy, nevertheless, is flickering. I can tell she's thrilled I'm home.

I stood up and tossed the mermaid's purse onto a dune. *Dammit fucking fuck fucks!* The sand would gobble it up, fertilizing the sea oats. I walked back to the house, where Mamo and my mother would act as if nothing had happened.

Now WHEN I WATCH digitized home movies of my mother on my phone, labels like C-PTSD, OCD, BPD, and narcissism evaporate—instead I see a basically good person. She was born at the end of World War II into a culture whose greatest aspirations for her were marriage, motherhood, and patriotic hyper-consumerism. She was overwhelmed with impossible standards, isolating her from common sense and herself. She was largely cut off from the wisdom of her body—of elders and fellow women—and the medicine of the natural world. All the while, deep down she and her fellow Americans knew their nuclear arsenal could destroy the biosphere of the earth many times over—that using the sky, soil, and ocean as open sewers can't end well. Go walk through your local Costco to see what over a half century of corn syrup, pointless wars, and screen time has done to us. We the people of Prozac, fracking, and Zoom.

My mother's unknown early trauma took place within that collective sickness, ultimately causing her maternal instincts, I think, to go into overdrive and turn pathological. To this day, it helps me to think of the abuse as a haywire purification ritual for us both—and even for our numb-from-the-neck-down, unsustainable civilization.

It might sound odd, but I see my family as a microcosm of that gimme-gimme, carbon-belching society. Our gleeful overcollecting of creatures in tide pools was an example of surplus killing, common to many predators: hyenas, honey badgers, zooplankton. But the prey my family and I gratuitously hunted was inedible. We felt special— the sensation, however bogus, of being one with nature. Denial kept us from imagining the agony they felt in the Florida sun. Denial also leads many Americans to tell themselves pollution is a sign of progress and climate change a hoax. It leads perpetrators to rebrand abuse as no-big-deal. Flashbacks as false memories.

Whether we're talking about abusers and victims—or people and the planet—it's all part of what's known as our extraction mindset. Pretend the interconnectedness of all beings is woke hogwash. That there will be no consequences for your crimes. Do what feels good, take what you want, and get out.

Cynical as I am sometimes, when I look back on the day I asked my mother who hurt her, I realize I was trying to bond with her as a fellow survivor: I wanted us both to be transformed by truth. To stop hating her, I thought I needed us to acknowledge together that ancestral trauma is self-perpetuating, passed down like a black-magic heirloom that makes us do things we later regret.

I never got an explanation for what she did to me—was she trying to wipe away her unspeakable past while also proving to herself that she could finally be in control of men's bodies, which, considering just my father, she saw as unsafe? Who early on in her life forced her into shallow water, demanding stillness and exacting humiliation? Who treated her like an object that needed to be scoured and bleached, only to be dirtied again? Who kept the karmic propeller spinning? I still want to know who hurt her. Even if I have to break into the underworld, I want to strangle them. To save the girl who was born innocent and stop the cycle.

If she kept me a dependent, self-hating infant, her traumatized brain perhaps reasoned, I wouldn't suffer as she had. And she wouldn't ever have to feel irrelevant. As she raised me, my mother was so triggered, so busy projecting her own sense of dirtiness onto me, she couldn't see the pain she was causing.

I wasn't real enough to her. Instead, I was whatever she needed me to be—a contaminated boogeyman one minute, her savior or coupon cutter the next. Limbic overdrive, amygdala hijack, panic attacks— whatever you want to attribute it to, her brain didn't allow her to be a rational, caring mother.

IN THE TWO DECADES of adulthood before I cut ties with my parents, more than anything I wanted a mother I could feel safe around. One who knew that to hurt your child is to hurt yourself. Which is to say, a mother more like Elliot's in *E.T.*, whose name, of all things, is Mary.

Abandoned by her husband, in much of the movie she's understandably frazzled and disengaged; her children don't exactly respect her. Later, though, we see her tenderly reading *Peter Pan* to her young daughter. Then, while holding Elliot close, she tries to protect her children from federal agents in spacesuits at the front door.

What kind of mother did Mary become after E.T. left? I see her breathing more deeply, hiking in the redwood forests nearby, eating less processed food, paying more attention to her children. I see her filled with wonder in the most ordinary of moments: glimpsing the mountains in her rearview mirror, washing her hands at the kitchen sink with water that's snowmelt. It's as if she's had a breakthrough psychedelic experience. Still, life isn't perfect. Her wakefulness often leaves her, but it always comes back. She's practicing what I like to call the three Ss: slowing down, softening, savoring. Rather than unwittingly traumatizing her children, which she never did anyway, she tries to meet them right where they are.

It's no accident that as she reads *Peter Pan* to her child ("Clap your hands if you believe!"), in a nearby closet, E.T. reaches his glowing finger toward Elliot's bleeding hand. "Ouuuuuch," E.T. says. "The wound is healed," the screenplay reads. To me, that's an analogy for parental love. The ouch, in being seen and accepted, is soothed. That healing resonance is pure magic for the child, who thought the pain would last forever. While she can't make bicycles fly in the air like E.T., a mother can be nurturing more often than not.

Yet even with the best of parents, beyond early childhood, no one in this life can hold your hand and make it all okay. No shrink or shaman can do that. And no climate scientist can flip a switch to refreeze the Arctic, bring back the Great Barrier Reef, and resurrect the extinct golden toad in Costa Rica. It's childish to wish for a Planet B or a new parent—for a pristine Mother Earth or healed human mama. While you do what you can to help, you know the limits of your influence.

When you're in kindergarten, though, your mother can work miracles. She can take you to the backyard to talk about death and the goddess holding it all. There, you and your mother can bury the toads. Afterwards she can hold you in her dirty arms.

And your wound? She can heal your wound.

AFTER MY MOTHER LOSES HER SHIT at the tide pools, my memory of that day sputters and stops. Destabilize time and space, cue the dreamscapes in time lapse.

MOTHERSHIP

I see the birth of the moon after the earth collides with the Mars-sized protoplanet Theia. The first oceans form from comet water. Our tide pools fill with water, but each one is a replica of the bathtub. Instead of steam, they're all outgassing faith in a happy future. They're chock-full of primordial ooze, the building blocks of multicellular life, the ingredients for human lunacy replicating and roiling. In the bathwater, Darwin's "warm little pond" where he thought life began, I see amino acids recombining until they're cells evolving into algae, a trilobite, an ichthyosaurus, a reptilian bird, a rat, an ape, a rough human slouching toward Jacksonville to throw back the Welch's grape juice on an altar and be damned.

What I know: Our species can make radioactive art out of insanity, entropy, and nanoplastics so small they cross the blood-brain barrier—can terrorize the closeted sixteen-year-old with antibacterial soap and hard water, the Formica countertop with Formula 409. It can declare sacks of Halloween candy a square meal; it can't stop playing fuck-me-now hopscotch with Grindr squares extending out to the orbit of Neptune until both hands are claws and the mind is a flapjack.

What I also know: the boon of being alive—with meteors, rubies, ferns, papayas, red-tailed hawks, Orion's belt, lava, purple coral, longleaf pines, and cashew butter—exceeds the misery of it.

Decay, annihilation, then maybe rewilding. Can't you smell the earth without us a million years from now?

Sea biscuits! The clerk back at our hotel said the six paunchy sand dollars my family and I had captured were called sea biscuits. I'd forgotten that one.

Embarrassed, I looked it up later at the library. Legend has it the five petals etched on the top of sea biscuits and sand dollars are the five wounds of Jesus: shake one after it's dead and you'll hear the brittle wings of angels rattling inside. Those dove-shaped mouthparts are called, incredibly, Aristotle's lantern, because almost twenty-four centuries ago he thought they looked like a five-sided lantern with the panes removed. The pentagon of teeth grinds up sediment, and the decaying organic bits are slurped up.

On top of a sea biscuit is a star-shaped plate called the madreporite. *Madre*, as in mother, *porite* as in pore, controlling the flow of water in and out. It's one word, almost theological, to describe my mother. She often seemed like a constellation not of stars but perforations in a thin firmament. She was a baffling shell that you, the alien astronaut, could lift from the water and hold up to the sun.

CHAPTER 4

Exultation

By the time I snorkeled my first reef, it was already sick. My family and I were at Dry Rocks Reef off Key Largo, not that long after visiting the tide pools. The year before, in 1987, the first mass coral bleaching was recorded off the Florida Keys.

The morning was overcast. My mother and I struggled in the waves, holding hands. Bubbles from the divers below effervesced around us, dozens of other snorkelers yelping and kicking nearby. Though our masks were leaking and visibility was poor, we could see a black fish, maybe a grouper, cruising out from a ledge. A barracuda sidled up beside us and flew off. Much of the coral was broken or discolored, smutches of blight covering overturned colonies.

Even as a fourth grader, I knew the reef was in trouble. But I didn't know what white band disease or global warming was. I couldn't fathom that the ocean absorbs 90 percent of the heat not radiated back into space—and that coral, hypersensitive to pollution and temperature changes, was a fortune teller. An underwater canary for the coal mine we call the earth.

Exultation

I let go of my mother's hand as we swam toward the statue of Jesus. *Christ of the Abyss*, a nine-foot-tall bronze ceremoniously sunk in 1965 on Dry Rocks, then one of the most sublime reefs in Florida. He was an exultant man, but there was no cross: he was looking up, his arms uplifted like the dying elkhorn coral around us, his robe cuffs furry with algae. This was a kind shepherd who dropped his crook to assume the pose of branching coral, imitating it to praise it, to think like it, to stop being human for a while and take on coral consciousness. It's said God sent Jesus to Earth to save humanity—but what about longsnout seahorses, mustard-hill coral, and purple sea fans with flamingo-tongue snails? What about the five-hundred-year-old brain coral a short swim from the statue—absolutely massive, still alive, slow-growing? It electrified me.

For thousands of years in the Florida Keys and across the Caribbean, seemingly endless thickets of marigold-yellow elkhorn and staghorn coral protected the coastline and provided habitat for countless creatures—snorkeling Dry Rocks in the 1800s, you might have gone blind from the apatite blue of stoplight parrotfish; the butter-and-eggs glare of French grunts, schoolmasters, scrawled cowfish, and rock beauties; the amethyst-plum of sea fans dotted with flamingo tongues. Dry Rocks also used to swarm with sharks and manatees, gargantuan barracuda and grouper, even playful Caribbean monk seals that went extinct in the 1950s. There were so many sea turtles that the first European sailors couldn't go net fishing; in places their ships were barely able to move.

But since 1975, the Florida Keys have lost over 90 percent of its live coral. At Dry Rocks today, the hard coral is virtually all dead, even the ancient brain coral near the statue. To put the staggering losses another way: in my lifetime, coral coverage in the Keys has dropped to 2 percent, the keystone species of elkhorn and staghorn coral having declined by about 97 percent. These two coral species, once the very building blocks of reefs in the Atlantic, are now critically endangered. On top of that, seawater increasingly acidic from absorbing our CO_2 is slowly eating away at the little remaining coral there, forty years earlier than expected. Imagine Yosemite's redwoods turning white and dying, the saplings too, with fewer and fewer seeds left to germinate, and you begin to get the idea. Think E.T. sick and white in the ditch.

THE JESUS DEPICTED in the statue wasn't the one weaponized to make me an abomination. To find that Jesus, look for the lighthouse in downtown Jacksonville, twenty miles from the ocean.

A fifty-foot concrete shaft with black stripes and three big picture windows, it stands beside Parking Garage 4 of the First Baptist Church. Until the bulb was replaced, it shone so brightly into the windows of nearby homes that residents complained it kept them up at night. FBC itself was the unfortunate guiding light of my birthplace, a mega-church taking up eleven city blocks, its Sunday school classes arranged by zip code.

It's not only known for the former pastor who after 9/11 called Mohammed "a demon-possessed pedophile." For years, FBC success-fully lobbied the city council to not pass a human rights ordinance and keep Jacksonville one of the only major US cities where, among other things, it was still legal to fire employees and refuse rental housing because of sexual orientation. Council members who voted no came to an FBC Sunday service to be applauded for voting against a bill that Pastor Mac Brunson said would "accommodate sexual orientation and sexual expression in the city." The word *accommodate* is not just a metaphor: the same Jacksonville motel that turned away a Black family in 1954 could legally refuse a night's rest to a married gay couple with children until the ordinance was finally signed into law in June 2020.

So is it any wonder that growing up I was called a faggot with impu-nity inside and outside of Jacksonville schools? My history teacher who emphasized past contributions of women told me after class, "Homosexuality is unnatural." I pointed out that it's been documented in dolphins and many other animals and that it puts species at an evolutionary advantage. "You aren't a dolphin," she snapped, to which I should have said, "It's people like you who make me wish I were."

When I returned as a first-year teacher to the school, a self-loathing former teacher of mine slapped me in the face beside our faculty mailboxes in the front office. *Pop.* He didn't like that I was out of the closet and teaching on his turf. Five years earlier he had required one of my friends to get parental permission to write a research paper on the 1968 Stonewall riots, the beginning of the modern gay rights movement. For many of those who said they loved me, I was a sinner who needed to be washed clean.

What I didn't know at eight or seventeen was that with joy I can hack into my brain. I can prove to myself, to every synapse, that I am neither a mistake nor a sodomite in need of an overlord's forced baptisms. I can climb every rung of my DNA and ask for help:

Thymines and adenines, unfasten, reshuffle, change your dance, reconfigure the double helix puzzle. My soul is as spick-and-span as eggs incubating in a male jawfish's mouth. Immaculate as the Orion Nebula's gas and dust, a nursery for baby stars.

Cytosines and guanines, revise yourselves and tell me I'm loved, that we are love itself.

Maybe my darkness couldn't be vaporized once and for all, but I could talk back to it, expose it patiently to the sunrise-red tail of a ringed pipefish, to periwinkle branches of staghorn tipped in damson plum.

The darkness wanted me to shoot myself, as it had for my great-grandfather, who was an MD in the US Naval Reserve Force. Orlando H. Petty wasn't drafted—he signed up to serve at age forty-one. He won a Medal of Honor for remaining on the battlefield without a gas mask to rescue and treat wounded soldiers in World War I. Suffering serious lung damage and probably PTSD, early in the Great Depression he shot himself in the Philadelphia row house where his twenty-one-year-old daughter—Mamo—still lived. No one ever spoke of this. I only learned it in 2009 after randomly googling his name and finding his obituary. He wasn't only a national hero when he died. He was the personal physician of Philly's mayor and a professor at the University of Pennsylvania's medical school, having published influential research on treating diabetes with cow insulin. He dedicated his life to teaching, writing, and healing.

The darkness also wanted me to hang myself, as it had for Brian, a troubled, Tolstoy-reading hunk I fell for in my thirties in California. After a few beers, we walked down a sycamore-lined street in my neighborhood, trading puns, teaching each other the names of Mediterranean plants. The interval between us was abuzz. I'm remembering his dark, deer-like eyes, his understated snowboarder masculinity—and the vastness between us, his frustrating unknowability. He took his life on a Kauai shoreline facing the same ocean as Raja's.

As I flirted with suicide in other ways as an adult, I began to see that nature, especially coral reefs before they perished, might save my life. And help me be useful to others. Whether CO_2 levels are at 280 or 2,800 parts per million, whether the planet is on fire or locked in ice, whether you and I are climate refugees in Canada or kings and queens safe on a Martian colony, a true curiosity about other beings can be awakened. Compassion, it's been said, is a verb. It quivers in response to suffering. And it takes direct action.

Raja Ampat was my wormhole back to Dry Rocks Reef in 1965, when the Keys had dazzling reefs and my mother was an undergrad nearby. I sought my own do-over. Physically traveling back to 1988 or 1996 to push my mother away from me—to save that little boy, that confused teenager—was impossible. But intentionally feeling exultation over and over like the statue's might ease my sorrow. On Raja's protected twenty-first-century reefs, I practiced feeling loved and whole, learned what inner safety felt like, and slowly changed my brain.

At night in Raja Ampat, beneath shackled Andromeda and the beating wings of Pegasus, Venus laying down a thin trail of light on the lagoon, I prayed to the Holy Ghost of Neuroplasticity, asking the brain regions involved in PTSD to be healed:

> O, fill my amygdala of unprocessed traumatic memories with the banded grandeur of a sea snake coiled in a limestone hollow.

> O, abide in my hippocampus of declarative memory consolidation as the tumbling teal of spaghetti sponges—animate, inspire, and guide my prefrontal cortex's every quark and quirk to give me more choices when I'm in distress.

> And You shall renew the bio-electric face of the earth.

I may not believe in a male Caucasian deity, but I am still a man of faith. In the sand forty feet down, an encrusted boulder as my altar, I've bowed down before the invisible good work of photosynthesis, which feeds coral and helps create an ecosystem that can be seen from space, one that covers less than 1 percent of the ocean floor but a quarter of all marine species depend on.

I glorify the Mother of All, whoever You are.

CHAPTER 5

Dieback

*"To stand at the ruins is to succumb to memory.
It is to be pierced, undone."*

—SOFIA SAMATAR, "Standing at the Ruins"

When I was growing up in the 1980s and '90s, we weren't afraid of the world ending like my students are today. The Cold War was over; 9/11 was unthinkable. Mainstream America wasn't concerned about a runaway greenhouse effect or another mass extinction. We couldn't conceive that because humanity was the dominant force on Earth, we had entered a new geological epoch: the Anthropocene. Indeed, *Wall-E* wouldn't be released until 2008, a movie that more than any other has helped shape my students' sense of doom.

Until my thirties, I thought I was personally doomed—but not humanity, at least not consciously. And yet, as at Dry Rocks Reef, deep down I knew we were in trouble. At an environmental summer camp, I was the weird one weeping during a slideshow of ecological devastation set to Bette Midler's "From a Distance." In fifth grade I won a poster contest with my entry, a drawing of the earth with glittery silver stars and angry orange letters that spelled out "Global Warming, Global Warning," but I didn't understand what it truly meant that the atmosphere was trapping more heat.

What was a greenhouse anyway? I lived in Florida, after all. How could it possibly get any hotter than that? Well, it can. Since I was born in 1979, CO_2 levels have risen by almost 25 percent, and now in Jacksonville there are twelve more days with a heat index of 90 degrees or more, with historically redlined, minority neighborhoods up to ten degrees hotter than "nicer" areas with extensive tree cover like where I grew up. Move over, peaches—it's gotten so warm that the Georgia Citrus Association, which includes growers in the Jacksonville area, was founded in 2016. "That was unheard of twenty years ago," Fred Gmitter, a University of Florida horticultural sciences professor told the Associated Press. "It's getting warmer up there and better for growing citrus." When I ask my students about their firsthand experiences with the climate crisis, as with wonder, the hands shoot up. Of course my students are afraid.

But their anxiety, at times immobilizing, isn't purely ecological. It's digital: my students are overstimulated and mentally imbalanced from mainlining social media. I shouldn't be offended when they ask me to create exam study guides for them—many of their brains, rewired by the likes of TikTok, can't keep up with the course material, or much of anything for that matter, heightening their anxiety. Since high school, TikTok has been barraging them with ten-second videos individually tailored to maximize the dopamine hit and the company's profits. They're hooked, as recent neuroscience research suggests, the parts of the brain involved in addiction lighting up as they watch content based on hyper-personalized algorithms.

Their anxiety is also sociological. Every semester when we discuss the EPA statistic that Americans spend about 90 percent of their lives indoors, I ask, "How many of you know a classmate who's afraid to walk to class?" We're in Harrisonburg, Virginia, a low-crime, semirural area, but nevertheless most of the hands go up. Many of them drive the half mile to campus instead of walking or taking the free shuttle bus that can be tracked in real time on an app. They think driving is safer and quicker, though in actuality the parking situation can be stressful. When I encourage them to take walks in local parks without their phones, they often look at me like I'm nuts and politely ask, "What if there's an emergency?" Drive through any neighborhood on a Saturday afternoon, even in rural Virginia, and you'd be lucky to see a single child playing outside, even in their yard. Even before COVID-19, it was as if we were in quarantine, afraid of leaving our homes, afraid of one another and the phantom child snatchers waiting to throw kids into vans.

Even my mother, when she wasn't exiling us to our rooms, let us play outside. I didn't grow up exploring forests and creeks like Rachel Carson on her sixty-five-acre family farm in Pennsylvania or living off the grid wearing natural bug spray like Cheryl Strayed in Minnesota, but being outdoors soothed me. At night as my parents argued in their bedroom, I would go into the backyard to look through my mail-order telescope at the open cluster Pleiades in Taurus. Was there a planet around one of those blue stars where families weren't scary? For a few moments, my wonder protected me like the shields around the USS *Enterprise*.

IN THE 1990S, as I grew older, I saw fewer stars. Light pollution increased as Florida's population soared, so far doubling to twenty million in my lifetime. We still took trips into nature on weekends, but beginning in middle school, I was in an overachieving rush and left behind my yard's muscadine grapes and the slugs in the smelly oak hollow. My family got a dial-up modem that gave me access to America

Online chat rooms and softcore GIFs that took an hour to load. I fell madly in love with a varsity baseball player named Jarrod in Oregon, but now I'm pretty sure I was being catfished by an imaginative geezer.

If my parents were out of town, entire weekends could evaporate as I sought love and oblivion as a closeted teen online. My brain was being rewired to be bored by simple pleasures like the clouds and the grass, and instead to seek out intense bursts of dopamine and irrelevant, unsettling info—and so was everyone else's. Wonder became at best a notion, not an experience. I began to lose what some of my students have never had.

As Glacier National Park continued melting in the 1990s, we were enthralled by Monica Lewinsky, Steve Urkel, and Tickle Me Elmo. Mass shootings became more commonplace. Social inequality continued to soar. Mobile phones proliferated. Walmart became the largest private employer in the world. We hadn't heard of Wi-Fi yet, or pocket-sized supercomputers for sending pics that disappear, reading *Beowulf*, and shopping for sneakers. Still, it was easy to forget my trauma with even slow computers.

MY CLASSMATES, BY AND LARGE, liked me, even as I thought they despised me. On autopilot, I tried to make everyone feel special—as with my mother, I became the person my classmates needed me to be as I worked overtime to feel safe and accepted. As Judith Herman writes, "In the effort to placate her abusers, the child victim often becomes a superb performer. She attempts to do whatever is required of her.... She brings to all these tasks a perfectionist zeal, driven by the desperate need to find favor." Many thought I was a kiss-up who did things just because they looked good on my résumé. Looking back, I know they were right. What they didn't understand was that as an impeccably programmed Golden Boy, I was covering for my parents—and ensuring myself more options after graduation so I could leave Florida for good.

MOTHERSHIP

Whatever can be said of my parents, they cared about my education. Thankfully, I wasn't allowed to watch much TV or play video games. A Nintendo system, my mother said, would break the TV, which gave me more time to read, write, and be outside. If I wanted a book, they took me to the library. Every afternoon, my mother asked me what we did in each class and what the homework was, and she remembered everything. The next morning on the breakfast table were sticky notes in her bubbly cursive cheering me on and reminding me of deadlines. She made teachers cry who graded me unfairly, for years in Publix trolling the woman who gave me my only B before college. How many mothers do that for their kids? I can still hear my mother quizzing me in the kitchen on my spelling words: *fisherman, laundry, eclipse.* You better know the difference between *bring* and *take.*

She might pretend to call me on the phone: "Is Gregory Pegory there?"

To prove to her I knew predicate nominatives take the subjective case, I'd answer, "This is he! May I help you?"

We learned the names of seashells together: *wentletrap, junonia, fighting conch, lettered olive, brown baby ear, cut-ribbed ark, Lady-in-waiting Venus, depressed slipper snail, sharp-rib drill...*

And my father? He fried eggs for me at 5:00 a.m. before the SATs and had a cold Mr. Pibb waiting when he picked me up from school. If he said he would be somewhere, he was always there at least five minutes early. He didn't shame me for not playing sports or watching football. He congratulated me on my academic success.

My grandfather, who invested much of his Army salary into the stock market, paid for me to go to college. He also funded my informal education: Space Camp and the life-changing eco-camp in the Withlacoochee State Forest, trips to Belize and other places with coral reefs, raising my ecological awareness and opening my mind. *There's a beautiful planet*, their gifts said, *beyond the house where you're kept.* They knew my mother was unstable and my father was trouble. Money was their rescue attempt.

IMAGINE IT JUST ONCE more and then never again: I'm fifteen, naked in the tub, and my mother is showering me—one minute over the noise of the spray, she's celebrating that I'm an alternate to the International Science Fair for my project on water pollution and telling me I'll be president of the United States and the next she's making inappropriate comments about my body as she scrubs it.

That was the mindfuck of my origins.

Here, life seemed to say, *grab the dark bottle, put a dropperful of this wildcrafted tincture blend under your tongue: abuse and privilege, mortification and hero worship.*

It will burn like a motherfucker—now swallow!

CHAPTER 6

Stone Foundation

In 1997, just before my senior year of high school, relations that weren't between a man and woman were still illegal. Several months before, Ellen DeGeneres came out on the cover of *Time*. Matthew Shepard was murdered in Wyoming a year later.

When I said the words, "I'm gay," my father went white and held his head in his hands. In the silence, I stared at the big, angry sores on his ankles that wouldn't heal. Oozing blood and clear fluid, they crackled purple-red like burns from a motorcycle tailpipe. He couldn't stop scratching.

"No, you're not," my mother said, her voice quavering.

"How can you be surprised? I've known since fifth grade. I was walking to my safety patrol locker, and it dawned on me. Remember Doug from Vero, I fell in love—"

"No one will want to be around you," she declared, after saying disgusting things I won't repeat. "Oh please, no one goes to a gay doctor or lawyer."

At the time, they didn't know anyone who was out, and besides, I didn't want to be a surgeon living on a golf course in the evangelical pressure cooker of Jacksonville anyway. Believe me, it may have an NFL team and a Mayo Clinic, but I still think of it as a big small town of closet cases, a place where dicks are called tallywackers and ordering unsweetened iced tea gets you side-eye. The minor league baseball team is called the Jumbo Shrimp. We had a city council member and Florida state representative, Kimberly Daniels, who doesn't buy candy around Halloween because it's been "prayed over by witches." She said in 2008, "If it wasn't for slavery, I might be somewhere in Africa worshiping a tree." An ordained minister and former sex worker, she also offers her services as an exorcist for gay demons.

"Did someone molest you?" my father asked me later when my mother was out of earshot. Barely able to find his words, he seemed wracked with guilt.

"No, of course not," I said. Today I wish I'd answered differently.

A week later, my father announced I needed a booster shot and drove me to a clinic whose waiting room held a complete woolly mammoth skeleton. Inside, the nurse instead actually drew my blood— to check testosterone levels. A physician my father knew from work told him, despite the utter lack of scientific evidence, that low levels of testosterone cause homosexuality. To be sure, that hypodermic needle stole a vial of my blood. Nevertheless, I'm thankful it did: it punctured my bloodline illusions, infected me with critical thinking.

COME BACK WITH ME to that crisp December day in 1997 when I first read *The Dream of a Common Language*, a poetry collection by Adrienne Rich. My friend Jeni gave it to me for my eighteenth birthday.

Sitting in the backyard of old oaks and pines, I thumbed the pages to release the new book smell. On the cover was a photograph of a tiny artist's studio looking toward the Brooklyn Bridge, which felt as far from Jacksonville as Alpha Centauri. *Could that be my room someday?* I wondered. *What's on the other side of the bridge?*

A week or so before, I had gotten into Harvard. And in September a girl named Dina outed me to the whole school, but when I confided in her, I was probably hoping she'd tell everyone and one of my born-again crushes would want me. Though my barely convincing disguise was torn off, I still felt like I had one on, as if I'd removed a tight Halloween mask and my face kept hurting.

I opened the book to the first poem, "Power," fifteen years before Cheryl Strayed made it famous in her memoir *Wild*. *"The Dream of a Common Language,"* Strayed writes, "was my religion," the one book she carried for her entire hike up the Pacific Crest Trail from Tehachapi Pass to the Bridge of the Gods. She was grieving the death of her mother and her marriage. Rubbing sage for energy like her mother taught her, Strayed spent a blustery night at Tehachapi reading "Power," which is about Marie Curie. I read the final stanza over and over:

> She died a famous woman denying
> her wounds
> denying
> her wounds came from the same source as her power

One of my mother's Diet Mountain Dews beside me for energy, Rich's words blew lightly, haltingly on my psyche. *Your pain*, Rich seemed to tell me that afternoon, *is a doorway to freedom and beauty. Be with it to tap into your power.*

"Greg! Greg!" my mother called out from the garage. "Come help me change a floodlight out front."

"Okay, later, I'm reading now."

"All right, but I'll need you soon!"

Legally an adult, I was no longer so quick to do her bidding, but I was careful because she'd ground me for weeks for one "rude" comment.

As I READ *The Dream of a Common Language* outdoors, my body was hurting. It wasn't just "growing pains," as my parents said. There in my backyard, Rich's words were making my body tingle and throb. The sensations, I see now, were trauma shudders—old wounds asking for acceptance. Emotional and physical pain were the same.

Turn to page forty-one of my senior yearbook to see the photo of me above the caption "Most Likely to Succeed." As I stand next to Leah Hodges, my right hip is higher than the left, my midline thrown way off: the side of my body that my mother faced as she washed me is perpetually tight. I'm standing in front of the school gymnasium, but at that moment, as always, part of me is still in the tub, veering away from her and the soap, no one to protect me. The flashbacks don't stop.

That side of my neck is especially tense and tender. Ever since puberty, I compulsively popped it with the heel of my hand against my chin. Hard, too hard. I was pushing down the flashbacks, the cathartic bawls that came in waves. Trying to short-circuit the SOS signals my body and my mind were sending one another. Look down at my legs, which might as well be stilts. The lower half of my body looks like it belongs to someone else—because until I leave for college, it does. Hypervigilant and panicking, I don't know where I am in space. I don't know how to stop feeling gross.

That was my C-PTSD body.

Why am I like this? My mind got tangled in that question during AP Calculus and play rehearsals, and as I showered myself in the tub that now had a curtain. To my mind, people could tell I was a victim just by looking at me. By hearing my occasional stutter and feeling my crooked pinkies.

DEAD SYCAMORE LEAVES scratching across the driveway behind me, the neighbor's kid dribbling a basketball, I turned to the final poem in *The Dream of the Common Language*, dedicated to Rich's life partner, Michelle

Cliff. "Transcendental Etude": the title immediately got my attention. To me, "transcendental" suggested the shedding of an old, inauthentic self, a declaration of independence, what she calls "pull[ing] back from the incantations, / rhythms we've moved to thoughtlessly."

I was writing a research paper on transpersonal psychologist Abraham Maslow and how peak experiences, especially mystical ones, help us reach our human potential. All the same, I misunderstood his notion of self-actualization as a one-off transcendence of all pain. As psychospiritual microwaving. Gremlin to Gizmo. Clark Kent walking in, Superman walking out. "It's not like you're launching the Space Shuttle," a therapist told me in college. To try and launch myself away from Florida, I often pointed my telescope toward a fuzzy splotch in Orion that appears in Rich's poem:

> We cut the wires,
> find ourselves in free-fall, as if
> our true home were the unidimensional
> solitudes, the rift
> in the Great Nebula.

What other wires did I need to cut to reveal my true self? What kind of life was possible beyond Jacksonville?

How could I heal?

That's where the word *etude* comes in, which is a musical exercise for practicing certain technical skills: Rich's poem planted the seeds of a practice that saved my life. She opens the poem by acknowledging societal and ecological suffering. Families of deer are shot. Children, even in pastoral Vermont, grow up in poor, violent homes. She notices the carcass of an elm, "this green world already sentimentalized, photographed, / advertised to death." Sitting on a stone wall at a farm, she ruminates on all those losses, as I do as an adult doomscrolling on the toilet.

She stops herself. She comes back, drops in, drops down. Cutting the wires binding her to suffering, she chooses to be here now, in nature, "in free-fall" with the insects, birds, slugs, and groundhogs, bringing her to the edge of transformation.

As her speaker comes into the present moment, my attention did too. I synchronized with her abiding in nature. In fits and starts I took in the turkey vultures above me, the mockingbirds and woodpeckers, the wooden fence streaked with lichen, the wolf spiders and acorns between blades of St. Augustine grass. I was calm. The trauma in my body became just another force in the ecosystem. All that subtropical green held my pain while my mother was inside dusting her Hummel figurine of a stargazing boy.

What I want to tell that teenager fresh out of the closet: *Don't you ever—ever—mistake mindfulness for helplessness. Notice the suffering and then change the direction, try a new translation.*

ART, RICH WOULD TEACH ME, is not only for our personal pleasure and personal growth. It's part of a larger effort that enlarges the collective heart and imagination, upending business as usual—essential if we're going to survive. And yet this is the kind of liberation maybe worked out over lifetimes, that no protest or pill—no coral reef or alien encounter, for that matter—can provide in one fell swoop. Making the most of the body, family, and planet you're born into is the challenge thrown down to us. It requires daily patience and follow-through, not doomed vows of sobriety made at 3:00 a.m. after deleting an addictive app for the 4,675th time.

The Buddha solved his problem, it's been said, so now solve yours.

Marrying a woman, "Transcendental Etude" confirmed, was not inevitable. I knew I could, without shame, be with a person who deserved me—we could be, as Rich writes of two lesbian soulmates, "eye to eye / measuring each other's spirit, each other's / limitless desire." What was dirty and what was clean didn't have to matter, just as it doesn't to radishes and star-nosed moles. I could pray to Ganesha, the Buddha, Jesus, even trees—or nothing at all. The hot, popular Young Life kids praying around the flagpole every morning could do their devotional thing and I'd do mine. For me, God was in the belted prayers of Andrew Lloyd Webber and Melissa Etheridge, the tropical sorcery of *The Golden Girls*, the spiral mandalas of lightning whelks and flyspeck ceriths, the hair whorls of my latest crush as I hummed the Indigo Girls song "Ghost" in the desk behind him.

In my future, I could have my own home, maybe with a desk by a window looking out onto a city of comrades, and with my own key, and bathroom and study doors that lock. My mother couldn't choose the clothes I wore each morning. I could, in time, stand up to my parents, even if I had no idea what that would look like. In the most ordinary of situations—by the ocean, in the grocery store, inside the voting booth—I could think and feel for myself. And perhaps the hollowness I felt would dissipate. Even if others scoffed, and they did, I could use my college education to become "just" a teacher.

Where can dreams take us? Rich at the end of "Transcendental Etude" imagines a woman who creates a collage from fabric, seaweed, milkweed, a wasp nest, a feather, a whisker, seashells. But her collage-making is not only a metaphor for poetry writing—it's also for defragmenting and healing the mind. The elements of the neurobiological collage I'm still assembling are internal, invisible. Consciousness is our workspace, Rich taught me, affirming what Thoreau calls "the unquestionable ability of man [*sic*] to elevate his life by conscious endeavor." My goal has been to befriend my terror and my joy: that would be wholeness. Forgiveness but not forgetting.

For Rich in this poem, this outlook is that of a compassionate woman with dragonfly-like vision. A subversive, prismatic agitator. A comforter and healer.

Is she modeling one possible next step in the evolution of human consciousness? And how can we get there? If we're going to survive, human nature itself might have to change, and the visualization and meditation practices I've sketched so far take time to work. Send a monolith from *2001: A Space Odyssey* to Earth to thicken our cerebral cortex and give us neurons that fire many more times per second. Expand our prefrontal cortex so we can keep our worst impulses in check, inclining us to take the long view, share rather than hoard, let go instead of holding on, and care for our unborn great-great-great grandchildren and our living children.

Often I've wished to be totally reprogrammed in mind, body, and soul—to be given a new neurobiology, one implanted with memories of different parents. For parts of my upbringing to be deleted. And yet here I am, at times still riding the struggle bus. Praying for technological breakthroughs that could restore the planet to even what it was when *E.T.* was first released.

Transformation, whether individual, species-wide, or planetary—there is no app for that. No incantation. It's as if we need an alien to be stranded on Earth to teach us a new way. To shuck our chromosomes and rewrite the code.

For now, we are left to slog through our pain and face our fears—consciously evolving consciousness, patiently overwriting the collective tapes of selfishness and lashing out. In the end, though, you can't make anyone do anything, even wear a mask during a pandemic. There will always be people who drive a stretch Hummer with big silicone testicles dangling from the back just to make a point.

Time and genetics are not on our side. No, we have forever. *All is illusion*, the ancient sages tell us. *Maya*. How many miles are there before we sleep?

CHAPTER 7

Adrienne

November 21, 2020

Dear Adrienne Rich,

I don't know if you ever got the letter I sent you in college. It was the one that ended like this: "I just wanted to share my thoughts with you, the one who has shaped me so." Of course you didn't mold me from the dust of the earth. But you gave me new eyes. Split the geode caught in my throat.

Just as my mother sang me "Row, Row, Row Your Boat" and I finally said my first word, I learned a new language from you. An uncommon one. Your words, filling my mouth every time I read "Transcendental Etude," became my own. What is a poem if not a set of new instructions for breathing, fresh possibilities for the tongue, jaw, and belly? "Change your syntax, change your life," I tell my poetry students.

I read your poem over and over in a whisper, my mouth forming the same sounds you made at your desk, cadences that dissolved my armor, conjuring hope where there was little. The songlines of manifesto, psalm, tent revival, and protest march to make profane love sacred, not only to come out but also to come forth, naysayers be damned. Teaching me to look inward and outward, building new neural pathways in the process. Not exactly telepathy like that between E.T. and Elliot but something akin to it. You were a mother I could trust, the caregiver I always wanted, your body to me made of phrases like *a dead elm raising bleached arms—lifted breathtaken on her breast—the very soul of light*. I know, I know, there's a long history of disembodied female muses, but I hope you can understand I could only think of you as soul-force music, without hands that could touch me, a goofy kid with a shell collection and terrible dandruff.

It felt like you were speaking to me instead of second-wave feminists. That attunement between writer and reader, I'll teach my undergrads two decades later, is why we come to literature in the first place and stay. It's the goosefleshy sensation of being seen, truly seen. Of being directly addressed from the void, of ringing sympathetically with the struck bells of Truth and Beauty. That resonance.

All great literature, like yours, is in essence self-help. As we read, we feel suppressed emotions, and feelings for which there aren't words. We clarify our values. Our conscience expands—you've taught me and many others to imagine the suffering of the voiceless and the powerless, and take direct action.

I know you would agree that we need to *mobilize*—reversing, not just slowing, the build-up of carbon in the skies, all hands on deck. With the entire biosphere in mind, present and future, we need to make hard choices. And we need to do it now. As a species—not only as artists and readers, or as Americans and Chinese—we must manifest the visionary spirit of Walt Whitman, who writes, "What is the count of the scores or hundreds of years between us? // I consider'd long and seriously of you before you were born." Couldn't the "you" in his poem be a redwood tree in 2108 that is drying out because fog appears too infrequently along the California coast? Or an eight-year-old boy in 2279 whose mother just told him the last wild orca has died, and he begins to write a poem?

It's better you never wrote me back. Years later I had the chance to talk to you after your reading in St. Louis, but I ran out after you finished. There are things about our mothers, biological and adopted, we never need to know. It's good for them to remain mythic and mysterious. Meeting you off the page, I would've lost you.

We're not dirty, we will transform our pain, you seemed to say to me—*but don't spend your life navel-gazing. Look outward. Give back to the world.*

Dive, dive into the wreck.

Your poetry began to reparent me. Twelve years ago you died and still your words hold me. With my full consent.

CHAPTER 8

Crazing Lake

I was in my dorm room. It was late Sunday morning, the fall semester of my sophomore year at Harvard. My roommate David handed me the cordless phone.

"It's your father," he mouthed.

Dad cleared his throat several times. "How I—how are you?"

"I'm reading *King Lear*."

He said my name with a squeak. Already I was floating, watching myself at my desk. "My immune system is shot."

"What does that mean? Is it cancer?" I asked. The wounds on his calves still hadn't healed. He was exhausted and had lost a lot of weight, this mild-mannered sales rep for Big Pharma who ate shredded wheat with blueberries for breakfast.

"I've had a problem for years," he said. The radiator clicked. "Now it's caught up with me. In the worst parts of Jacksonville, I went to the phone booth at Winn Dixies and flashed $20 bills. Once this lady went down on me and cut me. Then we had intercourse."

"Fucking God, what about Mother?"

"She's fine, I think. She's getting retested."

What else did he say? He proudly said he married her because he wanted her to be the mother of his children, as if she had been just an incubator and nanny to him. He said we should've gone to church as a family every week. I rolled my eyes, knowing all too well the hypocrisy of some Christians at my expense.

"I let your mother do the raising of you," he told me. "I couldn't file for divorce because I couldn't leave you alone with her. And I know—I know I didn't say much when you were growing up. I didn't know what to talk about. I'm heterosexual, okay?"

I asked my dad if he was dying. Yes, he said, he was, though he was on some drugs the doctor said might help.

I stayed polite. Before we hung up, I told him I loved him. What if he died before I spoke to him again?

Immediately afterwards, my mother called to divulge secrets, saying she couldn't have me thinking all this was her fault. He had recently admitted to cheating on her nearly every day of their twenty-six-year marriage. She also said they'd each been previously married, which she'd never told me, and the four of them had been best friends. Then both couples divorced. After her ex-husband went to live temporarily with my father, she wrote him off completely as a friend. But then my dad "coincidentally" moved into the apartment below hers, and they began to date, marrying in the early seventies.

As she jabbered on, sharing X-rated details about him that I'm still working to delete from my brain, I went blank. My teeth chattered. I hung up and stumbled into David's room, collapsing into a ball on his twin bed, making sounds like some harrowing of hell. He held me tightly for a long time. He didn't shush me or say it was all going to be okay. Afterwards, alone in my room, I swiveled my head side to side like a robot.

THAT NIGHT, WANDERING IN Cambridge along the Charles River, I found myself in a monastery's chapel. Up and down the stone walls I ran my hands, resting my head against the cold solidity, weeping. I was flooded with visions of the strangers my father had been with, their children.

A monk in a black robe startled me. Snot all over my face, in a few sentences I told him about my father. Not knowing what else to say to a man with a wizard's beard, I ended with, "He, he has committed—terrible sins."

"Pray for him," he said softly, handing me another tissue. "But careful, everyone sins, you know. Everyone."

SEVERAL WEEKS LATER at Thanksgiving, I went to see my father in a motel. He was sitting on the hideous floral bedspread, his boxes stacked high on one side. Even when I was little, I never wanted to be alone with him. He put me on high alert.

Under his eyes were white pouches; his eyebrows were electrocuted caterpillars. I handed him a Polaroid in a popsicle-stick frame I made at camp one summer: we're at the Alligator Farm in St. Augustine, in front of Maximo, a fifteen-foot crocodile from Australia. Thanking me for the gift, he started bawling, telling me he wanted to die.

Feeling silly, I took the Bible from the nightstand and read to him about Job on the dung heap; we had been discussing spiritual tests in my Bible as Literature course. He wasn't having it. Instead, he showed me photos he took of ducks in the retention pond outside, something he would've never done before. They mesmerized him. At its bleakest, life was finally precious to him. In crisis, he felt genuine wonder.

Suddenly he sat up straight. "You're going to get it, you know," he said, waving some pamphlet from his doctor, his hands scabby like a lobsterman's. I knew just by speaking I intimidated him.

"I use protection," I said.

"Forty percent of the men in San Francisco—"

"I don't live there!"

"Forty percent! You're going to get it," he said emphatically. "There's no way you won't."

Moving unnoticed through society, he could chat anyone up in his folksy way. He needed his wife and kids as virtue-signaling proof of his manhood—we were action figures in his Republican family-values diorama. To my father, we were each an "it" like the sea biscuits we collected, unreal and expedient. Remember this was a man who didn't stop his wife from molesting their son on a weekly basis. He let her worm her way into me and pulse there with mortifying intimacy.

"You're going to get it, you're going to get it:" in the years to come, what won't I do to lift his death spell? Maybe you can understand why it's been especially hard for me to get close to my students. They're the same age as I was when I was shattered. When I talk to them about their mental health struggles, I see myself in college and freeze.

THAT WINTER SOME NURSE PRACTITIONER put me on Zoloft, which didn't do a thing but space me out. After I quit cold turkey, I was beset by brain shivers and mood swings. I howled in a rainy city park for the Virgin Mary and spent the night in the hospital. Soon after, David's family put me in touch with a therapist named Holly who specialized in mothers and sons. Other than hanging out in chat rooms and watching porn—habits that got so addictive I ripped out the ethernet card from my laptop—I often didn't know what else to do with my free time. Cyberspace reliably drowned out what my parents had recently unloaded on me on the phone and at Thanksgiving. "Keep paying attention to your body," Holly said when I told her about my emerging compulsions, encouraging me to meditate and join clubs. Wasn't there something else she could do?

After some catatonic months I can't remember, I began writing poetry when I should've been doing my assigned reading. Other than going to class and tutoring at a prison, I mostly stayed in my dorm room with thin pillows and thin walls.

Numbness turned into grief-stricken restlessness. After therapy on Friday mornings, even if it was cold, I took public transportation to go on hikes in the Blue Hills Reservation and Arnold Arboretum. The trees made me feel a lot better, but I always held myself back emotionally as I hiked, worried someone would hear me. The intensifying nightmares and flashbacks needed more room.

So I took a bus alone to a yoga center in the Berkshires for a snowshoeing workshop. I thought I would shuffle out of earshot, up some snowy hill in a true wilderness, and from the cold summit, my pain would be sobbed out of me, out into the wild ether. Transcendental altitude.

By the end of the weekend, I hadn't gotten much alone time—there were too many people in the forest—and I disliked snowshoes. I certainly wasn't healed. Over a quinoa breakfast, I did meet a woman who came to the center after divorcing a man she called her "was-band." Priscilla felt uncannily familiar, and not just because she had my mother's name and blue eyes. Her vibe was possessive, but I didn't let myself get sucked in—the yoga, meditation, and time in nature had given me strength. After talking for hours about our problems, we walked to the frozen lake nearby and stood on the windy shore. She unwrapped a peppermint.

Suddenly, the lake made a noise, like a depth charge in a submarine movie but higher pitched, like a thin, long saw that wurbles when shaken. The lake, a big pond really, cracked. It cracked, it crazed, it hushed. What was once solid was splitting, melting in the February sun, setting off a chain reaction of noise. Thoreau heard it too once at Flint's Pond, asking, "Who would have suspected so large and cold and thick-skinned a thing to be so sensitive?" She and I looked at one another, astonished at the sound's unearthliness.

For a moment, we stopped feeling as though we and the lake were distinctly separate beings. Priscilla and I glimpsed our boundlessness. We walked the shore, circumambulating what we'd later call a symbol for a closed heart beginning to open. To help it along, we threw stones at the ice.

THOUGH IT MIGHT READ otherwise at this point, this book is about hope; it's not a tell-all of my family's transgressions—you wouldn't want to know the whole story anyway. But trust the piles of journals in my closet; the divorce papers and medical documents I saved; my first book of poetry with thinly veiled metaphors for my humiliation; the reams of notes in my therapists' locked cabinets; the warnings from teachers and the whispers at school and day camp; the solicitation scrawled by a relative in a public bathroom stall. Trust the flashbacks that I walked a suicidal path to try and blot out.

In college, I confided in a meditation teacher about my upbringing. It was all still fresh. His response was, "I've heard a lot worse," his voice without even a hint of the loving-kindness he taught us on Wednesday nights. "Well," I should've said, "so have I"—because of course we all have. His reaction was another version of "get over it"—if you keep suffering, it's your fault for not letting go, even if it's inconceivable under the circumstances at your age. His comment, rooted perhaps in his own bitterness, kept him feeling like an invincible spiritual referee in a North Face vest.

I WROTE MY WAY OUT of the worst of my devastation. I drafted poems about my parents but hid behind persona, allegory, and description. I wasn't about to remember my past without line breaks, to be literal and nakedly autobiographical, to trust more in sense than sound. In time, as my writing teachers had my work published in highly regarded magazines, I felt adopted by a new family. Writer was an identity apart from Golden Boy and Survivor Freak.

I almost left college but ended up graduating. By the time I was twenty-five, I had worked as a cashier at JCPenney's, waited tables at a sushi restaurant, taught at my old high school and a conservative Jewish middle school, trained as a yoga teacher and energy healer in India, taught "relaxation and breathing" at a homeless shelter, and worked as a temp at a mortgage company. I went to graduate school at Washington University in St. Louis and then on to Stanford University for a fellowship that in the wake of the Great Recession enabled me to finish my first book of poems. At first it was hard to feel excited about the move, since my father had me convinced that San Francisco was where I was going to die. In time, I stopped believing that. After the fellowship ended, I stayed on at Stanford to teach as a lecturer.

Around the same time, a grapefruit-sized tumor was found in my father's transverse colon. New drugs had turned his terminal illness into a manageable disease, but this time I thought he was going to die. My then-partner Chris suddenly broke up with me, saying he no longer had as much "conviction" about our relationship.

Right after we split, I got my first smartphone and downloaded Grindr. All that screen time and hooking up deadened my senses, making other people seem disposable and ghostlike—I had an extraction mindset of my own. I would excuse myself multiple times when out with friends to check my phone in the bathroom. Haunted by the past, I was using the Bay Area's screen-based, sexually liberated culture to numb my C-PTSD symptoms and retraumatize myself.

At the library without my phone, I read Cormac McCarthy's *The Road*, a novel that imagines a father and son journeying through a post-apocalyptic hellscape, the same East Tennessee mountains of my father and his ancestors. Other than T. S. Eliot's *The Waste Land*, I'd never read nothingness conveyed so powerfully. As scientists increasingly sounded the alarm about climate change, *The Road* made me long for nature and a male protector as Grindr took over my life. It became an addiction that got totally out of control. I knew I had to flee from California for remote wilderness where there was no Wi-Fi. Where I could connect with myself and nonhuman creatures apart from my drug of choice, as far away from my family as possible.

So in June 2013, subletting my studio apartment, racking up a credit card balance I couldn't pay off, I headed to the Southern Hemisphere, where the most pristine, accessible reefs were. I would dive the Great Barrier Reef before it was hit with devastating bleaching several years later, as well as the Coral Triangle—Raja Ampat, Komodo National Park, Papua New Guinea, and East Timor in particular. Reefs in the Western Hemisphere, such as in the Keys, had already been decimated, but I longed to return to some healthy version of them, even if they were in the Pacific.

My unconscious magical thinking: if I could dive a "virgin" reef, I would forgive my family and be purified. The trauma circuitry, as I imagined it, would be pulled out of my brain like copper wires from a wall.

Part Two

CHAPTER 9

Lag Time

"Recognition is famously a passage from ignorance
to knowledge."

—AMITAV GHOSH, *The Great Derangement:*
Climate Change and the Unthinkable

On May 9, 2013, one month before I left for my trip, the Mauna Loa Observatory in Hawaii announced that the daily average concentration of CO_2 had hit 400 ppm. By comparison, there was about a third less CO_2 in 1798 when William Blake was writing his famous poem "The Tyger." (Sidenote: more tigers are in captivity in the US than are in the wild on the whole planet.) The last time it was at 400 ppm, 3.5 million years ago, the Arctic had camels and no ice, and sea levels were at least thirty feet higher. Unlike then, global temperatures now are rising quickly over historical time scales rather than slowly over geological ones. In other words, you can see climate change happening with your own eyes, with your skin. Over the past sixty years, in fact, CO_2 levels have been increasing one hundred times faster than they did at the end of the Ice Age. Ecosystems like coral reefs can't adapt quickly enough.

As in the graph I showed my environmental lit students, global temperatures are playing catch-up with the rising CO_2 levels. In other words, the warming effect of a carbon emission might take decades to be felt, but it will be, like a thermostat whose set point is raised or a hot plate that takes time to boil water.

"We live in that lag time," I tell my students as we read the unthinkable future *The Road* imagines. We're flourishing in it—like swarms of mayflies blackening the sky, like a Death Valley superbloom after a wet winter. Deluded about what lies ahead if we don't act decisively, we're staring at screens for most of our waking hours.

Eventually, though, karma slices through self-deception. Our carbon is a set of largely unknown but scary promises, a commitment to an unthinkable future, not just that of distant descendants but also of my students and your children. If we don't act, Mother Nature will use far more than decimated reefs to make us wish we had. She is our teacher.

PROBABLY THE MOST AMAZING creatures I saw on my trip were manta rays. The first time was in the cool waters of Indonesia's Komodo National Park between the scrubby islands of Gili Lawa Laut and Gili Lawa. While I held on to a slimy rock, three or four of these huge cartilaginous fish, ten feet from wingtip to wingtip, were filter-feeding with their gaping mouths in the swift current. To hover, all they had to do was barely flap their wings. Their feeding was majestic. They embodied effortless surrender and patience.

Elsewhere, at my first dive site in Raja Ampat called Manta Sandy, eight of us kneeled side by side in the sand at fifty feet forming a wall of bubbles and waited. Garden eels poked their heads out of their holes and fed on drifting plankton—but I had seen them many times before.

Then I tried to get interested in a tiny pipefish darting its seahorsey eyes around as I peered into them, the equivalent of King Kong looking into a skyscraper window—but my regulator was irritating my gums, my right foot was cramping. Waiting there for twenty minutes, I was beginning to think the dive was hopeless.

Then one supersized manta, and then another, appeared in the distance and glided toward us, swooping above a huge coral head like a pelican passing at an angle over a navigational buoy. It was a cleaning station, consensual and peaceful, for the mantas. On their skin were parasites that butterflyfish rushed up to feast on.

The two mantas might also have been there to communicate. In fact, with the largest brain of any fish, mantas might be able to recognize themselves in mirrors, which experiments by Csilla Ari and Dominic D'Agostino indicate, suggesting self-awareness that even dogs and cats don't have. Before moving on to another huge coral head, they soared and somersaulted beside one another, describing infinity. Underneath my three-millimeter wetsuit, my body was all gooseflesh.

Some months later, I found a video online of Indonesia's Tanjung Luar market, notorious for selling meat from dolphins and other marine megafauna. Dead manta rays were laid out on the concrete floor; each one's huge triangular wings had been sliced off and placed beside the body. In Asia, manta gill rakers are bogusly peddled as an immune booster and cancer cure. The remaining cartilage is sold as cheap filler for shark-fin soup in China and elsewhere. Drift nets and other irresponsible fishing practices also cause large but unknown numbers of manta deaths per year.

For a time after seeing that upsetting footage, when I remembered the mantas soaring at 7:30 a.m., in my mind I could hear the fins slapping against a fiberglass deck, a club bashing the head, a machete slicing off the wings. It was a soundscape of our self-inflicted crisis. Everyone in this globalized economy, in a sense, was wielding those weapons, including me. I felt a sensation like when I was nine and a baseball hit my thumb as I swung. An uncanny pang—a trauma shudder?—ran through me.

ONE AFTERNOON THAT SUMMER off Madang, Papua New Guinea, a vast underwater hillside of scroll coral riddled with fairy basslets astounded me, though the big fish that made these waters famous weren't there. Sulfuric acid from the nearby Ramu Nico Basamuk chemical plant, the worried locals told me, was slowly poisoning Astrolabe Bay.

And any day fishermen might dynamite sections of the reef. They'd be looking to feed their communities, aspiring to the kind of high-consumption lifestyle that we enjoy in the developed world. Such a fishing method, common in the tropics, ruptures the swim bladders of fish and leaves slow-growing reefs in ruins. Even at legally protected reefs in Indonesia, I saw signs of dynamiting: dead fish, ominous rubble. Maybe bobtail squid were also blown to bits—they're bejeweled with symbiotic bioluminescent bacteria that glow like the moon so they don't cast shadows when hunting at night. Olive sea snakes that peer right into your mask as they ascend ninety feet to breathe air. Potato cod as big as my love seat. Bearded sharks. Three hundred bigeye trevally drifting in a channel, resolute as Yemanja's sentries. Acres of coral giving way to seagrass, where cuttlefish hold fast to their secrets.

My dives came to feel devotional. At Osprey Reef off the Great Barrier Reef, a safe distance from dynamite fishermen, one stand of bright-blue coral around a hollow of red anemones had me kneeling in the sand to pray. Feeling my wonder grow, feeling into the mortal threats that reefs face, I began to float away, my palms unclasping. My weight belt was too light.

Many of these creatures could be gone before my generation begins to collect what will be left of Social Security. As Charlie Veron, the world's foremost expert on coral, has said,

There is no hope of reefs surviving to even mid-century in any form that we now recognize. If, and when, they go, they will take with them about one-third of the world's marine biodiversity. Then there is a domino effect, as reefs fail so will other ecosystems. This is the path of a mass extinction event, when most life, especially tropical marine life, goes extinct.

When I floated above the reefs and found myself apologizing to them, the figure of 400 ppm of CO_2 drifting through my mind, I was crying tears of what's been called anticipatory grief. Sometimes I half-expected the reefs to disintegrate right in front of me like damp cotton candy. I know coral bleaching and ocean acidification don't work like that, but still, that's where my mind went.

AFTER A DAY OF DIVING the Great Barrier Reef, I stood on the liveaboard's deck facing the exposed coral of Ribbon Reef #3 at low tide. As I pondered my trip's obscene carbon footprint, my ex-boyfriend and my car came to mind.

A year into our relationship, I bought a used hybrid. When I drove it home, Chris did his best to be happy, despite being a devoted biker who for ethical reasons vowed to never own a car. On my twice-a-week commute to Palo Alto, the Honda got close to fifty miles per gallon. The rest of the time, though, it mostly stayed parked on the street—I felt too guilty to drive much. I did my best to make my purchase seem sweeter, less threatening to us both: I draped a juniper rosary around the rearview mirror; on car trips, we listened to Chris's favorite bands on the stereo when I'd rather have listened to Dolly Parton; and I christened the car "Lambcake."

For him and for me, I thought I had successfully rebranded the $17,000 automobile—which annually lets out about seven concert grand pianos' worth of CO_2—as cute, innocent. But the truth was more complicated. With every mile driven, nearly a half pound of trigonal, covalently bonded molecules called carbon dioxide was spewed out, infinitesimally nudging up global temperatures. By how many tenths of a nanosecond did each mile I drove accelerate the melting of Kilimanjaro's glaciers, the inundation of Battery Park and the Niger Delta, and the acidification of the Coral Sea, so that Ribbon Reef #3 and the rest of the Great Barrier Reef will be just a memory?

Some months later at a birthday party in downtown Oakland, I offhandedly referred to Lambcake as "our" car in front of a mutual acquaintance. "That's not ours," Chris said sternly. "It's *his*," he said, pointing right at me.

Living together at the time, we drove Lambcake to run faraway errands or to go up into the Oakland Hills for hiking. He had offered to pay, based on his use, for part of my car insurance and gas. So his rebuke took me aback.

In retrospect, though, his reaction wasn't a personal attack—it was a moral reflex with which many people, who instinctively understand that we're living on borrowed time, can empathize. Chris helped wake me up to the crisis; he was my eco-teacher, even if I often resisted his sometimes brusque style. Of course he was embarrassed to be named publicly as an accomplice to climate change. Given that our species is responsible for what should instead be called catastrophic planetary warming, melting, and flooding with a mass extinction to boot, how can I blame his defensiveness?

THAT SUMMER IN 2013, along with peer-reviewed research on climate change, I was reading the Transcendentalists, often just before dives. One quote I especially treasured was from the first section of "Nature," where Ralph Waldo Emerson asks, "If the stars should appear one night in a thousand years, how would men believe and adore; and preserve for many generations the remembrance of the city of God which had been shown!" Carson echoes him in the quote on my syllabus for Environmental Literature of Wonder and Crisis. "One way to open your eyes to unnoticed beauty is to ask yourself, 'What if I had never seen this before? What if I knew I would never see it again?'" To wake up from my residual smartphone trance and grow wonder, I asked variations on the same basic question in my mask and fins that summer.

What if once a century the moon, huge and golden during the night dive, showed itself for ten minutes and then disappeared? (In the shallows off East Timor, the moonlight was so bright I turned off my torch. The columns and plates of coral cast shadows. I ascended. I inflated my buoyancy vest and, while waiting for the others, floated on my back like an obese otter.)

How would I look at this whale shark if it were the last one left, not only in Cenderawasih Bay in New Guinea but the whole planet? (It was enormous. Its charcoal skin was splattered with white splotches like bark lichen, its huge dual-lobed caudal fin swishing side to side. I was still angry at the villagers for stealing our gasoline, which meant we had to leave the whale sharks early.)

How would you breathe your next breath if you knew it was your last? How far down would you let your diaphragm go as you inhaled? How long would you extend the exhale? (On land, hardwired fear causes me to hold my breath, activating the stress response: fight, flight, or freeze. But if I hold my breath on a sudden ascent, my lungs could collapse, so I have to keep breathing through my regulator and feel whatever comes up. Rest and digest. Undersea ease, queasiness. Checking my air gauge on the ocean floor, I always see I don't have forever.)

At my safety stops—the last three minutes of a dive spent at five meters to prevent decompression sickness—I often thought of the parable of the surfacing sea turtle. To be given a human life is to have won karmic Powerball. Angelic beings are too happy to want to work on themselves. Hungry ghosts and demons are in so much pain that they can't develop their minds and hearts. Sea biscuits, toads, and damselfish can't practice holding themselves and others in love, at least I don't think. A human life, caught between suffering and bliss, is ideal for awakening. That is one of the greatest gifts, I've come to believe, that you can give the world. At the same time, our very survival demands even more: nonviolent, boots-on-the-ground engagement with people and institutions, with inequality and injustice, as we race to somehow stabilize the planet's climate.

WELCOME TO YOUR DUALISTIC universe, where every moment is obliterated, and anything can happen and does. The castle needs a watchman. The comet hunter must be patient. Can you be there in soft readiness?

You've been marooned here in a body—I mean, did you really choose to be born and fucked with? Change course, let it run, watch the roles of castaway and victim disintegrate. All things degrade, give way to something else. Joy and loss—life and death—are like the algae that partner with coral polyps: one doesn't exist for long without the other. Beauty's mother is Death, poet Wallace Stevens observes. "God is Change," Octavia Butler writes in her novel *Parable of the Sower*. Impermanence is our queen. She astonishes and she slays, and we swoon as if we've just taken physical form, boggled to have fingers and toes. Wake up, wake up, soon we'll be bodiless again.

AS MY DIVE LOG FILLED with names of fantabulous critters I only got to spend seconds with—ghost pipefish with skin indistinguishable from algae, spotted eagle rays that jumped into warp when they saw me—it became even clearer that the degradation of our oceans is "anthropogenic," as the scientific euphemism goes. In other words, we're ruining it. Depending on the year, humans can cause a dead zone the size of New Jersey in the Gulf of Mexico around the Mississippi Delta. Since 1950, we've destroyed over half of the world's reefs, and reef-associated biodiversity has fallen 63 percent. We've pulled 90 percent of large fish from the water.

Several years later, during the back-to-back global bleaching events of 2016 and 2017, half the coral on the Great Barrier Reef died. Quoted in *The Atlantic* in 2018, Terry Hughes, director of the Australian government's coral research program, said, "You could say [the ecosystem] has collapsed. You could say it has degraded. I wouldn't say that's wrong." The chairman of the GBR Marine Park Authority, Ian Poiner, put it more succinctly: "The overall outlook for the Great Barrier Reef is very poor."

Toward the end of my trip, I wasn't just unsettled by my credit card balance. The crisis was viscerally real to me. Though my first book of poetry had been published several months earlier, I realized that as a poet I couldn't express what I was feeling after diving some of the last intact reefs on Earth. I had looked at seahorses, whale sharks, and mantas in the eye. Their vulnerability was unmistakable. Shaken by beauty under threat, I was learning to care about beings other than myself. As Craig Foster says of the cephalopod he befriends in the Netflix documentary *My Octopus Teacher*, "She was teaching me to become sensitive to the other, especially wild creatures."

In remote villages and on liveaboard boats, as I turned away from poetry and began journaling about climate change and nature, the little boy inside me, the one who killed the toads, spoke more loudly. As I recovered an inner sense of safety with the reefs' help, I remembered more and more. My childhood flashbacks and ecological flashforwards, in their entrapment, panic, and doom, felt eerily similar. My mother's emails, as many as five a day, infuriated me when I saw them. It felt impossible to write about climate change without discussing my upbringing, to meditate on our future without thinking about my past.

Economy, ecology, eco-friendly, eco-anxiety: the prefix "eco" comes from the Greek word *oikos* meaning "house" and "family," and by extension "Earth." Perhaps that's why years later I'll often tell my nature-writing undergrads in Virginia, "The ecological is personal, and the personal is ecological." What I won't tell them is how I've lived out those correspondences and why.

CHAPTER 10

Otter

I returned to the United States in August to teach another academic year. In my Bay Area neighborhood of baby strollers pushed by techies staring down at their phones, in the swipe-left world of cyberspace where I spent too much time, I was still hella lonely. The beauty of the coral pulsed in my teeth.

One night I looked at myself shirtless in the bathroom mirror, pushing back one love handle. I leaned to one side and heard my father say, "All my life I've wanted to belong to something." Remembered my Castro therapist telling me, "I don't think you know who you are." Her clothes, her hair, and her armchair were all black, so during our sessions, she was just a pale face—she said my climate pessimism was a projection rooted in my childhood. "If therapy hasn't ever really helped you," she asked after meeting me, "what makes you think I can?"

Then I raked at my chest hair and took a selfie with the phone I used for texting my mother, reading Virginia Woolf, and getting on Grindr. I stood up straight and scowled. My mind replayed the young Pacific Heights doctor recently telling me on a date while cradling my head, "You're so cute I should take a box cutter to your face—to bring you down some notches, Otter Boy."

Indeed, I wasn't a twink. A few years before, gay culture's label for a fairly slim, hairy fellow—"otter"—took off, a trimmer version of a cub or bear. In Northern California, I was a textbook example of one, I suppose. My beard was bigger than ever. I'd stopped shaving off my body hair, which had a lumbersexual power there that it didn't in the South.

After only a few months back, I had to get away from San Francisco—from touchscreens and men, the not-so-classy bars where I got drunk and wrote poems in my head as Miley Cyrus songs played—and go smell the cold ocean and put my arm in it. I missed the sea. I longed for solitude in nature, resonance like I felt sixteen years before with Adrienne Rich's poetry, surrounded by the creatures in my backyard. Dreaming of a common language, I wanted to see otters in the wild.

WHEN I WAS GROWING UP, everyone in my family but me had an animal. Not a pet, mind you—they were too much mess and fuss—but a goofy mascot, a cartoon character standing for either power or powerlessness. My father was a moose; my mother a sheep; Papo a bear; Mamo a mouse.

In ordinary ways, usually egged on by my mother, my family's animals expressed themselves. It began, maybe, when she was a child riding on Papo's back as he growled like a grizzly. My grandparents and I would *squeak* and *grrr* at one another over the phone, trying to express inexpressible affection, made urgent by Alzheimer's and Parkinson's. To acknowledge that for all the sweetness, we were still animals.

Every holiday my mother bought me a moose-themed Hallmark card to give my father. *Not a creature was stirring, not even a moose,* one card read. *Merry Kissmoose.* Another: *I moose say you're a great dad!* When pleased with a good grade or a passably immaculate room, she might *baaa* and exclaim, "Hoof check!" and I showed my "hooves," my hands making awkward Vulcan live-long-and-prosper signs. Even mint jelly made her grimace—a waiter would tell us about the mutton special, and she'd declare, as if we had religious objections, "Heavens, no, we don't eat *lamb*," and give us a wry, dire smile.

She even had a plush toy named Brownie. She was her lamb daughter, an ovine teddy bear bought at a Black Friday sale at JCPenney. Sometimes Brownie, who was in fact a light beige, would join us at the dinner table. My mother would make Brownie talk and move.

"You're stinky, Greg."

"I love apples."

"Ringo Starr is a hunk!"

My family members, I should make clear, never tried to resemble their animals, like the burly man I met in Papua New Guinea who was ritually scarred to resemble a crocodile, the most sacred creature of the Sepik River. Not part of some cosmic mythology, their five creatures were playful, necessary identities—masks to don when my family's more authentic selves were too scary. They were a way to pretend that abuse wasn't happening. To bring order to the chaos, to plaster camaraderie over distrust.

"So what's my animal?" I would ask Mother.

"You're Pegory, of course." Even with prodding, her answer never went beyond that. When I was a baby, a very big one, she bounced me on her knee and said in a halting, singsongy way, "GREgory—is PEgory—a bouncing baby BOY!" I'm told I would giggle. What this mythical creature Pegory looks like I still don't know, but I picture a mindless sprite with a pot belly and a few tentacles.

Needing, perhaps, to carry on the family tradition, I gave animal names to my three exes—Lemur, Raccoon, and Seahorse, respectively. Lemur called me Greggie. Seahorse called me Slugger (he was also Coach). Raccoon half-heartedly called me Giraffe but only to make me happy.

Really though, what was my animal?

I PLANNED A LONG WEEKEND south in Santa Cruz, where Adrienne Rich spent her final twenty years and had recently died. Observing sea otters cavorting in Monterey Bay, getting as close as the Marine Mammal Protection Act allowed, I hoped to better understand the animal label that men online and at bars were giving me.

When confronted with real sheep at a petting zoo, my mother was relatively unimpressed. The emblem, not the living animal, mattered. On my excursion, though, I wanted to get as close as possible to my potential animal mascot. I also hoped to meet, away from the Bay, an earthy, less jaded man. Someone wild yet reliable.

So I posted a Craigslist ad with the subject "Visiting Otter." In it I announced, "i'm coming to santa cruz next week to research sea otters and would like to meet good guys to get beers with and see what happens," and included a measurement I'd rather not repeat here. The first guy to respond was someone I'll call Jake:

> good luck trying to find all those things you want in this town, seriously... i have some body hair, but not as much as you may be looking for. i live in the mountains but can travel anywhere in the county. here's a picture. would be cool to hear back from you either way.

Jake was smoking hot. Behind him in his pic was the carved head of a pronghorn wearing a leather mask, and a tapestry of a big buck in a meadow.

I GOT TO THE NUDE BEACH early and felt as if I had entered a different dimension, one in which there is no cell service, and a few men, wandering the cliffs above, seemed on perpetual alert for enemy ships. *This town is weird for hooking up*, Jake texted me earlier. *I basically only have sex at the beach. lol.* As I sat in the sand waiting, a short man nearby was walking along the mouth of a river. Then he charged hundreds of gulls, scattering them. Keeping him in the corner of my eye, I scanned the sea: nothing but rough waves, spume, and the occasional drifting kelp bulb. The southern sea otter, I read, prefers calm waters.

Standing up to stretch, I saw a man with a swimsuit-calendar body walking down the dune path. It was Jake, frowning. *Am I too hairy?* I wondered. *Not fit enough?* Within the first ten minutes, as if to convince me to be wary, he told me that he couldn't work full-time because of a disability; he hadn't had a boyfriend in ten years; he grew and sold what he called his "medicine," which I can attest today is the dankest organic bud south of Mendocino. Nothing he said fazed me. We soon found a spot under a brambly cliff to sunbathe. "The rangers won't bother us here," he said, handing me a joint. I was fairly new to pot so I asked him to light it for me.

As I brought up my "research," he rubbed his tan, mostly smooth chest and stomach. Sea otters have the densest fur of any mammal, I told him, with up to a million hairs in a postage stamp-sized area. An entire human head typically has one hundred thousand. He fluffed the curly gray hairs between his pecs. "Months of dry brushing gave me those," he said, his voice cracking. After years of being rejected by men for being too smooth, he now avoids gatherings of hairy men—it's simply too painful. Of his older brother, who was considerably hairier, he simply said, "It's not fair." With a flourish of mild disgust, he gestured to little bumps I hadn't noticed on his sides. "Must be my well water," he said in his SoCal surfer way.

Then a clean-shaven man in only a black bomber jacket walked onto the beach, his blondish-gray hair carefully parted. "Watch your step," Jake told me, "that's Seaweed Man."

"Who?"

"He puts kelp bulbs in his butt."

"Gracious!"

"Then throws them back onto the sand."

Horrified, my mind churned, thinking of a documentary I'd seen on kelp and climate change. Without otters, the kelp that Seaweed Man collected for internal use would rarely wash ashore. Sea urchins, with their five self-sharpening teeth, eat away at the kelp holdfasts on the ocean floor, causing the one-hundred-foot plants to float away like balloons. The forest ecosystem collapses, and the virtual wasteland that's left is called an urchin barren.

Once otters return, though, the situation reverses: they crack open the urchins and eat up to a third of their body weight daily. Until 1938, when a small population was discovered under Bixby Bridge in Big Sur, sea otters were considered extinct in California due to overhunting. Since then, otter populations have rebounded, and so too have kelp forests, one of the most efficient absorbers of CO_2 around. Research by Chris Wilmers and colleagues indicates that kelp ecosystems absorb twelve times more greenhouse gases when otters are present. The extra carbon that North Pacific kelp forests sequester every year because of otters is equivalent to taking at least three million passenger cars off the road.

Given this research, I can't exactly judge Seaweed Man. I think he means well. He's an extreme example of biophilia, which biologist E. O. Wilson defined as "the innate tendency to focus on life and lifelike processes." Maybe he thought of the kelp as medicine for his childhood trauma. Maybe he wants to feel like less of a zombie in this culture— who wouldn't want to merge with something that pure when so much else is a scam? Or maybe all his family had plant names but him.

THE NEXT DAY I FANTASIZED about renting a tandem kayak with another otter dude at Elkhorn Slough, the best place in California to see wild otters. That didn't happen. Jake couldn't come, and no one else promising had responded to my ad. With cheap binoculars, I went alone.

Looming over the estuary were the tall, twin stacks of the Moss Landing Power Plant, which at the time emitted 3.5 megatons of CO_2 a year burning methane. But in a kelp ecosystem roughly the size of West Virginia, it's calculated that the presence of otters annually results in 4.4 to 8.7 more megatons of CO_2 being removed from the atmosphere. There's not that much difference between the two sets of figures; and global use of coal-fired electricity, driven by China, continues to grow even now in the 2020s.

Above me, Priuses whooshed over a bridge as I paddled against the tide into the estuary; a big rig blasted its horn. An unbearable smell blew in from the nearby dairy farms and from the stained dock where a seal colony lazed. I headed toward the opposite bank lined with eucalyptus, my paddle cutting through putrid froth.

Then to my left, I saw him: like a meerkat peeking from its burrow, a sea otter popped its head, and half of its body, out of the water. He—the estuary is overwhelmingly male—had a quizzical expression on his face, like a perplexed, bemused reference librarian, and proceeded to float on his back. In his paws he held a fat innkeeper, the pink worm Koreans eat raw. He tore into it like an overcooked corn dog.

How can I be with you without scaring you away? I silently asked him.

He dove and disappeared.

Several minutes later, a second otter popped up, this one whiter. Floating on his back, he rubbed his ears in circles, then scrubbed his diamond-shaped nose pad. He kicked his webbed hind feet, barrel-rolling as he swam away. Another otter bit his neck playfully and rolled on with him.

I kept paddling.

I came to Seal Bend, where I saw what looked like a partially submerged oyster bed. As I got closer, I realized it was forty or so otters congregating in what's called a raft. At Elkhorn Slough, rafts nearly always consist of males floating close together, often holding paws. It was an adorable sight. Down from a couple of beached seals, I paddled my kayak up onto a sandbar to watch the raft, a distant truck beeping as it backed up. One otter, perhaps the watchman, stared intently at me between his feet.

Pushing off from the sandbar, I paddled to the side of the raft, euphoric to see so many otters but still giving them a wide berth, and some lines from Whitman came to me, the otters swimming closer and closer to one another—

I will make inseparable cities with their arms about each other's necks,
By the love of comrades,
By the manly love of comrades.

Tenderness; acceptance; solidarity; safe, platonic touch; even basic safety—when had I truly felt them with a group of men?

Forty otters made me want something that seemed impossible: belonging. All at once they dove and were gone.

On my OkCupid profile, I joked that I wanted an otter as the ring bearer at my wedding—honestly, I wasn't serious. It was a wholesome, quirky image meant to liquefy the heart of a future boyfriend. *Imagine it padding down the aisle*, I wrote, *with a cushion on its back*. Though I wasn't ready for marriage, I did want to doze in safety with an equal. A comrade who wouldn't use me, who could love me just as I was.

AFTER I CAME BACK HOME, I found a research paper by Heather S. Harris and colleagues with the title "Lesions and Behavior Associated with Forced Copulation of Juvenile Pacific Harbor Seals (*Phoca vitulina richardsi*) by Southern Sea Otters (*Enhydra lutris nereis*)." It had been referenced in a slew of shocked blog posts and nature articles with titles like "Otter-be Ashamed of Yourself." It was found that male sea otters, to put it bluntly, are rapists. They will have intercourse with a baby seal, male or female, until it dies and hold on to the body for up to a week, using it from time to time for their own pleasure. Sometimes victims are female otters: a tenth of all mating attempts, in fact, are lethal for them.

In one horrific case observed by the researchers at Monterey in May 2011, a male otter went up to a male seal pup onshore and tried immobilizing him with his mouth and front paws. The pup soon escaped to the water, but the otter chased him and grabbed his head, chomping down on his nose again and cutting it badly. For a quarter of an hour, perpetrator and victim spun around in the water. After 105 minutes, the pup was dead. The otter released him and began grooming himself.

AFTER I FINISHED THE ARTICLE, the room was too small, and my body was a throbbing fist. I felt nauseated. Picked at my beard and eyebrows, swiveling my head. Wanted to get on Grindr. A familiar alarm was ringing through me. Still, I felt tenderness for the seal pup, identifying with it—with him—in ways I couldn't grasp.

I remembered the panic attack I had when Chris and I were in Los Angeles taking care of his brother's newborn twins. That afternoon, I wanted to scream or run or both. It was hard to breathe in that tiny, dark apartment of theirs. With two babies, not just one. Babies had always weirded me out, and I avoided them at all costs. ("The survivor's overriding fear is a repetition of the trauma," Judith Herman writes. "In early stages of recovery, the survivor often avoids the unbearable thought of repetition by shunning children.") I was sure we'd drop them and damage them for life. Maybe Chris wanted to test-drive us as married with children, but my parents seemed the only possible characters for us to play in such a dress rehearsal.

As Herman reminds me, the kind of terror I felt from simply being alive—sometimes called dysphoria or annihilation panic—"cannot be terminated by ordinary means of self-soothing." When I was in that kind of distress, I didn't have comforting internalized images of parents to rely on; instead, I felt like a disintegrating beanbag chair pimpled with pain. It took what she calls "a major jolt to the body" for me to come out of it. For those with C-PTSD, that could take such forms as self-mutilation, drug abuse, eating disorders, or sex. "I do it to prove I exist," said one survivor quoted by Herman.

After stretches of slutting it up in California, I retreated from the world, trying like some dead poet locked in a tower to write and "be spiritual." Once the loneliness got unbearable, I sought out once again the kaleidoscopic offerings of hooking up: pleasure, punishment, validation, and numbness. Living in that hamster wheel kept me from having to deal with my childhood.

Feeling doomed as I thought our planet was, I didn't know who I was. But I knew I wanted to belong to something, to stop bringing myself down so many notches. Could dry brushing help?

Otters repulsed me. The otters I saw in the wild didn't understand my self-involved questing, just as starfish don't know what Etsy is. They reminded me not to sentimentalize nature, which can be brutal, even by human standards. Coral polyps, for instance, sting other species of coral and expel their stomachs to digest them, the battle lines visible between colonies. Bumphead parrotfish ram their heads into live coral to feed more easily.

Let's hold hands and float together!

IN THE YEARS AFTER her divorce, my mother wasn't so interested in sheep. Brownie was put in a drawer. Instead, she had two tuxedo alley cats, Sylvester and Miri. She also took good care of the hedgehog boot brush I gave her one Christmas. Henrietta was her name, she decided. "Nein! Nein!" she made Henrietta shriek with a spot-on German accent.

Ever since I left for college, for months at a time I refused to speak to her, but I always came back. She didn't give me money, but she'd offer to take the two of us on luxury trips to places like the Galápagos.

In Bali, staying at both Four Seasons resorts, we had a private plunge pool and a butler who unpacked our luggage and put our neatly folded clothes in teak drawers. Initially, she demanded I always hold the door for her and pull out her chair at restaurants.

"No way, I'm not your gigolo," I finally had to say, practicing saying no to her. After every trip, I swore I'd never do it again. She liked to have me to herself.

One afternoon when my mother was visiting and we were walking along Monterey Bay, I offhandedly asked if she had long-term care insurance, which would defray the costs of a nursing home or home health nurse if she ever needed it. She had recently turned seventy. Whatever she did to me, I didn't want her to suffer. Her money wasn't limitless—she hadn't worked for pay in forty years.

Glaring at me, she said, "Do you think I have Alzheimer's? Because I don't." I tried to explain that wasn't what I meant, but she was furious.

Eventually we came to Lover's Point and shared an oceanside bench. She pulled her windbreaker hood over her head. She crossed her arms. In silence we watched the bobbing kelp bulbs.

"Hey, Mother, there's an otter!" I exclaimed, pointing to a big one.

"Looks like a log," she said, clearing her throat in her over-the-top way, as if a fishbone were caught in there.

My eyes blurred. "See, he's sleeping," I croaked.

"Ah, I—yes, I think I see it now."

I took several big breaths, staring at the clouds obscuring the sun. "Do I look like one?"

"Not really," she said, pulling her wool mittens tight over her hooves. "Why on earth do you ask?"

CHAPTER 11

Ice

Naturally, as marriage is about to be legalized for you and you're a bachelor, you might think about bodies in orbit, especially your favorite moon.

Enceladus, an icy satellite of Saturn, is mine. In my third-grade presentation on Saturn, though, I didn't mention it. It was just a white pinhead pricking my model's Styrofoam ring system. Years would pass until NASA discovered the subsurface ocean that made Enceladus famous. Liquid water, necessary for life as we know it, had never been detected on another world. Bursts of that salty sea, rich with organic compounds and all six elements required for life, are shot up into space from cryovolcanoes on Enceladus, creating Saturn's E ring.

Something's comforting about those ice geysers. They were erupting while Halley's comet burned in the Etruscan sky, causing panic and awe—as my great-great-great-great grandfather Rhodum taught his son Rhodum to plow the soil of Harrison County, Ohio—when my mother as the Big Bad Wolf and my father as Little Red Riding Hood won the costume contest on their honeymoon cruise—*guggagugga boom! Whoosh!*

And it was doing it when I left California for the summer of 2014 to sublet a friend's room in Brooklyn, attempting another geographical cure. Nico and Billy, two guys I was acquainted with from Florida, invited me over for the Fourth of July. After a round of bourbon, they showed me their wedding album. Six years earlier, though not legally recognized, they were married in Florida.

I studied the photos. Up at the makeshift altar, Nico is reading his vows to Billy, trying not to cry. Billy's brother plays the guitar next to some peace lilies. Later, Billy is dancing with his mother, who barely closes her eyes, as if she never wants to forget this moment with her son.

Thumbing through the album, I thought to myself: *I want that too.* Growing up in the Deep South, I hadn't ever wanted a husband. But then and there, when I was ready to see it, I realized I did; well, at least I wanted the option. Truth be told, I'd never even been to a gay wedding.

Like many partnered queer men in the Bay Area, Chris and I weren't monogamous. It had been at my urging, which was more about self-medicating than expressing freedom. On the other hand, Nico and Billy—like Galápagos albatrosses, *Schistosoma mansoni* flatworms, and shingleback skinks—were seemingly monogamous. I glanced up at them still playfully bantering after a decade together. They were best friends comfortable in each other's presence, with a large social support network, hobbies and passions, and meaningful work.

Not to turn Nico and Billy into a heteronormative PSA, but this is what hit me that night: it was time for me to grow up. I was thirty-four. Most of my friends were married with children, including the cheerful guy I met years ago on Manhunt.com who recently had adopted a daughter with his husband. It seemed even my mother might wed the short, wealthy birdwatcher she met on a European river cruise.

On the other sofa was our mutual friend Nick, a sarcastic, thoughtful guy I grew up with, his cancer in remission. Next to him was his boyfriend, who would take his last name when they later married.

MOTHERSHIP

As children, Nick and I reluctantly competed in potato sack races on our school baseball diamond; dodgeball frightened us. In high school, he drew hilarious cartoon pictures of me, and I'd write him thinly veiled love poems. When he came out soon after I did, we bitched for hours in his car about people thinking that being gay is a sinful choice instead of a superpower. Finally, a friend who truly understood, a cute, brilliant one at that. In a silly teenage way, I was convinced Nick and I would fall madly in love, but he didn't like me back. I wasn't jealous seeing him with his future husband, but I did want to know his secret for thriving in long-term relationships.

LATER THAT NIGHT in Brooklyn, we walked several blocks to Nick's apartment. After some Whitney Houston sing-a-longs, we climbed onto the roof to watch the fireworks over Manhattan. Something in me needed to detonate. I was the only single person there. Huddled together were Nico and Billy, and Nick and his boyfriend, and all the other couples lit by pyrotechnic stars arcing like the icy bits of ocean falling back to Enceladus, like the blood spurting from the neck of Chinnamasta, the self-capitated Tantric goddess who grants self-control to all who can receive it.

As we watched the fireworks, the center of my chest quivered. "Love does not consist of gazing at each other," Antoine de Saint-Exupéry writes, "but in looking outward together in the same direction"—but isn't it both? I was stuck in an episode of *Sex and the City*, without the money, svelte body, and readership of Sarah Jessica Parker's character. "Maybe some women aren't meant to be tamed," she says after her ex's engagement party. "Maybe they need to run free. Until they find someone just as wild to run with."

After the fireworks, I bolted. On the subway, I breathed in courage, breathed out self-hatred. Sitting with my annihilation panic, I watched it turning into yearning—the longing to create a family.

Ice

Was it any wonder I was single?

Even if it was irrational, I feared marriage because I didn't want to recreate some version of my parents' shitshow marriage, *Brokeback Mountain* meets *Mommy Dearest*. I was still beside myself, plagued with flashbacks and panic. I'd wake up from nightmares about my family and be consumed by gross feelings. When on a date or with friends, the slightest thing could get me feeling I might be in danger. Commitment for me meant entrapment and imprisonment—because when the excitement died down in a relationship, I once again became a humiliated child.

Days in Brooklyn were spent writing in my little room, trying to stay cool with flavored fizzy waters. My phone was in a lockbox timer. But around 5:00 p.m., the box unlocked, and I got online and Ubered all over Bushwick and Williamsburg to meet up with stoned, sleeve-tattooed hipsters. To them, I was a cliché—another sad, inconsequential writer trying to feel like Joan Didion in New York. I had to stop hooking up, but I didn't know how. The pressure was on.

Home one night from a bar where a Dutch naval officer rebuffed me, I watched an episode of *Obsessed*, an A&E documentary series in which a therapist works with OCD patients in their homes. Cindee, a wiry Wisconsin mother of five, exercises so obsessively that she can't care for her kids and her health is shaky. Over several weeks, Dr. Shana Doronn comes over to her house and establishes trust, slowly exposing her to triggers of greater intensity. This is called exposure therapy.

In the climactic scene, Dr. Doronn gives Cindee thirty-two minutes on the living-room treadmill, and that's it. They sit on the sofa, where Cindee is forced to feel what she's been numbing with endorphins and rushing. She wants to exercise, but she can't.

As her withdrawal intensifies, Cindee's hand raps uncontrollably against her water bottle. "Don't fight this," Dr. Doronn coaches her.

"Let this pass through you." Cindee glares ahead into space as if she's about to drive off a bridge.

After some minutes of pure agony, Cindee begins to soften. She starts weeping, remembering how her compulsions have hurt her kids and husband.

"When I saw the physical manifestations of Cindee's anxiety," Dr. Doronn tells the interviewer, "this told me that the exposure was working. She's just now learning to tolerate any emotion."

The episode had me fantasizing that Dr. Doronn could come to my apartment at 9:00 p.m. on Friday and Saturdays to coach me when I was most triggered. Regardless, the wisest part of me knew I needed an inner Dr. Doronn for C-PTSD so I could experience intolerable feelings without acting them out.

Diving underwater or teaching in my classroom, I wasn't triggered. But what about on cold, rainy days when I called friends and they didn't answer? What about those moments I told myself nothing mattered because we're all fucked anyway? Even with an accountability buddy to frantically text, blockers on my devices, and vows to myself to contribute $250 to repugnant conservative causes each time I acted out, I couldn't consistently resist my triggers. The Lt. Gen. Michael T. Flynn Legal Defense Fund was the richer for it.

Pain, Cindee and I will learn, does subside. We can rehearse feeling safe no matter what, like a stoplight parrotfish sleeping in the mucus bubble it belches for protection. Feeling safe when we're scared. When we're craving something that we've sworn off.

When I felt frozen in my bachelorhood, I sometimes thought of Enceladus: its commitment to Saturn, its water underneath so much ice.

ENCELADUS, I'M ALONE. Would you shine in my dark room tonight? Show me how to not scratch an itch. Restore me, not my phone, to my factory settings, before the compulsions began. Let me dive your virgin ocean, which has no microplastics or sewage.

Tugging on you, dividing the ice of your south pole, stretching you, squashing you, keeping the water liquid with the gigawatts of twenty power stations, Saturn's gravity is your master. Elliptical orbit, tidal heating—injury, relief, more injury—it all just happens. You didn't ask to live with huge, uncontrollable forces. ("Don't try to make things turn out your way," the Burmese monk told me at his monastery. "Know what is happening as it is.")

When you're closest to Saturn, your dark cracks called tiger stripes are at their narrowest; as you speed away, they widen. This causes your ice geysers to intensify at your south pole, spraying sno-cone grit that I can see backlit by the sun almost a billion miles away.

Enceladus, please dim for me slightly, so without squinting I can fly above Hassan and Samad and Julnar and craters not yet named, and touch down. So I can send and receive the needed telemetry. I don't care if I die trying to reach your center.

I've landed; I'm walking Dunyazad's snowy rim. Now I'm skidding across the finer-than-talcum Sarandib Planitia, looking up at Earth—home of dragaliciously Mardi Gras–colored peacock mantis shrimp and my father's tackle box—from the bottom of Daryabar Fossa. I leap into an ice chasm, Damascus Sulcus or Alexandria Sulcus, I'm not sure which, falling for miles through flurries until I hit water, swimming down, jetting down to the bottom of your ocean, where your silicate core begins and dissolves.

I switch on my torch: is that coral? I turn it off again. Orange specks and threads are glowing off and on. My instruments are sure: there are amino acids. Heartbeats. Enceladus, beneath your ice is life!

CHAPTER 12

Trees

Five o'clock in Oakland, almost a year after Brooklyn. After searching online all day for a husband, I finally left my apartment.

I was numb from exchanging messages with men like the Berkeley ski instructor with a Brachiosaurus tattoo on his neck. After some pleasantries, he told me he wanted to take me for a "test drive." With two taps on the screen, I blocked him.

I looked out the window at the withered poppies. This was California's worst year for drought in over a millennium, some rural counties almost running out of water. I was feeling parched too, thirsty for connection. My needs were clearer to me: I was ready to leave the Golden State for good, hopefully for a tenured professorship in a more affordable area. But there I was, trying to track down the man of my California dreams as if he were a rare, vintage E.T. toy on eBay.

Only the men who ignored me seemed marriageable, like the blond, ripped physician eleven miles away who in his shirtless profile pic was holding a puppy beside an alpine lake. He was, the app told me, one of its most popular members. With my muffin top, I'd never look as good as he did poolside in Palm Springs for his thousands of

Instagram followers. I bet his rent wasn't half his take-home pay. He was out of my league, even if I couldn't have said it at the time. By the time shadows stretched across my rug, I disliked myself even more.

I sat outside in the only place I knew to: near the big maple.

It was around this time I read *Buddha's Brain* by psychologist Rick Hanson, a senior fellow at the Greater Good Science Center at UC Berkeley. Rick's book turns the latest peer-reviewed neuroscience research into mental trainings such as the H.E.A.L. technique. H.E.A.L. stands for:

- Have a positive experience.
- Enrich it.
- Absorb it.
- Link it with negative material (optional).

It's not pseudoscience. It's a commonsense practice with ancient roots. In Patañjali's *Yoga Sutras* from about two millennia ago, it's called *pratipaksha bhavana*, the practice of gently, steadfastly replacing negative thoughts with positive ones. Positive experiences can be consciously recalled, Hanson reminds us, but they must also be installed, as neuroscience research into memory consolidation by Jonathan L. C. Lee and others suggests is possible. "Imagine or feel that the experience is entering deeply into your mind or body," Hanson writes in *Buddha's Brain*, "like the sun's warmth into a T-shirt, water into a sponge, or a jewel placed in a treasure chest in your heart." As I already knew, neurons that wire together fire together. With practice, sad memories—or frightening, humiliating ones—can be brightened, despite what our negativity tells us. We can get better and better at unconditionally accessing "the perfection underlying life"—those are painter Agnes Martin's words, pointing to the joy of what she calls "the untroubled mind."

Depressed on his couch, William Wordsworth unwittingly practices H.E.A.L. in his poem "I Wandered Lonely as a Cloud." He recalls the daffodils he saw with his sister Dorothy, and his "heart with pleasure fills." He allows himself to savor the feeling and install it more deeply in his brain. As those sad memories are reconsolidated in the hippocampus, they bring with them the happiness of seeing the daffodils. For years I'd been loosely practicing H.E.A.L. without realizing it: with the mantas in Komodo National Park, with the greenish waves I'd stare at as a teenager in Florida.

Neuroplasticity is my greatest hope. When I feel like a terrible person, I can call up a time when I felt upstanding, intensify that feeling, and imagine it seeping into my unworthiness. Over time, that inner sense of badness is eroded. H.E.A.L. works against the brain's built-in negativity bias, which leads us to downplay the positive and focus on the negative. For instance, I remember one student evaluation—"Wren [sic] tells you exactly what you should & shouldn't believe. Don't believe in global warming? Don't take it, you won't pass"—but I forget the many favorable ones. In other words, as Hanson puts it, we're "Velcro for the bad and Teflon for the good."

Since college, my mindfulness had been slowly strengthening—frankly, I'd wasted so much time online that I was often guilted into meditating. It was a binge-purge cycle of screen time and hooking up followed by digital detox and celibacy. Awareness of the problem wasn't enough to stop it. But what I could do was practice holding myself in compassion and H.E.A.L.-ing when I was triggered. I knew the social media apps, hacking into our need for connection, were painstakingly designed to be addictive. That porn, and presumably Grindr, is at least as addictive as cocaine. Nevertheless, it was my charge to figure out how to unhook. Consciousness is indeed our workspace.

SITTING NEAR THE MAPLE out back, I pretended the tree was one of Giotto's 700-year-old frescoes in the Scrovegni Chapel in Italy—once I passed through the airlock, they gave me only fifteen minutes to bask under the azurite blue of the vaulted ceilings. Then I pretended I was a curious eel that shimmied onshore to this backyard to experience the terrestrial unknown—you have five minutes, I told myself as the tree dazzled me, till you have to get back to San Francisco Bay or you'll asphyxiate.

The maple leaves looked greener. Sharper. My mindfulness deepened: I was more with the nuances of my breath, less with the idea of it, each leaf with its seven pointy lobes curling a bit. As I had this positive experience, I imagined the maple filling the husband-shaped hole in my heart, letting it link with my sense of defectiveness. In the gathering wind, the branches rose and fell. The whole tree, I sensed, was vibrating. Its leaves and limbs, phloem and xylem. Electrons and subquark strings.

Branches fell; branches rose; leaves quivered.

More than anything else, the many leaves reminded me of the multiverse theory, which postulates that there are an infinite number of universes. They're constantly being born, expanding, and dying out, like froth bubbles at the mouth of a fiddler crab. Because atoms can be arranged in only so many ways, stuff endlessly recurs in those universes.

Anything is possible.

In other words, infinite copies of the maple exist in the multiverse; that exact moment was happening an infinite number of times elsewhere. Right now, countless maples and Muppets and manatees are writing about a man in sweatpants typing this self-conscious sentence. In endless elsewheres, the maple is a pile of rotting logs after dying from decades of megadrought; essentially immortal, it's made of steel and home to thousands of winged, fire-breathing lemurs; able to speak English and Mandarin, it tells humanity how to change our ways.

In endless elsewheres, you are robber baron and Seaweed Man, caretaker and undertaker, nomad and homesteader—dynamite fisherman, grandmother, and hero. Adrienne Rich responds to my letter, and we correspond off and on for years. When I'm two, Dr. Doronn stages an intervention, coaching my parents to sit with their feelings and practice tolerating discomfort—we undergo remarkable healing. My father and I take camping trips; he teaches me what I'm having to teach myself now. You're me. I'm your mother. We're a raft of otters.

No moment is ever lost. Whatever you can imagine is true.

The multiverse theory says our fictions are someone else's facts: in a sense, what we imagine is documentary footage of other universes, unwitting reconnaissance of their multiplicities. In alternate universes, our visions of paradise and the underworld are realities; cavewomen ride pterodactyls, and mermen sing to sailors; our lives are someone else's admonishing fables. The laws of physics are rewritten over and over.

"If every second of our lives recurs an infinite number of times," writes Milan Kundera in *The Unbearable Lightness of Being*, "we are nailed to eternity as Jesus Christ was nailed to the cross." He goes on to declare that Nietzsche considered "the idea of eternal return the heaviest of burdens," but that kind of infinitude is reassuring: we don't have to be perfect this go-around.

I reached for my phone. *Dr. Adonis of the Alpine Lake*, I wondered, *did you hit me up?* No. And in the most obvious move, I turned it off.

With a weapon of mass distraction, it was all too easy to escape. When my rage toward super PAC-funded climate change deniers overwhelmed me, I could text a cuddle buddy. When I visualized my maple dying in the Bay Area's increasingly arid climate, I could binge on YouTube videos about the multiverse that implied endless copies of the tree are thriving—or I could imagine human beings whose circle of compassion includes not only loved ones and pets, but also strangers, human and nonhuman, across nations, habitats, and centuries.

Uncontaminated ecosystems exist on other copies of Earth, but not this one. *Yeah, but I don't want another Earth,* I said to myself as a squirrel raced up the trunk. *And Enceladus is way too cold.*

BACK INSIDE MY APARTMENT, I turned my phone back on to load a PDF of *Travels* by William Bartram, the British naturalist who explored the Florida wilderness before the Revolutionary War. Ignoring messages from two new dudes, I swiped to my favorite passage, when Billy is sitting by the St. Johns River at Lake George in 1766, only a hundred miles upstream from where I grew up.

After smoking some weed Jake had given me, I saw myself with Willy underneath a huge live oak. We've finished a supper of jerky and oranges. He pours me another glass of muscadine wine, and we're together in silence at twilight, slapping at mosquitoes. I pick a bit of moss from his shirt; he flicks an ant from mine. After a while he scribbles in his journal by candlelight—"the balmy winds breathed the animating odours of the groves around me; and as I reclined on the elevated banks of the lake, at the foot of a Live Oak, I enjoyed the prospect of its wide waters, its fringed coasts, and of the distant horizon"—until the nib of his quill pen breaks.

Resting my head on his shoulder, I show him my phone, which he says is magic, and explain the multiverse theory, which he says with a laugh is heresy. I teach him the basics of climate change, and eventually he gets it—the geophysics behind the greenhouse effect isn't new or all that difficult.

"Sometimes I wish I weren't alive, at least not in the twenty-first century," I say.

"On the contrary, the mere mention of victuals in thy era doth evoke my envy," Willy replies, burping loudly.

I don't think he can relate. As the starry scruffs of sky brighten and an alligator bellows like a husky-voiced engine, the live oak slowly shapeshifts into my maple, our backs adjusting to the new, miraculous bark.

Then, flying over us toward a palmetto, a whip-poor-will drops a note from its beak: *Come back home to visit*, my mother wrote in her bubbly cursive, *I'm worried about you.*

I'm too exhausted and weirdly happy to leave. Willy Bartram and I are, as he will later write, "lulled asleep by the mixed sounds of the wearied surf, lapsing on the hard beaten shore." As long as I can, I want to stay here having this positive experience, enriching it, absorbing it, linking it with my intimacy fears. Here in the imagination, where anything is possible and I think I've escaped the worst.

CHAPTER 13

Return

Hut's on fire!
Jolted awake, I heard my hut on stilts crackling. My mosquito net blew about as if birds were trying to escape. It was the end of 2016, my first night back to Raja Ampat in a year. I smelled lightning.

I switched on my headlamp. No fire I could see. Through gaps in the floorboards, I saw the lagoon below. High tide. The wind was gusting harder. Storm surge and thunderclaps. Part of the thatched roof came loose, smacking the rafters and exposing the black sky. The door banged open. I thought I felt the hut pitching a bit to one side. *Shit.* If one stilt gave way, the whole thing could collapse with me into the waves.

Drizzle started, then thwashes of rain. I raced out to the uncovered porch to grab my clothes and yoga mat on the bamboo railing. Gone. My latest contribution to the Great Pacific Garbage Patch. And where the hell was my wetsuit? Looking around frantically, I found it on the ladder down near the water and grabbed it, the waves soaking my arm. Racing back inside, I stuffed my wetsuit, books, and underwater slate into my rubbery duffel. I twined the door shut as tightly as I could and crawled back into my sleeping bag. The short bridge to the island might still be intact, but I didn't want to check, fearing flying debris.

Where could I run to anyhow? I got here late yesterday believing I was the only person spending the night on this spit of an island. The closest village was a mile or more away, on the main island of Gam. No phone signal. Seawater splashed up between the floorboards. Rain started to drip on my face, so I moved over. It fell on my shoulder instead.

Am I going to die? I asked myself, the hut shuddering some more. Pulling the soggy sleeping bag over my head, I balled up and froze, not knowing what was next. My life didn't flash before me or anything. I didn't think of my family or past loves. No, I felt like I did the month before when we woke up to President-elect Trump.

Until falling asleep, I heard him ranting at one of his cuckoo-for-Cocoa-Puffs propaganda rallies that global warming was a Chinese hoax. Promising to pull out of the Paris Climate Agreement, gut the Environmental Protection Agency, and bring back coal. How fitting that his first secretary of state had been the CEO of Exxon Mobil, which had bankrolled climate change deniers since I was a toddler. Back then, when there was still time to truly do something, strong storms like this one were less common—because the world wasn't as warm.

I also had a dream. It was dusk by an Arctic river in Canada. I was in the future, maybe two centuries from now. The year 2250? 2317? The sky was orange. Billions of mosquito drones were flocking in joyless murmurations. No computer screens or flying cars anywhere. Just rushing water. Lizards. Neat rows of gingko trees everywhere.

There was a very thin girl sitting on a rock. She had my mother's nose and chin, but her skin was brown, not white, and her dark hair was in a braid. I knew she was my descendant, my great-niece many times over. She was drawing something. Crayon noise and river noise:

the sound of time looping. She handed me a drawing of a pony with a seahorse head.

"What was the ocean like," she asked, "when there were fish?"

I WOKE UP WAY TOO LATE, after sunrise. Since on the equator there are always twelve hours of light, I liked to get up when it was dark to meditate and plan my day underwater. Every second was precious, but I wasn't here to rush. I was practicing my 3 S's—slowing down, softening, savoring—to unravel the C-PTSD that had kept me an adult child. While there was still time, I was here to spend time with these miraculously intact reefs, all the creatures I was unintentionally helping to destroy, and still am.

I stepped on the porch in only a towel. The hole in the roof was the only damage. The new day was clean. Inlaid with pink cirrus. Into the glassy lagoon I wrung out my Hanes underwear, which were also my PJs, the drops rippling toward the mangroves. It was as if I were wringing out my life in California, which I'd recently left for the professorship in Virginia, and releasing the pain of seeing my parents at Thanksgiving.

I sat on the edge of the porch, my feet dangling over the water, and looked out at the wilderness. If it hadn't been for the hornbills and cockatoos passing over me, or the angler flounder in the shallows below, I would have yodeled.

This was where I'd meditate.

I saw it: I was here. I was still alive. In a wilderness that felt like some safer version of Florida. Hot, humid, and salt-scented like summers in Jacksonville but with rainforested peaks, sublime reefs, and few people. In my solitude here, I believed no one could hurt me. Five times I'd come to Raja Ampat to flee my triggers and write about natural beauty. Ten thousand miles from Florida, these reefs held my panic like nowhere else.

Then all of a sudden, well-being enveloped me. There was a voice in my head saying, *Trust in the care.* I felt embraced by the ring of karst islands and mangroves that had protected me the night before from the worst of the storm. It was like a benevolent soul taking me in its arms. Was this the spirit of my grandmother Mamo? Some ancestor I didn't know about?

The hug was maternal, not erotic, a distinction that couldn't be more important to me. It was different from Edward Abbey taking in the Utah wilderness and desiring to "possess it all, embrace the entire scene intimately, deeply, totally, as a man desires a beautiful woman." I didn't want to possess that swath of Mother Earth—or be possessed by it. I wanted to stay open to it wholeheartedly, radically, as when you let the rain on your face be enough. All the hookups in the world couldn't give me this: being held as a trustworthy mother holds her son.

I could remember this happening clearly once before. I was a back-packer renting a trailer at a deserted campground in Europe, feeling rotten about myself. The air was electric and cool. A chubby white dog followed me wherever I went, as if he knew me, as if in some other lifetime I had rescued him. We were inseparable.

One day I swam naked in the river that felt like a lake. The mountain behind was thickly forested with holm oaks. Amber was the dusklight. *Amazeballs.* Chomping at his reflection on the surface, the dog paddled beside me.

There was a moment while swimming I won't forget, the kind you can count on one hand in a life, with fingers to spare: the curving land and water were *holding* me. Caring for me in my self-loathing. Utter love I thought required NSFW apps and marijuana. Which is to say, one knot of many in my being undid itself; the ready-to-punch fist of my heart unclenched, and for a moment I felt forgiven and forgiving.

As the sprawling bay in Raja Ampat similarly embraced me, I saw absolutely no evidence of humanity. It was 2016, not some dreadful year like 2216 when Adara will be alive. Obama would be president for a few more weeks, having just created an ocean sanctuary in the Pacific twice the size of Texas. There were still fish in the sea, like the blood-beaked needlefish around the hut's stilts. There were still reefs, like the ones in front of me that have more species of fish and coral than the entire Caribbean and contain an astounding 75 percent of all known hard coral species. And there were still rainforests, like the ones breathing on the misty mountains along the bay. No wonder international scientists have raced to protect these islands.

This was where I'd meditate. *Have this positive experience. Enrich it, absorb it with abandon.*

SPREAD YOUR OSPREY WINGS—no one can catch you!—and see the jungle spreading across roadless Gam, then all over Waigeo, where you'll hear pink-spotted fruit doves, imperial pigeons, mustached treeswifts, mimic honeyeaters, and, of course, male red birds of paradise, which every morning perform a noisy, flamboyant courtship dance with pompoms, plumes, and tail wires to maybe get lucky. Follow the karst fjords with *sarang semut,* ant-riddled plants for what one local called "Viagra tea." But be careful. Saltwater crocodiles are watching. Healing journeys mean nothing to them.

Drop your past into a sinkhole, slip out of self-defeating stories like armor you always thought was your skin—let it all fly off and dissolve.

Get yourself to Aljui Bay, whose protected waters are home to zany, fragile creatures not often seen in the shallows, entheogenically colored as the fraggles on *Fraggle Rock.* Glide past magenta barrel sponges getting down with Lambert's sea cucumbers with frilly mouths that seem to say, *If you can't accept me at my Blanche Devereaux, you don't deserve me at my Jacques Cousteau.* You aren't tripping: those really are orangutan crabs with swaying orange fur. Werk it, werk it! Nearby is a secret cove draped with carnivorous pitcher plants, watched over by a white-bellied sea eagle—spy on the crowds of golden stingless jellyfish catching sunlight at the surface. Like coral polyps, giant clams, and spotted salamander eggs, they're gorging on sugars from the photosynthesizing algae in their flesh.

Then whoosh over to the pipefish of Fincok and the pregnant male seahorses stalked by cranes and frogfish at Ayai, toward the friendly village of Selpele where for an afternoon Mama Eti, cooking the best coconut curry chicken and fish soup this side of the Mississippi, makes you feel like you're her son. Eventually you'll come to the famed limestone pinnacles of Wayag that guard a nursery for baby manta rays. If you still feel like it, fling yourself southeast to Kali Beru, a kingfisher-stitched river that's clear and blue even on cloudy days.

Row, row, row! O frabjous Raja! Callay! Callooh!

My soul returned to the hut. The breath was breathing me. I was water, we're all water, the tides that advance forty-five minutes a day. Or was I a brazzle-dazzle sprig of bottlebrush coral taking in all this majesty to fortify my skeleton?

Then when I couldn't stand how happy I was, it came to me: *Adara*. That's what I would name my seventh or seventeenth great-niece from my dystopian dream. It's the name of a fishing village in East Timor. For several days on my 2013 trip to the Southern Hemisphere, I camped there on the beach and dived. The people were like family. We ate papaya flower salads. An elder named Antonio gave me goggles he made from a coconut shell, and showed me his storehouse of dried parrotfish for hard times. At one sunset I watched with his family, a lavender-fire cloud wisped over the ocean like a dope rift in the space-time continuum.

Adara. Blending in my ear "avatar" and "adore," it was what I'd call the daughter I'll never have. There are already way too many people.

I WAS GRATEFUL WHEN INDEXIA, wife of my host Pelos, brought break-fast to my hut instead of to the shared table. She felt bad about last night's storm, I figured, and wanted me to feel welcome. As she walked over the little bridge and smiled, I saw her teeth stained red from the betel nut that she and everyone else chewed. She was plump and dark-skinned, with deep dimples. She was a proud, relaxed Papuan woman, a mother of two. I had met her briefly the day before.

"*Selamat tinggal!*" I said, thinking I was saying "Good morning." Oops, I told her goodbye.

She laughed hysterically, warmly correcting me, "*Selamat pagi*, Greck!" She handed me a plate of fried rice with a side of papaya.

"Ahhhh...*pagi, pagi, pagi!*" I said like a jetlagged cartoon character, my blood sugar getting low.

"Mister Bean!" she teased me, calling me the British comedian I'd been unfortunately said to resemble for years overseas. She knew only a few English words, about as many as I knew in Biak and Indonesian.

"Indexia! No, no, I'm Greg!"

"Greck!"

"Call me Large Marge," I said huskily with bug eyes, my hand over my heart. "Bea Arthur."

Though she didn't understand, we giggled for a long time. When I don't speak the local language while traveling, my rubbery face defuses tension and creates intense, temporary bonds that feel familial.

As I scarfed down the food, Pelos was already repairing the roof. Sneaking past me into the hut, Indexia dragged out the thin mattress to dry it out. She swept out the water and sand, and tidied everything up.

"I can help you," I offered a few times, but she wouldn't let me. For a moment I was back with my mother in the kitchen as she scrubbed the floor with her beet-red hands, but the lagoon sounds brought me back to Raja Ampat in 2016.

Indexia and I were fast friends who reveled in one another's silliness. Whatever guilt I felt about my carbon footprint, I told myself I wasn't colonizing her ancestral territory. The only thing I was taking were photographs, with my cameras and mind's eye. I was compensating her family well to stay here; conservation tourism, after all, has kept these reefs from being destroyed by dynamite and overfishing, just as it's saved Rwanda's mountain gorillas from extinction and Costa Rica's rainforests from being slashed and burned. Even if what she and Pelos earned from my stay wouldn't ultimately go far, Indexia wanted me here.

Before she left, she asked mischievously, "Married? Babies?"

I shook my head and sashayed toward her like Backwoods Barbie on the catwalk to hand her my plate. We laughed till we cried. Maybe she understood my fabulous answer to her personal questions as only a mother can.

BY THE TIME MY BREAKFAST settled, it was drizzling again. I quickly suited up and went down the ladder to snorkel, not scuba dive, since air compressors were too expensive for local families. (Coral is always prettiest in the first fifteen feet anyhow, below which the color red starts disappearing.)

I left the bay for the ocean and dove down to soar above stunning coral gardens. I snorkeled for some time, minding my own business. And then cruising along was a—no, it couldn't be. Yes! Cowabunga! There was just one, quite large I'd say, maybe nine feet long. A dugong.

Around the sea cow's snout were convict tangs schooling for protection and food. The tail was fluked like a dolphin's, not paddle-shaped like that of a manatee. Along its back were bright-white mating scars from the tusks of competing males or of a much older female. As a reminder of my own invisible scars, it barely registered.

As the dugong swam twenty feet in front of me, to be less threatening I feigned disinterest, angling my body slightly away. It circled back around to approach. Definitely curious, it got closer and closer. The fifth grader inside me was giddy, as if it were 1990 again and the school bus was pulling up to Marineland. Would the dugong nuzzle me like the manatee that came up to me at summer camp?

Ten seconds later it whipped around, headed toward the other entrance to the bay, fading into the blue: I'd been ghosted by a four-hundred-pound sea cow. But it was a wild animal. And if it knew Europeans needed only twenty-seven years to hunt its close relative Steller's sea cow to extinction—if it understood that dugongs are still hunted for their meat, their tears bottled up and sold as an aphrodisiac in Sorong and Jakarta—and if it knew the climate science I taught my students with its projections about sea level rise and ocean acidification—not only would the dugong have bolted the second it noticed me, but it would've wished we'd all go extinct.

Even here in the solitude of the tropics, don't seek validation from strangers. It only ends in disappointment.

At the same time, since dugongs are skittish and rarely seen, I got superstitious about the sighting. Was the dugong a reincarnation of Willy Bartram who came to comfort me, a sign that my soulmate would be coming soon? Or after last night's scary visions and dream, perhaps I manifested an underwater symbol that meant, even if I stayed personally stuck, everything was going to work out environmentally? A combination of human ingenuity and nature's resilience will restore the earth! Climate scientists are hysterical liars! Adara was a random figment of a girl in a stress dream, right?

All that was the blah-blah-blah of a fool who needed to be dunked in ice-cold water. Recall the arrogant Russian snorkeler killed by crocodiles in these waters the April before. Recite the very end of *The Road*, where on the backs of extinct trout are "maps of the world in its becoming. Maps and mazes. Of a thing which could not be put back. Not be made right again." Feel eco-grief but not for too long. Remember Miranda Hobbes declaring on *Sex in the City*, "Soulmates only exist in the Hallmark aisle at Duane Reid Drugs."

HOPING TO SPOT ANOTHER DUGONG, I turned around and swam to the edge of the thick mangrove forest along the coast of Gam. The sun was out. In three feet of water, plankton-filled shafts of cathedral light were falling around me. Flying buttresses of mangrove roots were anchored in the sand, which I'd never seen underwater before coming to Raja Ampat. To be sure, Florida's mangroves were murky and full of stingrays.

I looked up and saw the mangrove leaves—I marveled at how these forests are four times as efficient as rainforests at sucking up carbon. Looking down and seeing tentacles of leather coral swaying, I cherished shallow areas like this one because heat-adapted zooxanthellae evolved here, one of the keys to the resilience of Raja's reefs.

Then enormous, fanged snapper swam through the maze of mangrove roots, and for a nanosecond I wished my father was here with me. Astounded by their size, he'd want to cast a line; the only mangrove snapper we ever caught at the Key Largo Holiday Inn were tiny.

Trying to get my parents out of my head, I pondered the fact that mangrove trees give birth to live young. Then I closed my eyes tightly, forgetting the potential for crocodiles to show up, and hugged my legs to my chest. Bobbing in darkness, I heard the *pop-pop* of pistol shrimp snapping their claws. The croaks and grunts of morning fish choruses. It was downright noisy.

Soon I felt like I was in a womb, which has an ambient sound of ninety decibels, the same as in an apartment next to an elevated train. What would I have heard inside my mother in 1979? Her heartbeat after a sip of iced coffee, the forgettable songs from Ringo Starr's *Bad Boy*. Her declaring as she cradled Kermit the Frog above her enormous belly, *Greg, I love you, but golly day it's time to be born!*

Try as I may, fourteen time zones between us, I realized there was no hiding from my family or the planetary crisis. Life is impeccable. It has a way of bringing you the very thing you're running from and holding it up as a mirror. As psychotherapist Esther Perel puts it, "Trauma doesn't like to be touched." But it will be. What seems like an escape might be a confrontation. In what you thought was a refuge, you might really be more vulnerable to change.

COMING BACK FROM THE MANGROVES, I heard some high-pitched commotion. Lifting my head, I saw a young woman splish-splashing around in a string bikini. She looked almost computer generated, with her thin, almost orange body. Breasts so big even I noticed them. She was in water up to her knees, grazing her fingertips over the water, throwing her head back and blissfully laughing. A mustached hunk with a tatted face was photographing her with his enormous camera. *In a decade*, I thought, *he'll be washed up.*

"So you're the bloke who lives here," he said as I threw my flippers onto my hut's porch from the water.

She pursed her lips. "With the view, this would go for hundreds a night somewhere else. If you weren't here, this would be our bungalow."

"Is that right?" I said curtly, as if I were avoiding confrontation with a saucy student. "Welcome to Raja Ampat. How did you ever find this place?"

"We have connections," she spat. "We live in Indo when we're not on the Gold Coast." They were from Brisbane, Australia. Bananaland, it's called. "Jimmy is going to open a restaurant in Bali," parts of which are the Down Under's equivalent of Daytona Beach. "I'm an influencer model on Insta." She should go star in a Gen-Z remake of *Clueless*.

"She's up to one hundred K followers, mate."

"Never been on there. I just have the Facebook."

"Then what do you do?" he asked, realizing I was older than I looked.

"I'm a writer."

"You must be American," she said. "Trump! Isn't that adorbs?"

"Yes," I said, stepping up the ladder onto the porch, "and this American needs to get dry."

"Any idea when you're leaving?" Jimmy asked.

I ignored him. After I dried myself off with a rag, Indexia brought me a new thermos for coffee. Katya and Jimmy were still having their photo shoot next to my hut, occasionally making out.

"Just look at the water and mountains," Katya said too loudly so I'd hear her, motioning toward the sweep of the bay. "Gorg. Perf."

Indexia looked over at them, shaking her head.

"No good," she whispered, "no good." Bikinis, along with public displays of affection, were offensive to her and her culture. Even for a bikini, Katya's was skimpy.

After Indexia left to make lunch, I got a headache. I knew my solitude was over. I was the weird dork they wanted to swipe left into oblivion.

I paced inside my hut, hearing that basic bitch hissing, "If you weren't here, this would be our bungalow." I took my journal out of its Ziploc bag so I could vent. "She isn't real," I wrote. "She won't even look like the pics after he photoshops in a thigh gap and touches up her scaly skin." And then to soothe myself further, I got all fancy-pants and self-righteous: "Beauty—that isn't the sort I came here for. Hers is a vacuous beauty not found in the wild. It is as manufactured as Styrofoam or propaganda."

I can see today that my misogyny was rooted in envy. She was gorgeous, in a way, on the tall side and thin, with what my mother and I longingly called "small bones." I'll admit I was jealous of Katya's hot body, jealous she had a boyfriend she could travel with, jealous of all the attention she was getting from him, jealous that she didn't find life so triggering she had to live alone. And as for her Instagram presence—I too have offered buckets of pics to get validation from strangers, sending them shirtless selfies that only showed me well above where my fat tends to settle. Our online followers were seduced by photographic lies.

Partly because of this phenomenon, a sense of falseness and unlovability has permeated our culture. It's one reason my students kill themselves, one reason there's collective nihilism. You're not imagining it. As I learned from the documentary *The Social Dilemma*, the suicide rate for girls aged fifteen to nineteen has risen 70 percent since social media apps first appeared on smartphones in 2009, 151 percent for girls ten to fourteen. Remember, too, that my now-deleted Grindr and Katya's Instagram weren't free platforms; we'd been working unpaid for them, raising ad revenue with our content. Meanwhile, we grew shallower and more addicted.

MEDITATING SEVERAL MORNINGS LATER, I heard buzzing nearby. It sounded like a swarm of angry hornets. Stepping outside in my underwear, I looked around but didn't see anything. The sound got louder and zoomed about.

Then above my hut I saw a toy car with four helicopter propellers. A drone. I'd only ever seen one in a *Black Mirror* episode called "Shut Up and Dance." It slowly descended below the eaves to eye level, maneuvering back and forth to tease me, and then zipped away.

I rushed out over the little bridge to get a better look. It was high up in the air by now. Jimmy was holding the controller, oohing and ahhing with Katya about the footage he was getting. I stood there fuming, wondering how many likes and mean comments the video of me on my porch would get. Soon the drone crashed into a coconut palm and fell to the ground.

Please, drone, I thought, *please be broken*. Not saying a word, I went back to the hut to pack up my things. I waved to the spider as big as my fist in the corner. Bowed to the python hidden in the thatching. Blew a kiss to the reefs and the mountains. Then I asked Pelos to take me north on Gam to a place where, even for Raja Ampat, there was heart-stopping coral I remembered from the year before.

"Soon our phones will be floating on our eyeballs as smart contact lenses, and then they'll be chips implanted in our brains," I ranted in my journal once I got to the next hut. "If you don't like this world, you can always immerse yourself in another virtual one. Then what happens to empathy? Would you even care what happens to mangroves and dugongs?"

Katya and Jimmy in paradise could go to hell. That night I began drafting a long letter to Adara. I needed to talk to someone.

CHAPTER 14

Adara

December 2016

Dear Adara,

When I taught creative writing to kids your age one summer, they wrote weird essays for *Smiggle Wiggle*, our class magazine. *What did your face look like before your parents were born?* was an assignment. One kid said she was a green-eyed forest spirit with a mouth full of unsayable words. Another said her eyes lit up the galaxy and her golden hair held winter stars. One jokester said his primordial face looked like a cupcake baby panda alien's and that mine did too. They were a brilliant class; most of them hadn't even made it to sixth grade yet, so about your age.

I sort of remember your face. A bit like my mother when she was a girl. But different. You drew me a picture. You asked me what the ocean was like when there was coral.

You felt real, Adara, but I'm not sure I believe in prophetic dreams. I believe more in science, its predictive power, that as CO_2 increases, the temperature and acidity of the ocean do too—you roll a boulder into your river, and it won't float. We reach tipping points, and there's no going back for thousands of years.

Maybe as I was falling asleep the night I dreamed of you, I remembered the words of Oren Lyons, the Iroquois Faithkeeper—"What about the seventh generation? Where are you taking them? What will they have?"—and my mind created you. Maybe for my puny life to have meaning, I need to know you'll exist. That humanity will continue on. Less stupidly, I hope.

I'm living less than a degree south of the equator, in Raja Ampat. I sleep on the floor of a thatched hut and breakfast on banana fritters. As coral elsewhere is bleaching and dying, I'm here to document reefs that are still healthy and gorgeous. Patrol boats shoot dynamite fishermen on sight and sink their boats. Large-scale commercial fishing is illegal. Village chiefs, with evidence-based advice from Conservation International scientists like my hero Dr. Mark Erdmann, enforce no-take zones in marine protected areas. In the coming decades, Mark proudly predicts that people may be harvesting corals from Raja Ampat to reseed other reefs.

My carbon from my flights on this trip will melt Arctic sea ice about the size of my office on campus. I did that to you, Adara. No one made me. No apology I could offer would be enough, but I want you to know I'm sorry. Sorry and ashamed you inherited the planet you did because of our inaction. You deserve an answer to the question you asked me about my oceans, and so much more I can't give you.

It seems useless to write down a time capsule of underwater beauty—will it ever reach you? Will you ever be born?—but as the tide flows over hedgehog coral in this bay, my right hand on my journal, I vow to respond to you.

PACKING UP THE LAST of my childhood stuff from my mom's house before this trip, I found an old album. Inside were photographs I'd taken as a kid in the Florida Keys with a disposable underwater camera. The edges of the pages were stained.

Toward the middle were three photos I took when I was about your age. They were of elkhorn coral. I was obsessed with finding coral that was still alive, especially elkhorn. I'd stay out snorkeling until the captain had to blow his airhorn to get me to swim back. Before not too long, elkhorn coral—the giant redwoods of the reef, scientists have called it—was decimated. Now in its place are rubble and slime.

Those photos of elkhorn felt like a message to me from my worried childhood self. The child cared. The child was telling the man to do something, anything.

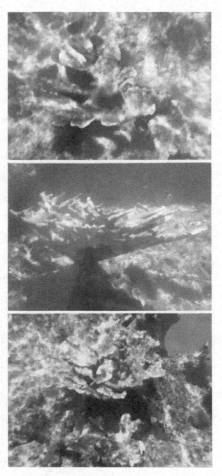

LET'S TRAVEL BACK IN TIME to the reefs here off Gam, between Yenbeser and Batu Lima, on December 21, 2015. It's my second trip to Raja Ampat. The higher sea temperatures of El Niño seem to have set in, the first foot of water so hot at noon that it blurs our vision—three days later in Central Park, on Christmas Eve, it will be sixty-six degrees at half past midnight; Albany, New York, will have a high of seventy-two, which was warmer than Phoenix. But the reef is astounding, seemingly impervious to heat.

Together let's snorkel over the healthiest, weirdest coral imaginable, to right before the drop-off, stopping at a huge coral mound. There sleeping in a hollow is a young tasseled wobbegong shark: brownish, well-camouflaged, usually nocturnal. You'd yelp, I bet, once your eyes could make out the flat cartilaginous fish, pumping water over its gills with its cheeks. Look at the whiskers on the front of the head. Those dermal lobes, as they're called, aren't sensitive like a catfish's—instead, they're fake worms that bring hungry fish close.

Its corkscrew tail with false eyes is also a decoy—have you ever pretended to be something you're not? Watch the wobbie beginning to wave it, mimicking a distressed fish, and a huge cloud of bluestreak fusiliers surges close to check it out. All this tail wagging is called caudal luring, the secret weapon of ambush predators like rattlesnakes and copperheads.

Suddenly the shark lunges up at the fish and, with a loud pop, snaps open its jaws. We see the pasty beige insides of the mouth, but it all happens so fast we can't tell if the wobbie got a snack. If you're ever bitten, Adara, don't worry—in the village there's a needle and thread. If you ate one, a local told me, your whole body would itch for days but you'd be fine. I'll keep you safe.

I'm sorry if I go overboard with my poetry, but the sneaky freaky tail, for me at least, is the most beautiful part of the wobbegong. It's a star chart from another arm of the galaxy, where interstellar dust, lit by brown dwarves, turns the sky an army beige. It's an atlas page, alive, furling, sweet in the mouth, bitter in the belly—take and eat, it says, this is love, even if you break out in hives. Or is it a sacred map not meant for me, that I'll never truly understand, like a dot painting on eucalyptus bark locating the Mirramina water hole where the mighty python of the Liagallawumirri lives? I'm a man crunk on beauty. Might it all be a code that, once unlocked, could help us sequester carbon, deacidify the ocean, and develop stable fusion power? It's so pretty, Adara, I almost think so.

Anyhow, around the shark is staghorn coral in crowded branches like the curved points of an antler. The pink, avocado, and tan batons are abundant as ferns in a redwood forest, sea oats on a dune. Sheltered there are fish like moon and bird wrasses, damsels, and sergeants. Many different types of shrimp and crabs are hiding here too: when I point my light at staghorn during night dives, the red crustacean eyeshine is like a scattering of garnets. *Crunch, crunch* fills our ears: we look up at the thousands of parrotfish rushing past, stopping now and then to nibble on coral.

Memorize that stream of fish, I tell myself, etch the shark and the coral into your mind's eye. Hold those memories close like the philosopher's stone for when you're an old man and the ocean isn't the same. Share them with anyone who will listen and believe.

SEVERAL DAYS AGO, taking a longboat back to Gam, I snorkeled the same reef. The shark was gone. So were most of the fusiliers. A few small parrotfish winged by, along with some foxface rabbitfish. In places the wobbegong's coral mound had begun to bleach. And the swaths of staghorn coral? Some branches were bleached white, others were covered in an ogre's snot—largely smothered by algae, a lot of coral was dead. I swam as fast as I could to get an overall sense of things. Algae was glowing Astroturf green on the bottom. Fields of large table corals, many of them toppled, were dying.

The reef, I'm trying to tell you, Adara, was unrecognizable. Mark told me that in his experience Raja Ampat's reefs, when they do bleach, quickly bounce back. But with all due respect, this is a different year, during a global mass bleaching of corals, the third in recorded history.

Had the high temperatures of El Niño been too much for even Raja Ampat's coral? They certainly had been for reefs most everywhere else.

STARING DOWN IN DISBELIEF at all the dead and dying coral, I thought back to the photo two tourists had shown me of a nearby villager holding up an enormous red fish by its lower jaw. A mature twin-spot snapper half as tall as the Papuan man proudly holding it. He was about to cook for the couple one of this reef's largest remaining predators. Even if this seemed akin to serving a grilled cheetah dinner on a Serengeti safari, I wouldn't dare admonish the villager. These were his ancestral waters, not mine. He was trying to do right by these rich, friendly Australian tourists, his honored guests. Like my friend Indexia, he wanted to attract more tourists to Raja Ampat, I would guess, so he could send his kids to school and pay his family's medical bills when someone gets sick.

In the coming decades as the climate dramatically shifts, where will his children and grandchildren and great-nieces go? Who are the leaders imagining his reef-bound culture's future and making reloca-tion plans? Are his descendants with you in Canada? Trying to imagine myself in his position, I'd serve the snapper.

I hope this isn't going too far afield, Adara—but the problem is that overfishing, still a documented problem in some parts of Raja Ampat, tends to cause algae blooms, hurting the ecosystem that's his main source of income. Coral and macroalgae are in a delicate balance on reefs: the algae is always growing, but grazers like parrotfish keep it in check. Overfishing of those grazers, though, and of apex predators like the large snapper, has also been shown to contribute to the decline of coral and the rise of algae and coral diseases. Overall, Mark told me, fish stocks are better than when he first started diving here fifteen years ago. But in the past two decades, Raja Ampat's population has increased by almost two-thirds, and now thousands of tourists come here every year, up from only a handful in the early 1990s when the first dive resort opened.

These visitors expect to eat fresh fish—most days I've been here, my local hosts have served it to me, sometimes open-water fish like tuna or mackerel, sometimes reef fish. And I've eaten it every time. How many hundreds of thousands of fish are caught here every year, not to mention the fish caught illegally and sold on the mainland? How much fishing pressure can the area take? What has happened to most other reefs, I fear, is beginning to happen in Raja Ampat because of population growth and climate change.

No wonder you asked me your startling question. My aim isn't to scare or depress you with all this—but to tell you about the beauty, I must also speak of threat.

I COME APART WHEN I think of my grandma. Mamo loved me unconditionally, I think, when no one else seemed to. We'd walk down her street, Reef Road, taking the path through the dunes to beachcomb at the tideline. Cowrie, conch, scotch bonnet, Humphrey's wentletrap—in the den we'd sift through her shell collection and eat chocolate and gossip about the hermit behind her house who kept a raccoon as a pet.

The coral here sometimes reminds me of her—she was beautiful, old yet vibrant, but I knew at some point she would pass away, making our time together precious. Her beauty would end. But the comparison between her and coral is overall fairly tenuous: my carbon wasn't partially responsible for her slow decline; she was bedridden and dazed the last five years of her life, until her heart stopped at age ninety-six. After she died, I felt grief, not guilt.

Most of her ashes were scattered by a fisherman in the Atlantic, but I keep some in a small urn at home between my chambered nautilus and a framed photograph of her. In the grainy shot, she and her brother have just reunited after years of estrangement. A portrait of reconciliation. She's radiant, as if she came back to life. You're their descendants too, you know.

WHO IS A MORAL INSPIRATION for you? Who makes you tear up when you think of them?

BEFORE I SIGN OFF, I want to tell you about Christmas night a few days ago. I was in the outrigger canoe, heading back from services in the village. The moonless evening wasn't pitch black: by starlight alone I could still see the canoe's stabilizers causing bioluminescent plankton to shimmer like emerald flecks suddenly backlit by flames.

Beyond our wake, the five stars of Cassiopeia's chair were reflected in the flat bay. The Gemini twins Castor and Pollux were too, Sirius so bright that it burned a hole in the lagoon. How was such a perfect mirror possible?

I thought of you then, and I'm not just saying that—I was sure the canoe, with stars streaking past its hull, was a starship about to go through a temporal portal, and we would be spit out into your century. Looking down from orbit, we'd see Florida was a smattering of islands. Jacksonville, my city, would be submerged. Only the highlands of Raja Ampat would be visible, the reefs long dead. Hudson Bay in Canada, near your house, would be larger, much larger, shimmering brown. Greenland would have forests; Iceland wouldn't have much ice.

I'd feel sick, of course I would. I'd find a way to get down to you, Adara. To meet you, once and for all. To give you a Christmas stocking filled with my grandma's shells and draw you a real seahorse.

CHAPTER 15

Purple

After seeing the dying reef off Gam, I set out for the island of Manyaifun to the northwest. There one afternoon, right after the sun went behind the mountain, I dove into the water. That time I snorkeled to the left instead of the right, past panda butterflyfish in pairs and a pufferfish of acid-drawn maps. Silverside minnows streamed around me like flocking pulses of mica. I kicked faster and faster, as if I were racing someone I hated.

Beyond the coconut grove, in the shallows in front of where the rainforest came down to the beach, were a few thickets of purple coral. They startled me. They were *looking* at me. I heard Shug in Alice Walker's novel saying, "I think it pisses off God if you walk by the color purple in a field somewhere and don't notice it."

I stopped swimming. Low tide: my chest was a few inches above the purple branches where spaghetti sponges were tangled. The next moment, and the next, had never happened before in this universe. Would never happen again. Every breath and bubble was utterly unique, unrepeatable. Hundreds of small fish blew about in a kaleidoscopic cloud.

MOTHERSHIP

The purple throbbed, it called me by my secret name.

LOOKING DOWN AT THE CORAL reminded me of looking up at a fresco by Francisco Goya. The one inside the dome of the Church of San Antonio de la Florida, the Sistine Chapel of Madrid. Women across Spain make a pilgrimage there every June 13 to pray to Saint Anthony for a husband.

I came in July. On a bench in the empty church, I lay on my back: hills and sky filled most of the painted dome, but along its equator was the bustle of eighteenth-century Madrid, including a saint pointing two fingers at a murdered man to raise him from the dead.

Though some people on the crowded street don't seem to care, others are amazed at the spectacle, including a man traditionally known as the toothless beggar. His gums hurt, I imagined. He's hungry and sleeps on the street, where he's chased by strays, spat on, and taunted. His spine is painfully curved and twisted, so he holds a cane in one hand and with the other grips the railing to watch the miracle, instead of looking down at his feet in shame. His eyes are tender. Despite his pain, wonder radiates from him as naturally as light from an anglerfish in the abyss.

Embedded in his miracle-inspired wow is longing: *could you heal me too, Anthony? Could you?* If a murdered son can be resurrected to clear his father's name, a spine can be straightened and teeth replaced. A homeless man can be sheltered, Antarctica can stay frozen, dead reefs can come back to life.

GAZING AT THE PURPLE CORAL like the toothless man looks at the miracle, I softened until I almost had no edges. I imagined him floating beside me with waterwings, and my jaw relaxed while the tip of my tongue stayed behind my teeth. Then I could see, really see, the purple coral.

Purple

I tried to photograph the scene cellularly, with my whole being, as if my wetsuit were a peacock mantis shrimp's retina, which is studded with up to sixteen different color-receptive cones instead of our human three. Slow your breathing to four breaths a minute. Are you relaxed yet? Aware? Look softly and stay still—more difficult underwater than in a church because of the current and your leaky mask.

This is the best I can do: in places the coral was the dark purple of a berry-gorging grizzly's scat—in others it was like the eggplant grown in the local village, or juniper berries floating in a Spanish gin and tonic, or the McDonald's character Grimace. The Smucker's grape jelly my mother spread on biscuits. Dusty amethyst or whatnot.

Buck up, no, buck down. Like scrub pinecones that burst open only when wildfires melt their wax, so much inside you lies dormant waiting for beauty. Tear open your wetsuit! Imagine the purple of the coral shining into your brain and onto the misfiring neurons that keep you small. Undergo the beauty, let it change you, don't just glance. You chose this water—now you choose what to pay attention to. Look and look, until the victim inside you is asleep and you're a dreamy stranger to yourself.

Had I been more devout, I would've called myself a magus and each polyp a holy child in a limestone manger. Still, I was giddy like it was Christmas Eve—it felt good to gush, to create the sacred while discovering it. Adoration that day meant feeling wonder, which is unbidden but snuffed out by hurrying.

The coral didn't need me. It didn't even know what wonder was, or permafrost, or suicide. I was the one who needed wonder, to feel as though I were coming back to life. My wonder was a small, futile attempt by one of the 108 billion who have ever lived to atone for the Sixth Mass Extinction. I alone cannot stop it. At this point, it may be unstoppable:

Autumn of autumns, arouse in me an allegiance, unshakable and brave, to the dying sea, to cuttlefish and lightning whelks, to barracuda, diatoms, krill.

Look long enough at any creature and the universal fact of change, of withering, knocks the breath out of you. Resurrection, outside of frescoes, comes when flies hatch from your corpse. This island's reefs by and large were thriving, so it was easy to forget that most of the others around the globe were dying.

I remembered the ruined reef I wrote to Adara about. Over the sound of stareye parrotfish munching, I could've sworn I heard the West Antarctic Ice Sheet buckling and sighing: after it melts, nine feet of water could slosh inside what remains of the Doge's Palace in Venice and Battle Ground Baptist Church in the Ninth Ward of New Orleans.

Eventually, though, my future-tripping stopped. My assumptions about the coral unfastened. I was looking at it—but was it also looking back at me with eyespots of uric acid? Or was it tasting me instead, my pheromones, my nontoxic sunscreen? Did it understand me as a fellow colony, made of 30 trillion human cells and about as many bacteria? Was it telegraphing to me chemical cries, as it does to fish when algae begin to smother it? Or was I as imperceptible to it as mermen were to me? 95 percent of the universe consists of undetectable dark matter and dark energy. Is that darkness really just packing peanuts in the shipping crate we're stuffed into? Ashes in the cosmic urn and we're the bone bits?

Is the darkness actually wonder contemplating itself as wonder?

"PEOPLE THINK PLEASING GOD is all God care about," Shug goes on to tell Celie. "But any fool living in the world can see it always trying to please us back." It pleases us, yes—but it also horrifies us, baffles us, and is usually a blur, all of which Goya's fresco shows. There may be a miracle happening in it, but a woman leaning on the railing is staring off into space; the murderer is running away before his resurrected victim can implicate him; and a yellow-hooded, evil hag looks down at us, her back to the saint. She means the world harm—speaking to her from the heart or whatever won't stop her.

And after fifteen minutes with the coral, I was the daydreaming maiden with the white scarf: I was guessing how much whiskey was left in my bottle and craving ice cubes, which I hadn't seen in weeks. Squeamishness with the present moment is partly what makes us human. Ego's grand lie: resistance will keep you safe. Meanwhile, bracken ferns blowing at the edge of a spruce grove—or the smell of creosote after a desert thunderstorm, or the feel of a sea cucumber's knobby leather—go unnoticed.

If you cling, you'll suffer, but if you don't appreciate in your bones the coral while it's still alive, you'll regret it.

BEFORE GETTING OUT OF THE WATER, I saw a sea slug on some rubble. The oval-shaped body was covered in tubercles, closely bunched cones that looked like stupas made from lunar bricks. Had it been still, I wouldn't have noticed it, but it was inching along sniffing with its rhinophores, feeling with its spotted underside for sponges to eat, and the tassels of its external lungs swayed. *Dendrodoris tuberculosa*: the goddess of oceanic fertility dwells in these warty trees. It did what it needed to survive, but it wasn't in a hurry; it had no tension. Neurotic restlessness wasn't in its DNA, just as abiding continuously in the beauty of nature isn't in mine. (*Abiding*, I once heard it explained to a Frenchman, means "resting with trust.")

As I stood up to take off my mask, I saw the nearby island the village had forbidden me to snorkel around. It was their cemetery. Beyond was a much larger island, Batang Pele, charred from a fire accidentally set by a child. Other than its mangroves, the island was toast.

MOTHERSHIP

The view reminded me of a sign I once saw driving through Florida on my way to my mother's house: IF YOU DIED TODAY, DO YOU KNOW WHERE YOU'D SPEND ETERNITY? I hoped my afterlife, if it comes, would be in some imperishable version of Raja Ampat. I would slide like a slug across that bay, and then one bay over, and so on, until I knew every coral polyp in the archipelago, on Earth, on every exoplanet with brine.

May the past and future fall away.
May the present be a safe harbor.
May the afterworld be an eternity of unceasing wonder, of intimacy
*   with all things.*
In fields where in a few places there's still purple coral.

I prayed all of that, more or less, and removed my fins. I rubbed my eyes and went to go find my bourbon.

CHAPTER 16

Rehab

In August 2017, I was in silence when I got the call at the meditation center. My mother, who had faced sky-high blood pressure most of her life, had suffered a terrible stroke.

I rushed to Florida. My mother, covered in tubes and electrodes, was in the ICU in Jacksonville. When she saw me, she let out a barely audible groan. The right side of her body was paralyzed, and she was right-handed. If someone hadn't been driving to see her when she had the massive brain bleed, the doctors said, she could have easily died alone on her bedroom floor.

Over the next several months, she lived in physical rehab centers that took care of her every need. I was thankful to get a partial leave from my university so I could fly down to see her often. I dealt with her doctors and nurses and orderlies. Her lawyer, financial advisor, and insurance company. Her pharmacists, physical therapists, occupational therapists, and nutritionists. Her lawn guy, her pool boy, her handyman. Everyone. I shopped for diapers and incontinence pads and big tubs of wet wipes. With help from her bank, I was handling all her bills. I may have left Florida with hives all over my body and spent my thirty-eighth birthday alone washing her bras while drinking cheap wine from the bottle, but her mobility was improving. It felt worth it. By October, she could speak intelligibly and wiggle her fingers and toes. With therapists on either side of her, she was slowly learning to walk again.

At long last, she and I could sit and connect. We were kinder. At the long-term rehab center where she lived temporarily, I wheeled her out to the pond with the fountain in the center, and we watched the ducks as the other patients with their adult children passed by. I learned to cradle her body so she could get into the car, and we'd go out to dinner. Before she returned home, I hired her caregivers, doing background checks, calling references, and negotiating salaries and hours. My relationship with my mother felt relatively transformed.

But after coming home in December, she no longer had a team of people looking after her all at once. Instead, she usually only had one person there at a time, and her money was paying them now, not Medicare. She became particularly demanding and unreasonable, barking at them to let her disinfect the dryer before it was run, to only run the washer once a month and, even then, only on the rinse cycle. She only allowed her dishwasher to run every two weeks, but handwashing dishes was forbidden. She would swear I had snuck someone sketchy into the house while she was asleep, which wasn't true. After all, she lived, finally, in a gated community with security guards at the checkpoint who answered to her.

Paying round-the-clock, at-home caregivers was burning through her money. Long-term care insurance would have come in handy. In several years, her financial advisor and I calculated, she would have nothing left. He and I created a plan so she could live the rest of her life without depleting her savings—I even offered to have her live near me in Virginia in an assisted living apartment—but she rejected it at once. She said she would stay in her home, which she had bought a couple years earlier, forever. What were we going to do? Or I should say, what was I going to do? I was in charge and didn't make the kind of money she would need.

I understood the stroke was traumatic for her, that her unresolved trauma, which wasn't her fault, helped cause it—and that coming back to her house made her shocking disability even more real. I had compassion for her. I did. But it felt all too familiar: helplessness alongside obsessive, rude attempts at absolute control. Forgive me if I sound self-righteous, but remember I was taking care of her despite our history. On her behalf, I had sold the house I grew up in. Before listing it, I came to Jacksonville in my free time to deep clean bedrooms and bathrooms where abuse had gone down, to sort through decades of fingerpainted artwork, legal papers, and trash. I was a resentful mess, a wad of annihilation panic, but I had no other choice but to help her. As her son, it was my moral duty. My obligations were not lost on me.

ONE DAY, AN OLDER FRIEND told me, "I don't know how you stand it, but if I spoke like that to my son, you best believe he'd never talk to me again." She had overheard a conversation my mother and I had on speakerphone. Nothing had registered as particularly cruel to me in the exchange. It felt normal—because it was. It took a caring, straight-talking third party to wake me up. No one else had ever quite heard my mother's uncensored berating and needling of me. People only knew her public self, bubbly and measured, with occasional flashes of prima-donna edginess she quickly laughed off.

"You're so touchy," she'd told me forever. "Too sensitive." When I tried talking with her about my childhood, she'd say, "I've done nothing wrong—you have no reason to be mad at me! Stop raking me over the coals!" She made me doubt my instincts, keeping our relationship going well into my adulthood. I'm easily manipulated, and she knew that.

"It would be different if she treated you like a person," my friend added at the end of our conversation.

BEFORE THE STROKE, my mother and I had shared some incredible times together. Earlier that year, she took me on a ten-day snorkeling safari in Raja Ampat to far-flung islands I'd never visited. On the schooner deck one night, fireflies flashing up and down Wayag's peaks, I wrote in my journal, "The past—it's time to let it go—and forgive her; I can feel her love for me: *it's real*—I'm lucky to have a mother who wants to spend time with me." On the top bunk above her in our cabin, I reminded myself over and over that both she and the reefs were still alive—that she was with me in my favorite place on earth.

I still savor snorkeling at Yangeffo and explaining the clear-water mangrove ecosystem to her, pointing out pig tunicates and soft coral on the submerged roots. I remember we held hands off Yenbuba as huge schools of barracuda and trevally rushed past us—despite the many places we had snorkeled together, neither of us had ever seen so many fish. Floating in the ocean brought us peace we could find nowhere else.

Even so, happy times with my mother weren't to be trusted. They were an essential part of the old rinse-and-repeat cycles of humiliation and expensive peacemaking. Somehow I could trust more in her cruelty, her pummeling domination of me, her hissy fits over crumbs and house keys and insurance that made me feel like a terrible person. She was at her most authentic, I often thought, when she was iron-fisted and obnoxious.

After my mother was back home from rehab, she told me she was working hard in physical and occupational therapy and exercising between sessions. But I couldn't see much progress. In time, I learned that my mother had been lying to me: when the physical therapist came over, they were both content to goof off; she was largely refusing to do any exercises, take showers, or even leave the house.

"She could be walking," one of her nurses told me, fed up with her, thinking of her less well-off clients with far fewer resources. "She doesn't have to stay in bed."

It wasn't only her ignorance of neuroplasticity that kept her largely bedridden. In a kind of role reversal from my childhood, my recovering mother wanted to be babied. She couldn't bother getting out of bed to use the toilet—she was content to go in her diapers, which given the extent of her recovery, she had no business wearing any longer. That unfortunate habit, along with her stubborn refusal to hydrate or let laundry be done more than once a month, resulted in urinary tract infections that frequently had her in the hospital.

Although my mother was seventy-four and otherwise very physically healthy, with no cognitive decline, I quickly learned that UTIs in the elderly can cause temporary delirium and seizures. After an ambulance brought my mother to the ER for the fourth time, she told me on the phone, "I don't like water. Stop bossing me around. Who are you, my father?" Standing in the living room of my closest friends in Jacksonville, I begged her, half-yelping, to drink more water.

"If you can't do it for yourself," I roared, "do it for your goddamn child!" I hung up. As my friends Zac and Scott bear-hugged me, I saw that my mother was traumatizing me again. This time around, though, I was choosing to be held captive.

CHAPTER 17

Dayan

"I'm an activist so my grandchildren can have fish."

—LEONARDO SALEO (1968–2010),
Conservation International ranger and Konstan's father

Row, row away from Jacksonville, the traditional land of the Timucua's thirty-five chiefdoms, and toward Indonesia off the western end of New Guinea, to Raja Ampat's southwest corner.

There's an hourglass-shaped island called Dayan where manta rays congregate at cleaning stations and blue starfish hold fast to mangrove roots. I remember standing there on the beach beside a whale backbone and my host, Konstan. Twenty-three years old, with a curly black beard and perfect teeth, he was kind and calm, with undercurrents of sadness. Though I was nearly a foot taller, I felt small. I was thirty-eight, but I looked younger without a beard or mustache—I shaved it to keep my mask from leaking. I was about to return to the United States and my housebound mother.

At Dayan, I had been healing in the element in which I was traumatized. The murky waters of Jacksonville Beach wouldn't do. Way too close to home. I didn't yet believe Frances Hodgson Burnett in *The Secret Garden*: "If you look the right way, you can see that the whole world is a garden." I came instead to Raja's reefs, among the world's most protected and pristine. Whatever they really mean, those two adjectives were talismanic for me.

After weeks at other sites, I spent the last ten days of my trip snorkeling Konstan's reefs most of the day and some of the night, jotting down field notes on the underwater slate strapped to my wrist. It all felt urgent because it was. In my lifetime, we will probably lose coral reefs. Konstan and his family depend on them for their survival. They are their seawall, pantry, and 401(k).

I didn't want to leave that diva of a giant clam, the one I don't tell my students about on the first day of Environmental Literature of Wonder and Crisis. As I dove down to her the morning before, she was too fat to close all the way. She listened as I asked for help with my troubles, and she answered with funky beauty and fierce regard.

With hundreds of pinhole eyes, she saw me the way a saint sees— beyond masks and into the indestructible sincerity.

If you ever find her, lightly blow bubbles across her bottle-green mantle, into her incurrent and excurrent siphons. Make a wish. It couldn't hurt to try. Tremble in awe, it's okay. Being torn apart by gorgeousness is your birthright. Like coral, algae called zooxanthellae lived in her tissues, making food from sunlight. Now that's fabulous. Shantay, you stay. Bye, Felicia; Hello, RuPaul, who always asks at the end of *Drag Race*, "If you can't love yourself, how in the hell are you gonna love somebody else?"

Neither did I want to leave the cloudy-eyed moray eel, thick as my thigh, that swam in the cove like a ribbon of emerald gravitational waves. I would miss the razorfish that schooled like upright knives. The mantas.

MOTHERSHIP

It was time to leave. Konstan's ancestral reefs had been my Secret Garden in a Walden Pond. They let the trauma breathe. Was there a way to press it all into an amulet and wear it home?

AFTER I PUT MY BAGS in his longboat, Konstan handed me a paddle. "I found a boat on the ocean two years ago," he said, flashing an adorable smile. "I made this for it."

Even though I was hot, it made me shiver, this gift meant to seal our friendship. I felt the ellipse of the blade and ran my fingers down along the shaft to the T-grip shaped like the tail of a surgeonfish. Except for the pinpricks from woodboring beetles, the handle was smooth, in places worn down by his hands to a glossy amber. Up on the blade, the tree rings looked like one half of Saturn's rings seen from an angle. Like ripples from a pebble thrown into the slack tide. One side of the blade was whitish from the salt air and sun. The other side, face down in the perpetually beached canoe, was brown. You row with oars and paddle with paddles, but my whole being still said *row, row*.

"Thank you," I said, dissociating off and on, lifting my sweaty baseball cap, "but don't you need it?" The paddle was against me, the handle in the sand.

Shaking his head, pointing to the longboat with a motor, he simply said, "Faster."

As I wobbled into the boat, I asked Konstan about the paddle's wood—photosynthesis is an obsession of mine. *Brar*, he called the tree in Biak, his endangered language. *Kayu susu* in Indonesian. *Alstonia scholaris*. It can reach a height of 130 feet; the big leaves radiate out in threes and tens; too light for heavy-duty construction, the wood is used for corks, coffins, pencils, and school chalkboards. Tradition elsewhere has it that the first of the twenty-eight Buddhas achieved enlightenment in the shade of this species.

His father, Leo, Konstan told me, was ambushed and murdered trying to defend trees like this one from illegal loggers, four of whom he confronted alone one morning in 2010. The motherfuckers sliced his right arm with a machete and speared him in the back, clear through his chest. I never asked Konstan how he copes, though he told me he believes in prayer. If we talked in depth about his pain, I might have opened up about mine. My mental health in the United States was shaky. I like diving because it's in silence.

With a pole, he pushed us from shore. We glided over the reef to deeper water, then zoomed north toward the main island, where I would take a public ferry and then head to the airport for home.

Now that Konstan no longer used a paddle and relied instead on his Yamaha motor, his family was getting richer in West Papua, one of the poorest provinces of Indonesia. A quarter of its people earned less than a dollar a day in 2016, about the price of a liter of fuel. The engine allowed him to bring occasional tourists like me to his remote wilderness, enabling his family to visit the doctor, send their children to school, buy food, and have mobile phones. As I well knew, even with a motor, the trip to Raja's remote islands could be long and dangerous.

Konstan was trying to speed into a better future. Like most of us, he has sought greater security as our planetary emergency continues to unfold. At least one village I visited, Arefi, had already raised their seawall, and salt water had infiltrated their well. Joy, the manager of the nearby pearl farm, told me Raja Ampat's climate was changing. It's getting hotter, he told me. He said there hadn't been a true dry season since 2015, which was unheard of; there were fewer fish to catch.

And yet what has Konstan lost in replacing his paddle with a motor? As he pulled on the cord to start the engine, it was a romantic, even colonialist question I couldn't help but ask myself. The slap-splash of waves against the hull, the sound of the breeze, rhythmic paddling, endorphin highs, greater strength and stamina, the melding of body and canoe, slowness itself as normal, boredom—for thousands of years those were the essential elements of ocean travel. When he told me on the beach one night, "The ocean is our mattress, the waves our pillows, the wind our blanket," I heard a hint of the nostalgia tourists like me love. His cracked smartphone was glowing in his hand.

But even better questions might be: What have we as Earthlings already lost? What future losses have we already committed to? Konstan, in using a motor, grew his carbon footprint. But the amount was minuscule—positively infinitesimal—compared to mine. I was responsible for two tons of carbon from my roundtrip flights, far more than Konstan's family emits in a year. How many brar trees would have to be planted to suck that up? How many brar paddles would that equal? Konstan gave me the ironic present of unburned carbon, safely locked away as wood. But since 1751, what has the industrialized world gifted him and his people? Over three quadrillion pounds of carbon, raising average global temperatures by about two degrees Fahrenheit.

Our collective future worries me to no end, though Konstan's is far bleaker: I live in a mountain valley 150 miles from the coast in a nuclear-armed superpower; he's maybe a foot above sea level on the equator in a nation with an almost nonexistent social safety net. By the end of this century or even sooner, research shows, it could be too hot to live in the tropics. And unless we take drastic action immediately, in his lifetime his reefs will likely die, his village inundated.

It will be our carbon, not his, that will be resoundingly culpable. I knew what I was: a sunburned emissary from the West, the birthplace of the chainsaw and Agent Orange, of the electric SuperPretzel Soft Pretzel Maker with a cheese-melting pod—of Exxon and Trump and other trademarks that will be curse words on the lips of our descendants. I felt ridiculous and gross.

WE STOPPED AT THE ISLAND of Mansuar so that Konstan could check his texts and get motor oil. There was an old-fashioned cellular signal, no data. I turned on my phone. "*Please call ASAP* 😈 😔," my mother had texted. I groaned loudly.

"I don't know how I can go on," my mother said. "If only I could get up on a step stool. I'm so depressed, Greg."

I stared down at minnows. She resented that I was "on vacation" without her. The few times on my trip I found a signal to call her, she had a caregiver read me her concerningly high blood pressure as if to say my distance was going to give her another stroke. Ten thousand miles away wasn't far enough.

"Remember how strong Mamo was," I told my mother. "Call on her spirit."

"How do I do that? Please help me, Greg." For as long as I could remember, way before the stroke that almost killed her, I had been her therapist, confessor, girlfriend, and punching bag.

"Talk to her just like she's there in front of you. You believe in guardian angels, right?"

"I want you to teach me meditation when you get back. I still don't understand."

Several times I'd tried teaching her, but she'd snap and say she didn't know how to focus on her breath.

"How do you watch it?" she would ask. "It's invisible."

I told her I had to go. Konstan was starting up the motor again, and I didn't want to get cut off mid-conversation and then have to rush to call her back once we got back to chaotic Waisai, the capital of Raja Ampat.

"You've got to persevere," I said, hanging up, trying not to condescend.

AFTER A WHILE, KONSTAN and I hit some rough waters. With the paddle across my lap, a freak wave soaked us. He cut the motor. There were no towels. Just the sun, trained on us like a heat lamp. Like the eye of a terrible god to be worshiped and appeased generations from now.

Speeding along sopping wet, I realized that for my C-PTSD brain, Konstan's paddle was a larger version of my mother's Walmart spoon. Her weapon was the same color as the bleached side of his gift and a similar shape. It was also made from a light tropical wood, akin to *brar*, without the extraordinary grain and grooves. No wonder his gift felt so urgently uncanny in my hands and across my lap. Why I felt so intensely ambivalent about it. It was a symbol of my personal trauma, which the reefs had stirred up and begun to heal, and a reminder of the planetary crisis underway. As for anyone, it could be both at the same time.

We arrived at the big dock in Waisai. I hugged Konstan, but it was awkward. Men don't really embrace like that in his culture, or so I believed. I guess part of me felt he was almost the younger brother I never had. We wordlessly shared so much. Sometimes I found myself assuming people were family when they weren't. I didn't intend to do it, but it helped me feel less lonely.

I stepped off his boat and onto a ferry to the mainland. At the airport I found someone to wrap the paddle in plastic, my second piece of checked baggage. In a couple of days, I'd be home, whatever that meant.

AFTER I RETURNED TO VIRGINIA, I had a burst of self-respect. Which is to say that cutting ties with my family wasn't exactly a decision. It was a primal moment of surrender. I'd seen myself turning suicidal after she had another series of outrageous breakdowns and preventable hospitalizations. Sometimes your moral duty to stay alive and the one to help your family can't be fulfilled at the same time. My mother didn't have Alzheimer's—her antics were timeless. I knew that if I remained in contact with her, I'd harm myself. A son divorcing his mother, to my mind, was a shameful taboo. Maybe others in my situation would have chosen differently—or they would've "peaced out" the day they turned eighteen and never looked back.

The next day, humming Madonna's "Borderline," I sent a letter to her and her bank resigning as trustee and giving up my power of attorney. From now on, a trust officer at her bank would manage her affairs. I also stopped speaking to my father, which should've happened long ago.

That was it—the clean break. Like a spaceship trying to leave a planet's orbit, it took time for me to reach escape velocity.

CHAPTER 18

A Joy Forever

Ever since leaving Dayan and cutting ties with my family, I better understand what John Keats meant when he wrote, "A thing of beauty is a joy forever." It's not sentimental to me anymore—it's essential wisdom for living on a dying planet. For becoming more an author of one's happiness and less a victim. A prevailer instead of a survivor.

Sometimes when I think about my parents, I'll use H.E.A.L. to gladden the sad memories as they're reconsolidated in my brain. To that end, I recall the night I walked alone in my wetsuit on Konstan's moonlit beach. Like rocks on a dimly lit asteroid, dead coral and plastic cast shadows across the sand. I waddled with my mask like some marooned alien to the ruined pier Leo built for the conservation post.

I slipped into the water. Submerged on a piling was a white, doily-like creature opening its petals the way a chameleon tongue unrolls. It was an echinoderm called a basket star, but to me it was a lotus blossom I saw frescoed once in a cave. It was a woven, living SETI dish broadcasting goodwill messages and listening intently. A mycelial antenna conveying chatter and nourishment not among brar trees in Konstan's rainforest but to alien worlds in our curving arm of the Milky Way.

Across the light years, the dark years, I trusted the creature could hear my mother telling me, *You have no reason to be mad at me*, my father saying, *You're going to get it, you know*—and that it was beaming back to them loving defiance, frequencies higher than incest and bigotry, repeating ones and zeros of new-covenant rainbows and my bedfellow Whitman's voice: "I am enamoured of growing outdoors, / Of men that live among cattle or taste of the ocean or woods... / I am the poet of the body / And I am the poet of the soul." My mother would say, *Night dives are dangerous, get out of the water*, but my need to internalize the grace of this animal was stronger. I stayed with the basket star, I breathed slowly, I didn't have to keep running. What happened to me wasn't my fault, but now it's my responsibility.

When I'm having another traumatic flashback, I practice over-writing them with memories of one especially astonishing section of Konstan's reef, if even for three seconds, MC Hammer singing "U Can't Touch This" in the background. I focus on the coral species that dominated the reef, *Isopora palifera*, which is roughly shaped like paddles. They didn't scare me; they were the bajillion daffodils mesmerizing siblings Dorothy and William Wordsworth. "We saw that there was a long belt of them along the shore," she would later write of the flowers. "I never saw daffodils so beautiful." I visualize those paddles of coral propagating inside a much deeper version of my childhood bathtub—the pickle-and-pear, green-and-pale-red colonies accreting and thriving along the ceramic-coated steel, sheltering sweepers in galactic starling flocks. Inlaid with brain coral the color of real brains.

I float above it all, swimming by myself, whole and complete. I am not the terrible memory—I am its witness. Panic going, despair gone, gently down the stream. The water of that cove-sized bathtub is stunningly clear.

In the imagination, no one can hurt that child again. You are safe. Little Greg is safe. He's in his skin, not dissociating, not waiting for anyone to degrade him.

In the imagination, the reef is safe; there it can never bleach and die—beauty thrives forever in the mind's eye, where no species is endangered and safety can be conjured as if from a spell. In *The Sense of Wonder*, Rachel Carson says of nature lovers, "Whatever the vexations or concerns of their personal lives, their thoughts can find paths that lead to inner contentment and to renewed excitement in living. Those who contemplate the beauty of the earth find reserves of strength that will endure as long as life lasts." I'm learning to rely on that storehouse instead of acting out my despair. When I'm eighty-five in the year 2064, there may be little else to comfort me but memories of living reefs. Perhaps just looking at the ocean will be too upsetting. Going outside might be unwise.

I don't know, but I'll try to remember the black manta—you must come early in the morning with Konstan to see her, after the hornbills have stopped honking and sunlight has caused plankton to rise up from the deep. She was jet-black with a few white patches, her mouth open to strain the water for food, her gills undulating. She was much bigger than I was, fifteen feet across, soaring in my presence like a badass starship on a science mission. On her back was a furry, bulbous scar it hurt to look at. In the strong current I stretched out my arms, trying to fly into it like she was.

Then she swam up. Her wingtip touched my fingertip once, then she veered away, down to the bottom of the channel. Joy filled me, and also sadness. That moment of contact was like a tuning fork barely placed against your thumbnail and you say to your friend, "Mercy, I feel it all the way down to my feet."

How many times in this life had she been a mother?

BACK IN VIRGINIA, after I unwrapped the obscene amount of plastic mummifying the paddle, it seemed dull. My new friend AJ, who lived a mile down the road toward West Virginia, tried restoring it in his woodshop. He waxed it first, but it didn't change much. He sanded that off and coated it instead with polyurethane. Oily stains, likely Konstan's fingerprints, were revealed in the process. They're permanent. It's still not all that shiny. But now it sort of radiates.

The night AJ returned it to me, we climbed up onto his roof to smoke a fat joint. It hit me hard. The cloudy sky, peach-colored from the lights of our town, seemed to swirl, and I thought we were going to slide off.

"Don't be such a pussy," he said, feeling my bicep. "You're swole!"

"Well," I said, "you're a damn dingleberry."

Getting more and more stoned, I thought he looked like Galahad, then Bradley Cooper, then a strapping version of Abe Lincoln. I wanted to kiss him—but he had a girlfriend I adored. He wasn't into me like that anyway. To distract myself, I stared at the city jail and the old courthouse with its corroded dome.

He must have felt me pulling inward. "What's your mother like?" he asked. "Your father?"

I kept it vague. I told him I recently decided to never speak to my family again and that I felt alone, even doomed, as I entered middle age. And yet, pre-pandemic at least, I loved living in Virginia. It was slower; warmhearted people and I looked each other in the eye and smiled; I took fuller breaths; after two months here, I had more friends than I did after six years in California.

AJ told me he's always lived in the area. He loves his family, but he can't stand most people. He's off social media. When his anxiety gets too intense, he tells his girlfriend goodbye and bikes up into the desolate mountains to camp alone. It's one of the perks of living in the Shenandoah Valley between a national forest and a national park. When you're losing your mind, which is easy these days, ten or fifteen miles away, past the turnoff to Rawley Springs, is a ravine where you can holler as loudly as you want. If someone can hear you, they probably get it.

I've asked but he still won't tell me what he does out there to calm down. I'm looking for new techniques. I know he cares about me, but like some people, he's hard to get a hold of—texts are answered after a week, as if he were somewhere beyond the solar system.

Does he lie back on a bed of ferns and imagine the maples brushing the angst off his being?

Does he read quotes from Edward Abbey, his favorite nature writer, to a waterfall? I can hear AJ reading aloud from a mist-soaked page of *Desert Solitaire*: "I am here not only to evade for a while the clamor and filth and confusion of the cultural apparatus but also to confront, immediately and directly if it's possible, the bare bones of existence, the elemental and fundamental, the bedrock which sustains us."

Does he squeeze his eyes shut and take a hammer to a rock? That's his preferred task when he's out working as a wilderness trail builder, grateful there's no phone signal. As he pounds away, does he curse society and his triggers, and the fact that he was born at all?

Does he rename the plants and animals to pretend he's on a different planet?

Maybe he doesn't do anything in particular—and that's the point. Run for the hills! Nature for nature's sake! Not everyone sees life as a therapeutic quest, or should.

Before coming down from the roof like spider crabs, he and I agreed: the future scares us. Sometimes there's nothing to do but get the hell out and go into nature.

Part Three

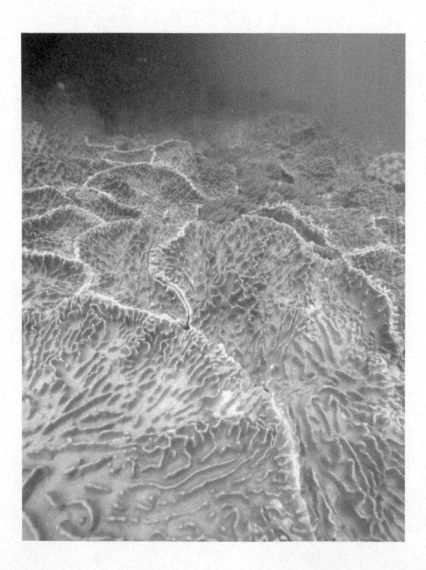

CHAPTER 19

Change Your Mind

"Normal waking consciousness feels perfectly transparent,
and yet it is less a window on reality than the product of
our imaginations—a kind of controlled hallucination."

—MICHAEL POLLAN, *How to Change Your Mind*

A round the time Konstan gave me the paddle, Michael Pollan's book on the therapeutic potential of psychedelics, *How to Change Your Mind*, was published. A *New York Times* #1 bestseller, it marked a huge shift in the culture and my own life. It showed me I shouldn't have scoffed at Jake in Santa Cruz calling his cannabis "medicine"— like me, he was a commitment-phobic trauma survivor with no good mainstream options for treatment.

If sober, sensible Michael Pollan tried psychedelics, I wondered after finishing the book, *why can't I?*

As you well know by now, cyberspace had been my speed and weed; it wasn't until after moving to California in my thirties that I smoked cannabis or even drank booze with any regularity. Other substances had been unthinkable, which is how I was thankfully raised. The few times growing up I saw my dad order a Bud Light, my mother gasped with horror as if he'd told the waiter to dust his fried shrimp with cocaine. "Are you alright?" she asked.

Nevertheless, seventeen days before Pollan's book was released—a week before I left for Raja Ampat to stay with Konstan—I had my first psychedelic experience.

I was in Tennessee at a multiday gathering of Radical Faeries, a group of back-to-nature queer folks, some in drag, some naked, some like me in a jackalope mask and jockstrap. Hundreds of us camped in tents, danced around an enormous fire, and cried together in heart circles. Just being there, we had stepped outside consensus reality, deliciously, unsettlingly so. It was my attempt to meet outdoorsy, free-thinking men not on Grindr but in person, which was tough where I lived in the hinterlands. It felt like progress to be there and celebrate May Day with twinks, bears, chub chasers, otters, pre- and post-op transmen, rednecks with meathook scars, Marxist furries with butt-plug puppy tails. The gathering on Short Mountain was a safe space if there ever was one.

Soon after I arrived, I saw a shirtless, shaggy guy in a leather vest and Indiana Jones hat, claw marks tattooed on his chest. He put out zero sexual energy.

Already stoned and tipsy, I walked up to him and blurted, "Hey there! Are you a shaman?"

"Actually, yes," he said softly, calling himself Hogan. As we chatted, I followed him to a boulder on a thickly forested hillside away from the campsites. It was a clear day. He said he'd like to share a low dose of DMT, which he explained we already produce in our bodies. He didn't want any money.

What he didn't tell me was that DMT is one of the most powerful psychedelics of all. A substance possibly released as we die.

"I'll try it," I said, noticing the sunlight on his stubble, "but you've got to hold my hand."

He lit a pipe filled with bits of shredded plant matter.

Oh, did I inhale. My body dispersed like dandelion fluff.

As I looked up at the trees, their new leaves turned into green fractals. And from them, like a Magic Eye poster, emerged a green face—was it a female Buddha? She was gentle, with the most serene, pleased smile.

Being itself rang as it never had on silent meditation retreats. It was like a monk who had meditated for decades in a cave was sharing his mind with me. Reality came into focus: *we're living in a simulation.*

But that isn't the right word; it makes our reality sound inconsequential and manipulative, almost evil. We are not virtual lab monkeys trapped on an alien server. Spitting on my Harvard education, I saw the universe had been created.

Time and space are a gift. So is having a body, even if it doesn't seem like it. Moving forward is an illusion. Holding on is useless.

Looking up at the Green Face, in the periphery I saw the stitchwork and scaffolding of so-called reality. It wasn't a cage. It was form that had arisen miraculously, sassily, from formlessness. It was a classroom. It was art. The Green Face was the Creator. The Engineer. Guru, Goddess, Mother of All.

As I held Hogan's hand and looked up at her, I tasted what I'd really been looking for: unconditional love. The words of Kentucky mystic Thomas Merton might as well have been mine: "Life is this simple: we are living in a world that is absolutely transparent and the divine is shining through it all the time. This is not just a nice story or a fable; it is true." I realized I could weirdly relax, even as the country and the planet were in crisis: I was in a baffling illusion that could be trusted. It was clear to me, at least then, that our destiny was bound up in rejoicing.

I carried the memory of the Green Face with me from Tennessee to Konstan's reefs—to the morning mantas, the giant clam, the paddle-shaped coral thriving during a global mass bleaching event. When I met the basket star and when blacktip sharks were patrolling near me, I felt her smile. Even as my biological mother provoked me in those moments I had a signal out at sea, in the back of my mind, the Green Face stayed with me, comforted me. This experience with DMT enabled me to see Raja Ampat's reefs more clearly than ever. Afterwards, I was brought to a tipping point in self-compassion, and I cut ties with my family.

Your life—your well-being—matters.

STILL, AFTER TRYING DMT and then orphaning myself in June 2018, I was as depressed as I'd ever been. I told a local psychiatrist I felt suicidal sometimes but that the antidepressants I'd taken since college—high doses of selective serotonin reuptake inhibitors (SSRIs) like Zoloft, Celexa, and Prozac—hadn't ever helped. It turns out 60–70 percent of patients on SSRIs don't experience remission, and 30–40 percent don't meaningfully respond to them. Given conflicting research studies, some of which are funded by pharmaceutical companies, whether SSRIs offer more relief than a placebo sugar pill is still an open question.

"No," I assured him, "I'm not a danger to myself or others."

Seemingly stumped, he prescribed me Ritalin of all things, which I guess as a stimulant was supposed to lift me up enough until our next frightfully expensive session.

I didn't go back. Instead of outright taking my life, I acted out my death wish by mixing Ritalin with weed, alcohol, Viagra, and poppers. With all of that in my system, often looking down at my phone, I drove on dark, winding mountain roads in West Virginia to meet up with strangers, almost getting into serious accidents several times. I hooked up with closeted homophobes in their Ford F-150s on pitch-black national forest roads, by railroad tracks and abandoned barns. When we heard a car approaching, we froze. Sometimes during sex the men got violent, whispering the crimes they'd gotten away with. I knew they were carrying guns.

When one especially charming guy offered me crystal meth—a chemical cousin of Ritalin—I almost took it. I became truly frightened after I scrolled through heartbreaking before-and-after photos of meth addicts and still considered obliterating my pain that way.

Something stopped me. I'd remember things like hiking the week before with my married friends Rob and Chip. We saw blue crayfish and orange-tipped oakworm moths. We tasted wild black raspberries, sniffed the flowering, coral-like stems of black cohosh. I'd remember the warmth of our friendship.

What also stopped me was seeing the Green Face in my mind. DMT wasn't some cool party drug that launched me into hyperspace so I could tweet about it. It was medicine.

Had I not taken it, I might be dead. A 2020 study published in the *Journal of Psychopharmacology* out of Johns Hopkins found that 90 percent of people reported in a survey said that their well-being and life satisfaction improved after using DMT. Half of respondents no longer identified as agnostic or atheist. In the first clinical trials in 2021, administering one intravenous dose of DMT in a clinical therapeutic setting to treat major depressive disorder resulted in an astounding remission rate of 57 percent. Losing neural structures called dendritic spines is a sign of depression, but in mature rats, DMT causes the number of spines—and the number of neural connections overall—to increase. DMT quickly promotes neuroplasticity, but what you do with that more malleable, coachable brain is up to you.

Why didn't that one puff of DMT cure me? For one, it wasn't a large dose. And depression wasn't the only mental health challenge

I was facing—it's called complex PTSD for a reason. On top of that, psychedelics can't transform you "bibbidi-bobbidi-boo" into a Prince Charming–ready angel. In the beginning, I didn't know that.

How to Change Your Mind introduced me to recent research into the therapeutic—as opposed to recreational—value of psychedelics. One paper in particular that Michael Pollan highlighted stood out to me. A 2009 smoking-cessation study directed by Matthew Johnson, psychiatry professor at Johns Hopkins, showed that after several doses of psilocybin (the active ingredient in "magic" mushrooms) and a brief period of therapy, 80 percent of participants had given up smoking after six months, 67 percent after a year. The more profound participants rated the mystical experience, the better the outcome. By comparison, a 2021 study published in the Journal of the American Medicine Association found that Chantix, a popular anti-smoking pill, had a success rate of approximately 25 percent after a year, even when combined with a nicotine patch.

Though researchers like to compare the mind on psychedelics to a shaken snow globe, Johnson has another analogy: it's "a reboot of the system—a biological control-alt-delete." The mental pliability that psychedelics foster, Johnson theorizes, gives people a chance to revise the rigid, self-centered stories that underlie their addictions. Could it help with mine?

Googling "PTSD psychedelics," I found a research paper by Antonio Inserra, a neuroscientist at McGill University, that changed my life: "Hypothesis: The Psychedelic Ayahuasca Heals Traumatic Memories via a Sigma 1 Receptor-Mediated Epigenetic-Mnemonic Progress." Ex-squeeze me? A sentence on the first page leapt out:

> Ayahuasca could come to represent the only standing pharmacological treatment which targets traumatic memories in PTSD.

Though the complex neurochemical processes Inserra laid out were beyond me, I took away that ayahuasca—an Amazonian psychoactive tea that's a mix of a vine (confusingly also called ayahuasca) and the leaves of the DMT-rich chacruna bush—was powerful. The MAO inhibitors in the vine prevent the gut from breaking down the DMT, keeping the difficult, potentially life-changing trip going for hours, causing cathartic purging. No "gold-standard" clinical trials with humans had confirmed ayahuasca as a PTSD treatment, though strong anecdotal evidence from ayahuasca-ingesting veterans and others had been around for some time. And while it's been in documented use by Indigenous South American tribes since the conquistadors wrote about it, ayahuasca has probably been used for thousands of years.

In any case, Inserra's paper taught me that ayahuasca stimulates the sigma-1, an important receptor in every cell—this interaction, Inserra proposes, is one key to its potential to heal PTSD. Siggy, as I began to refer to the sigma-1 receptor, became my homeboy. I pictured him as a cute, grinning puzzle piece that ayahuasca's DMT fit perfectly into. Soulmates. Two peas in a stress-responsive pod. Setting up his hypothesis, in the paper Inserra makes it clear that stimulating Siggy had already been experimentally shown to:

- Increase neuroplasticity and, by increasing brain-derived neurotrophic factor (BDNF), cause new neurons to be born.
- Have an "anti-amnesic" effect—it causes repressed traumatic memories to surface.
- Dissipate the fear associated with such memories.
- Disrupt the reconsolidation of traumatic memories.
- Change gene expression.

All these changes except the last can be seen on brain scans. Though Inserra's paper was technically a hypothesis, it was supported by a slew of neurochemical studies. It seemed, in theory at least, ayahuasca could help me.

Pollan's groundbreaking book and Inserra's riveting paper gave me hope. My species might be on a suicide mission, I came to see, but I didn't have to be on a personal one.

AROUND THIS TIME, I became especially good friends with a young woman named Kathryn. Curvy with big round glasses, she burped loudly and unapologetically; her belly laughs shook the walls. With a friend, she published an environmental magazine with pieces written by local gardeners, activists, and witches. A button on her backpack read FIND YOUR INNER CLIT. We understood each other.

Barely acquainted, one day we saw one another in the old cemetery at the end of Water Street in Harrisonburg. Under a spruce we shared our thoughts on men, food, and the nature of reality. We were both struggling. Over the weeks and months of this dark time in our lives, we lifted one another up—we knew we weren't the only people struggling with self-harm in this town.

I remember Kathryn working on me once—she's an extraordinary massage therapist—and I started weeping; she had another client waiting downstairs, but she kept her hand on my chest until I was finished. Then she struck her animal-skin drum above various places on my body—it felt as if she were shattering our compulsions, as if the egg where she and I were incubating had begun to crack. For weeks afterward, when I felt trapped and hopeless, I would consciously recall that feeling of breaking free, of a fresh start.

Yes, in Virginia I had a "social support system," as it's called, as never before. But in time, those friends—and the Green Face and the vast forests surrounding us—couldn't stop my downward spiral. I was on a collision course with the past.

As LUCK WOULD HAVE IT, I started therapy in February 2019 with a therapist I'll call James who took my insurance; the co-pay was only $25. My age and married to a man, he seemed like someone I could trust. He diagnosed me with C-PTSD, though he prefers the term "complex trauma." Familiar with the essence of Hanson's H.E.A.L. technique, he was also supportive of therapeutic psychedelic use. Instead of focusing on the past, he had me talk about what I was feeling in the moment, encouraging me to let go of thinking.

In moments of optimism, I printed out peer-reviewed research studies from Google Scholar and put them in a red folder. It would be my Bible. Papers like the one by Rafael Faria Sanches and colleagues showed ayahuasca was a fast-acting treatment for depressed patients like me who don't get relief from Big Pharma antidepressants. Study after study showed that ayahuasca was an effective intervention for addiction and was itself nonaddictive and well-tolerated. One showed that it led to increased mindfulness. Others pointed to its capacity to spark "divergent creative thinking"—thinking outside the box—and to enhance overall mental health and well-being. No studies indicated that ayahuasca was dangerous or toxic, though individuals with a history of psychosis and bipolar disorder shouldn't ingest it, and finding a trained, safe facilitator is absolutely positively essential.

I studied the research late into the night, Grindr flashing beside me, invitations to party with meth piling up. I meditated like hell, sending love to Siggy and his trillions of buddies in my brain—for the time being, I would aim to make him my one and only.

By the end of the spring semester of 2019, I didn't know what else to do but give ayahuasca a shot. But I wasn't about to solicit recommendations from the mob called Facebook, since ayahuasca was technically illegal in the United States. I didn't know how to contact Hogan or if that was even his real name.

Where could I turn?

Reddit, of course, considerably more trustworthy than the one-eyed oracles standing by on Chatroulette. A place called Dreamglade in Peru was recommended with a good number of up-votes. Their prices, at the time around $700 for three ceremonies and five nights in a hut, were the lowest of any I had found. They had a lake to swim in, and supposedly there weren't many mosquitoes.

With James's blessing, I booked the trip. I'd been to the Amazon of the ocean to dive its depths and now I was going to the actual Amazon to dive the wreck of my mind. To test Inserra's hypothesis for myself. What could possibly go wrong?

CHAPTER 20

Dreamglade

Heading to Dreamglade, the seven of us rode in a 4x4 from the airport in Iquitos, a sketchy city of almost four hundred thousand on the west bank of the Amazon River in Peru. In the truck bed I introduced myself to a barista and an Energizer Bunny of a banker, all of us clinging to the luggage. Stace, Dreamglade's big-hearted founder, was driving. To avoid adverse reactions during the ayahuasca ceremonies, we'd been asked to avoid alcohol, sex, weed, and salt for the last couple of weeks, so there was an unusual intensity to our shouted small talk. Alternating between worry and hope, I said as little as possible as we approached the jungle on the potholed dirt road. I told myself, *I'm not here to make friends.*

WELL AFTER DARK, around 8:00 p.m., we assembled in a huge circular hut called a *maloca* that looked like a thatched spaceship. Each of us had a foam mattress and a purge bucket. After a reassuring orientation of dos and don'ts, the space was cleansed with smoking pieces of palo santo. The vibe was solemn and austere. No Enya was playing; we weren't made to *Om*. The set and setting, in other words, felt spot on.

Raul and Lidia, the two *curanderos* (shamanic healer-doctors) facing the door, commanded our respect immediately. They are half-siblings from villages outside Pucallpa, the beating heart of the Indigenous Shipibo culture, eight days from here by boat. Sometimes Raul was summoned to the regional hospital there to heal patients who weren't responding to conventional medical treatments. Best friends, he and Lidia have each been working with the medicine for over forty years, having studied under master teachers like Raul's grandfather and Lidia's grandmother. For months at a time, they live as hermits in the rainforest to work with the plants.

Sitting on a colorful textile embroidered with what looked like Pac-Man mazes, Raul blew the smoke of jungle tobacco called *mapacho* into the bottle of ayahuasca, softly whispering a song to evoke its power. One by one we went up to receive our dose poured from a plastic pitcher.

As Stace handed me the shot glass, I remembered why I was in the middle of the rainforest a few miles from the Amazon River: I needed help. I was a patient, not a thrill-seeking tourist blind to the realities of cultural appropriation. Raul and Lidia were the doctors, generously offering their ancestral medicine to descendants of those who had tried to destroy their culture through mission work, corporate greed, and outright genocide.

As I brought the dose to my lips, my mouth trembled, then my whole head, and for a moment I felt like some super basic gringo on *Fear Factor*. Bottoms up! Though Jay Griffiths writes in *Wild* that ayahuasca tastes like "hemlock and stars; as foul as one, as brilliant as the other," I tasted no brilliance in this brown bitterness. Heavens to Betsy! It was a mix of—and I mean no disrespect—decaying bark, shoe polish, and toe jam. Swallowing hard to get it all down, I scurried back to my spot.

When the fire was put out, the maloca went pitch-black. Lying back on the mattress, I felt the medicine oozing its way down my esophagus like in the Pepto-Bismol commercials. Meditating with one hand on my puke bucket, I might have thought we were in a primordial void if it weren't for the singing male frogs hoping to breed outside in the lake. *This isn't doing anything*, I thought.

I checked that my headlamp was still around my neck. I picked at my eyebrows. Mouthed the loving-kindness chant. Felt for the folder of peer-reviewed ayahuasca studies to remind myself of the encouraging science.

This is a scam, I thought, *and I'm an idiot. What's wrong with me?*

Then it crept up: my body was softening into dough. The night passed over me in disorienting waves—this was going to be a very different trip from the one I took with Hogan's DMT. Behind my eyelids was diffuse light. Time absorbed me into its bloodstream. I was a cluster of lava-lamp blobs on the floor, a mass of cannonball jellyfish stranded on the beach.

Was I about to cross over into some dimensionless no-man's-land? In the rapture of near-total concentration, I was primally scared but also weirdly sedated.

Then Raul started singing an *icaro*, a healing song channeled from the plant spirits in the brew. "Whenever you're afraid," Stace told us in the earlier orientation, "take a deep breath and listen to the icaro." Days later I asked Raul in Spanish about the songs. Plant spirits are called upon during a ceremony, he said, and each icaro is a different plant's song channeled through him. The ayahuasca spirit singing through him is the ultimate source of healing.

Feeling like a seasick garden of smeared goo, I listened to his staccato icaro. As Raul sang, he became a huge, extradimensional beetle-king singing skull-penetrating incantations that rotated my brain cells ninety degrees like Tetris pieces with each quick, sharply separated note. He was conducting the trillions of cells in my body like an orchestra. The banker was screaming puke. The barista was giggling. Groaning, I sensed a Möbius strip of superintelligence humming above, as if we were in a terrarium and some Great Eye were peering down. It was like a first contact meeting between two vastly different intelligent species.

After the second dose, I felt a different form of sentience here, a nurturing female presence. Maternal love. Like all mammals, I know it when I feel it. She was in my cells, which was scientifically true since DMT molecules had attached to some of my Siggies. She used my body to communicate with me, uncomfortably at times, our language consisting of interactive sensations and emotions. Wordlessly testing and teasing one another, she was the parent, and I was her newborn.

Unable to walk, I crawled to Lidia. It was time for my *limpieza*, Spanish for "cleaning." Doctor and patient sat facing one another, knees touching.

Her icaro for me was at times high-pitched, almost squeaky, but then she'd drop down into the back of her throat, almost growling, kicking around spit until her lungs emptied and she gulped more air. As she sang, I remembered Mamo at ninety-five laboring to sing me "Happy Birthday" on her deathbed. I thought something like, *Lidia, a mother and grandmother herself, thinks I'm worthy—wants me to get better.* Whooshing my forehead with quick exhales, she sent me back to my spot in the circle.

AYAHUASCA MAKES YOU FACE what you most fear, and you don't get to decide for how long. Sometimes, you're even transformed into it.

Babies, as I've said, freaked me out. Triggered me as little else could. In my first ceremony I turned into one, neurologically at least. Research by Robin Carhart-Harris, a neuroscientist at Imperial College London, indicates that in brain scans, an adult brain on LSD looks like a typical baby's brain. (LSD is chemically very similar to DMT.) Importantly, Carhart-Harris found that, when faced with a task, an adult brain on a placebo depends on one main brain region, but the LSD-tripping brain, like a baby's, uses many different areas at once.

Given this lack of compartmentalization, UC Berkeley psychologist Alison Gopnik told Michael Pollan in *How to Change Your Mind*, "Babies and children are basically tripping all the time." They are free of the rigid thinking, linguistic constraints, and laser focus that bedevil adults. Emotional ups-and-downs, imaginativeness, intense wonder: babies and psychonauts have a lot in common.

Also like a baby, in the ceremony I was on my back, as in a crib, utterly dependent on strange caregivers to keep me safe in the darkness; I couldn't walk without help. I was often in a preverbal state, with bile, farts, burps, tears, groans, and giggles as my expressive language.

Moreover, at times I was overcome with an experience readily felt by babies: the "oceanic feeling" of oneness with eternity. "A feeling as if something limitless, unbounded" is how French writer Romain Rolland described it to Sigmund Freud, who of course replied that it was a primitive holdover from infancy when the baby assumed he was all that existed. No. The oceanic feeling in adults isn't a form of narcissism; it loosens the grip of the egoic self, releasing the heart so we're more available to the miracle of existence. Rolland called it "a source of vital renewal" in his personal life, and I suspect it's a big part of the healing that both psychedelics and nature offer. Perhaps my dives in the salty womb of the Pacific were attempts to recover the oceanic feeling.

Think of Thoreau playing his flute on his boat, looking down at thousands of moonlit fish and a drowned forest on the bottom of Walden Pond. Recall my father, near death, photographing ducks at the extended-stay motel, appreciating Mother Earth like the child of hers that he was. Remember the purple coral.

FIVE DAYS LATER, in the third and final ceremony, a high-speed montage of flashbacks too upsetting to watch rocketed through me. I must have blacked out—next thing I knew, I was about to barf, the only person who hadn't yet. Putting my head over the bucket, I retched. Nothing. Again I dry-heaved. Something awful nestled inside me had been disturbed. It loathed the ayahuasca and all the goodwill. I lay back, trying to belly breathe. I curled up on my side, shutting down, unable to breathe into the terror and be with it. There was nowhere to run.

In my limpieza that night, Raul sang forever, sounding like he was sternly lecturing the gnarliness inside me, reciting the galactic statutes it was breaking by staying inside me. The icaro was torture for my repressed memories. Thanks to the medicine's anti-amnesic effect that Inserra's paper emphasizes, traumatic memories were surfacing, but I couldn't make them out visually. Raul's singing was a battle hymn of a general telling his foe, *It's time.*

When the icaro ended, I pulled away from the bucket. He moved closer. And closer still. I didn't want to be this close in the dark to a man my father's age. My neck involuntarily twisted, my head cocking to one side with reptilian alarm—I was a lizard about to cough up a fat parasite.

"*Tengo miedo,*" I said through my hands.

"*No preocupes. Está bien, Gregorio,*" he said, cradling my head with his thumbs on my temples. For some time, he sucked air from my crown and blew it to the side like a stank burp.

"*Listo,*" he whispered.

I had to go to the toilet. As I slouched toward the door with a helper, Raul affectionately shouted in a whisper, "*Macho!*" His Peruvian way of reminding me I was strong.

"*Macho!*" he said again, making those whooshing noises.

WHEN I LEFT THE BATHROOM, Stace was sitting nearby in a chair. I sat next to him, keeping the bucket in my lap, and we got to talking. I told him about my family, at times dissociating and forgetting what I was even saying. Sounding as if I were auditioning for *The Jerry Springer Show*, I told him some of what I'd been telling my therapists for two decades.

"I've heard it all," he said, apologizing for seeming distant. He had also taken the medicine tonight, and it had been rough.

"I can't even imagine," I said. "This is honorable work, so courageous." You don't open a center like this in Peru to get rich. You do it to help a world in crisis.

"Who are you without your stories?" he asked.

"A freaking white witch!" I joked. "Mike Pence, watch out!"

Eventually Drew, one of the ceremony helpers, took Stace's place. I gave Drew the CliffsNotes version of what I'd already said.

"I see The Door," I said, pressing into the corners of my eyes.

"What did you say, amigo?" Drew asked with his slight Texan accent.

"I'm not opening The Door. Girlfriend, I would die." I twisted some of my arm hair into tornadoes.

"What do you think happened to you?"

"I think, you know, something with my dad."

I told him what my father asked me when I came out.

"The, um," I sobbed, "it was when I was very, very young. I've known it in my body forever, I just haven't mentally seen the clear footage of what he did, if that makes sense."

"You'll see it when you need to, if you need to," he said.

"Do you judge me for cutting off my family?"

"No—most people would do the same thing."

"I go back and forth sometimes. Honor thy mother and father. What about sacrifice? Duty? Nonviolence?"

"There are lots of different ways to look at it. But if you can get to the point of forgiving your parents, of looking them in the eye and saying, 'I forgive you, and I ask you to forgive me—we're good, Mom and Dad,' you'll be bulletproof. Bulletproof!"

"What if they chew me out? I also don't want to give them false hope that I'm going to pretend nothing happened."

"It doesn't matter what they say. You forgive your parents for yourself. Not to necessarily restart a relationship." The fact that he sounded like Dr. Phil made me squirm. Probably because that night, a straight-talking Southerner was exactly who I needed to talk to.

"Forgiveness is for you," he said, pointing right at my heart.

Several participants, an elfish psychiatrist and a lesbian couple, were dancing and running through the forest beside us. "Bally-hoo-hoo-hoo!" they chanted like young children, bringing to mind Carhart-Harris's research on the child-like brains of adults on psychedelics.

"I'm sorry to be taking up so much time," I said.

"This is what I'm here for," he said. "I'll stay with you until you come down a little more." Twirling, the three of them laughed, carefree as enchanted lovers in *A Midsummer Night's Dream*.

"Do you think time travel is possible?" I blabbed, feeling another mental control-alt-delete.

"Like with a time machine?"

"No, with the mind, on ayahuasca, through like an astral trap door or wormhole or whatever. *Donnie Darko* is one of my favorite movies."

"Yes, I most certainly do," he said with a sly smile.

"Can I go back in time and save my parents when they were young so the other bad stuff won't happen?"

"Maybe some part of you already has," he said, getting all *Interstellar* and ten-dimensional on me.

"Before the ceremony tonight, I looked at a photo of myself when I was five. I'm leaning back on a big sofa like a *Muppet Babies* version of John Wayne. The smile! The light! What happened to him?"

"I'm sitting right next to him, minus most of the Muppet. He grew up and became a man."

"Well, you're great too," I said, getting uncomfortable with the one-sidedness of our exchange. "I'm never going to forget you—I'm going to pay it forward."

"You give everyone a lot of compliments. But what about you? Do you say those things to yourself?"

"Not really."

"I want to tell you a story." He took a breath as if he were about to blow out birthday candles. "An army was about to attack a village, so the abbots in the monastery covered their huge Buddha with mud to make it ugly to the invaders. Years and years passed, and everyone forgot the statue was covered in dirt. Imagine one monk's surprise when he cleaned it."

Greenish geometry tattooed the air. Memories streaked through my mind, glittering and foundering like aborted timelines.

"Now look right into my eyes, Greg," he said softly.

Cringing, I darted up my eyes.

"The statue was pure—pure gold! Remember, no matter what you feel or what you've done, you're gold."

"C'mon, you're the twenty-four-karat one, Drew! I'm more of a silver guy myself. And I'm still not opening The Door tonight," I said, laughing.

It was 4:30 a.m. We trudged back to our huts to fall asleep before sunrise.

THE MONEY I SPENT that week was a pittance compared to a hypothetical $40,000 stint in rehab and the cost of lifetime therapy. I had to regress to progress—bear with me as I clarify what I mean. This is important.

We know that mother and baby regulate one another's emotions. This is called co-regulation. In the nursery, the mother coos, the child smiles, then she coos again, and he giggles back. After a crack of lightning, she cradles him, and his crying eventually dies down; her heart rate slows and so does his, and after a while he begins to fall asleep. This back-and-forth bonding—this synchrony, this resonance—gets us feeling safe in any given moment. We do it all the time with one another, usually unconsciously. It's like E.T. and Elliot mimicking one another's gestures to show neither of them is a threat: after coaxing him inside his room with a Hansel-and-Gretel trail of Reese's Pieces, Elliot rubs his nose and so does E.T., setting off a virtuous cycle of mirroring and trust.

For a baby, co-regulation creates a foundation of safety, greatly influencing the child's destiny. Co-regulation early on is priceless, slowly teaching you to self-regulate. Those nurturing memories are the bedrock of resilience; they gift you with an inner parent who can soothe you even when they aren't there. Then as an adult, you feel less compelled to do stupid shit. Simply put, our mothers are our first and most powerful teachers in relating to ourselves with kindness.

But what happens when co-regulation never quite develops between mother and child? For example, when a newborn looks away—one of the first ways that children learn to self-soothe—a narcissistic mother can feel rejected. She tightens up and ignores him when he looks back. Unconscious microexpressions of anger or disgust ripple across her face. Using what's called neuroception, a child senses danger and remembers it. Internalizes it. Over time, the child associates boundary-setting with abandonment, bonding with fear.

Something must be wrong with me, he comes to believe, and as he grows older, she will reinforce his mistaken belief. He develops a life strategy based on distrust and isolation. Of course, mothers, as mine liked to constantly remind me, can't be perfect; child psychologist

D. W. Winnicott famously said that a mother only needs to be "good enough."

What's important, though, my therapist James told me, is that after ruptures there is repair. In my case, there wasn't enough repair for me to internalize a soothing mother figure. That's a recipe for compulsions and addictions, the adult child's best attempt to feel okay in the absence of internalized love. They also provide familiar, reliable hits of unlovability.

Taking me back in time to my first year, Madre Ayahuasca practiced co-regulating with me at Dreamglade, replacing some of my maternal imprinting with hers. I responded to her with retching and bark-peeling sharts and writhing and yawning and stretching and joy and absolute terror—and she responded with surges of emotions, fresh maelstroms of nausea, flares of joy and love. I practiced staying present as I felt loved by this new mother, uplifted by her rather than steamrolled. Even the hardest moments at Dreamglade were offered in love, as love—the medicine was deconditioning me of fear so that I might be more capable of bonding.

I'm still coming to terms with it, but at Dreamglade, Madre Ayahuasca began to deeply re-mother me. As psychologist Rachel Harris writes in *Listening to Ayahuasca*, "the experience of feeling loved by her will both deepen and expand.... What sometimes follows is a gradual rearrangement of inner architecture with a new benchmark for feeling loved." That's exactly what my therapists had hoped to give me: a corrective experience. They set out to replace my flawed benchmark for love with their own. But I resisted; it felt invasive and scary; most of them needed more help than I did, like the therapist who "intuited" I wanted her to "penetrate" me or the one who wondered if I was gay because she said it was easier to find men to have sex with than women. Even far less damaging moves, like canceling a session last-minute because of a Halloween party or forgetting key details of my life might cause me to leave a therapist.

This is why C-PTSD, a disorder of trust, is hard to treat. When sessions get too intense, the client finds—or is confronted with—a reason to distrust the therapist. For a client like me with C-PTSD, no therapist ultimately seems trustworthy enough because, as James put it, imperfection signals danger, a reminder of the inescapable, traumatizing relationship from childhood. "Clients aren't looking for a new idea," it's been said, "they're looking for a new experience."

Here's the experience that I'd been seeking: feeling the panic of bonding with a safe therapist alongside the panic of remembering the past. Over twenty years of therapy, I hadn't truly found this clinician. (James was wonderful but wasn't quite this.) Madre Ayahuasca, I was realizing, might be that truly trustworthy, transformative figure. As if she were my inner Dr. Doronn, I began to receive the C-PTSD treatment I needed all along, supporting Inserra's hypothesis anecdotally at least. At Dreamglade she laid down another stone foundation—a new benchmark for love—for the trials ahead.

"Over and over, the answer is the same, isn't it?" Stephanie Foo writes in her C-PTSD memoir *What My Bones Know*. "Love, love, love. The salve and the cure."

CHAPTER 21

Tahuayo

Overjoyed after Dreamglade, I traveled by boat six hours south to the Amazon Research Center in the Tamshiyacu Tahuayo Regional Conservation Area. Larger than Rhode Island, it's one of the most biodiverse sections of the staggeringly diverse Amazon. Manatees, pink and gray dolphins, and giant otters swim in the rivers. I would end up spotting pygmy marmosets, capuchin monkeys, saki monkeys, spider monkeys, and mustached tamarins—more primate species live here than in any other protected area in the world. Despite my last name, I'm not much of a birder, but the churring blue-crowned trogons did astound me. I didn't come here for the animals, though.

"Bodacious," I murmured as I looked up.

"This is a lupuna," my stocky guide Manuel said as he paddled us toward the gigantic tree coming out of the water. Some distance from it, he tied the canoe to some branches poking out of the water. It was the wet season. The rainforest was flooded with six feet of the swollen Tahuayo River, a fifty mile-long tributary of the Amazon.

"¡Qué gigante!" I exclaimed. Manuel didn't know how tall this lupuna was—measuring it would require special equipment—but the species, the tallest in the Amazon, can reach 240 feet; its crown can stretch out 200 feet; and the oldest approach a millennium in age. With exposed buttress roots resembling rocket fins, it felt like it might lift off any minute.

The branches were dripping with bromeliads and orchids. On the bark were bumps, thorns, and camo-colored lichen. Fish that Manuel called sardines puckered the water. My long legs hanging over the bow, I lay back in the canoe, a life jacket as my pillow. Manuel dozed off, and I set my phone timer for one hour.

By now, having taken me to meditate underneath some of the largest, oldest trees in Tahuayo—giants of the forest like the quinilla, paranari, ojé, and machimango—Manuel was more comfortable around me. When I told him I'd just left an ayahuasca retreat, he looked at me a bit suspiciously—too many foreign "medicine men" have caused big problems in local communities in Peru, like the Canadian guy the year before who murdered the Shipibo's spiritual mother, then was lynched afterwards by villagers. And as Manuel was quick to point out, some shamans, Peruvian and gringo, have bad intentions. In Peru, *brujería*—black magic—is not woo-woo. It's considered by many people to be a real danger.

But I knew why I was here. Given how malleable the brain is after psychedelics, this was a precious window of time I wasn't going to waste.

A FEW YEARS LATER, I learned just how special the psychedelic afterglow is from the work of Johns Hopkins researcher Gül Dölen. Giving MDMA ("molly") to octopuses and rats led her to an astounding finding: psychedelics reopen the critical period for social reward learning. Marked by heightened neuroplasticity, a critical period is when certain experiences are needed by a child for normal development to occur. If the child doesn't receive the right "inputs" during that window of time, it may have long-lasting effects on development. Think of a five-year-old on TikTok for hours most days instead of bonding with family and friends, or a male zebra finch exposed to rock music instead of an elder's birdsong. If the bird hasn't learned to sing by day 65 after hatching, he never will.

Maybe give that finch a thimbleful of aya? A psychedelic experience, Dölen theorizes, *is* the experience of critical periods reopening—this, I think, partly explains ayahuasca's re-mothering of me at Dreamglade and why Amazonian cultures call the brew a teacher. Echoing Carhart-Harris's research on the childlike brains of tripping adults, ayahuasca primes us for new learning, especially around social rewards. Happiness requires connection, so if you don't know how to connect with yourself and others, you've been set up for misery.

At Tahuayo, with critical periods reopened, the first lessons of Madre Ayahuasca were instilled in my brain. I practiced relating with myself more cheerfully and rationally. Research, I've already said, indicates ayahuasca strengthens mindfulness. And mindfulness diminishes addictive cravings, boosts impulse control, and promotes neuroplasticity. Just as I had done underwater in Raja Ampat, it seemed like a good time to meditate intensively in nature, away from screens that could reinforce behaviors I was trying to end. As motivation, I remembered the two most inspiring words in the English language, ones Rick Hanson taught me. *Neurogenesis*: new neurons being born in the brain. *Neuroplasticity*: neurons growing new branches and pruning others, some of the 125 trillion synapses in the brain switching off and others switching on.

As I MEDITATED on my back in the canoe, my propped-up legs were spread apart, my most vulnerable parts facing the lupuna. With every exhale, my body sank further into the canoe, briefly reactivating the ayahuasca. In my mind's eye, I grew lupuna roots. Became the tree's twin. With no up or down, we were floating in outer space, our roots almost touching, like two neurons forming a synapse. My brain was replaced with a lupuna's crown. I felt as tall as the tree, and as patient and strong. Lupunas survive, no, thrive as they're inundated by seasonal floods.

I'd stepped into a universal archetype, the Tree of Life. *My brownish-white fruit isn't forbidden*, it seemed to say. *Chill out, won't you?*

As my mindfulness deepened, the late afternoon sun, suddenly breaking through the canopy, shone into my brain. I had no skull or skin. Looking up at a triangle of sky shaped like a manta's wing, I kept silently saying, *I praise you, I love you, whatever you are.*

In *Pilgrim at Tinker Creek*, Annie Dillard famously sees "the tree with the lights in it." For a half second, the lupuna and I flickered like that, spitting like a pair of pilot lights in a draft. "It was less like seeing than like being for the first time seen," she writes, "knocked breathless by a powerful glance." As at Dreamglade, flashbacks sped through me so fast I could barely see glimpses of the circus animals on my nursery wallpaper. But I stayed calm and centered, guarded by this tree and the research binder in my backpack.

I had made myself Dr. Inserra's guinea pig: Repressed memories were surfacing. Fear was being driven out of them. The memories couldn't be erased, but as they reconsolidated, I trusted they were incorporating memories of this tree. I had faith I'd be able to tolerate them whenever they resurfaced. They'd be less frightening then. With less fear, there's less need to medicate and it's easier to connect with others.

"Macho!" I heard Raul say, making me smile. "Macho!"

As I MEDITATED and H.E.A.L.-ed under the lupuna, I was, unwittingly, forest bathing. *Shinrin-yoku*, the Japanese call it. Since the 1980s, Japanese doctors had been prescribing slow, unplugged walks in nature to their stressed-out urban patients. In a wide variety of studies, forest bathing has been shown to lower blood pressure, reduce the stress hormone cortisol, diminish psychological stress, and boost mood. A godsend for those of us on constant red alert. Even when we're indoors, vegetation boosts well-being. One famous study found that hospital patients recovering from gallbladder surgery healed more quickly and needed fewer pain meds when greenery rather than a brick wall was visible out the window.

These studies confirm common sense: spending time outdoors makes us feel better. Perhaps this is one reason Konstan's father Leo was willing to die trying to protect his rainforests in Raja Ampat from illegal loggers. I knew I was happier living in Virginia where I could get in my car and be hiking in twenty minutes. The traffic, difficult parking, and crowded trails kept me from doing this in California.

In the Amazon, instead of being forcibly bathed in Jacksonville's tap water—or immersing myself in the clear water mangroves of Raja Ampat or being consensually bathed by Raul and Lidia's icaros during ayahuasca limpiezas—I was bathing in forest air. Bathing in rainforest air, that is, as a rainforest medicine was still in my system. But there were other medicines of sorts I was inhaling that scientists say could be behind shinrin-yoku's effectiveness:

- Phytoncides, which are antimicrobial essential oils released by trees that scientists believe are responsible for positive psychological effects.

- Negative air ions, which have been most conclusively linked to lower depression scores. (These particles are found in higher concentrations near forests and bodies of water like rivers, waterfalls, and the ocean.)

- Bacteria, which can find their way into the gut. A healthy, diverse microbiome has been linked to better mental and physical health.

The more biodiverse a forest is, the wider the array of phytoncides and bacteria, and as research is beginning to indicate, the greater the psychological boost. In Amazonian wetland forests like the one in Tahuayo, there are 3,688 recorded tree species. In the entire Amazon, there are an estimated sixteen thousand species; in Shenandoah National Park, there are only 331; in the woods of my neighborhood in Florida, I'd guess a couple dozen. It stands to reason that, given Tahuayo's tree density and diversity, this might be one of the best places on earth to forest bathe. (I should add that breathing clean air rich with microbes, as we did to varying degrees for thousands of years, should be a birthright. Biodiversity must be protected. Access to wilderness can't only be for the privileged, affluent, adventurous, able-bodied, and lucky.)

In the canoe, by simply breathing, the rainforest was medicating me with dozens of different phytoncides. With tiny flecks of lichen from the lupuna. Pollen from the orchids a hundred feet above. Capuchin monkey dander. Bacteria that only live in the buttholes of giant river otters and in the blowholes of pink dolphins. Helicopter dragonfly scat, mites falling from slate-colored hawks, and bits of bark from the hundreds of tree species within an acre of us. With thousands of different types of fungal spores.

All this was raining down on me, clinging to my nasal passages and throat, some of it bypassing the blood brain barrier altogether and entering my brain. (This is why air pollution is so dangerous.) Some of this would make it down my esophagus, eventually enriching my gut bacteria, which produce 95 percent of the body's mood-regulating serotonin. A 2015 study in *Science Advances* showed that uncontacted tribes in the Amazon had the greatest diversity in gut bacteria ever recorded, Americans among the lowest.

Might this be one definition of great modern mothering, to dirty your children? The bottle formula I drank as a baby instead of breast milk, my mother's constant use of wet wipes, the antibiotics samples my Big Pharma rep father slipped us for our chronic ear and sinus infections, the Pringles, Cheerios, and canned waxed beans we ate—according to what's known as the hygiene hypothesis, all these well-intentioned aspects of my upbringing may have undermined my family's microbiome, making us more susceptible to mental and physical illness. Within a decade or two, as the climate and mental health crises worsen and the brain-gut connection is researched further, microbiome-enhancing poop transplants—and ayahuasca, for that matter—will likely go mainstream.

"Okay if I jump in the river?" I asked Manuel after the timer rang. Scarlet macaws squawked in the distance. Cicadas and katydids fiddled. Manuel blew a snot rocket.

"Yeah, man, take care with the branches and thorns."

My mind raced with the aquatic dangers I read about—freshwater stingrays, electric eels, the fish that swims up your urethra. Bull sharks, I recalled, can be found 2,500 miles up the Amazon.

"If a black caiman bothers you," he said, referring to the alligator-like reptile, the largest predator in the Amazon, "I'll jump in and break its neck."

"What about piranhas?"

"The people eaters aren't here. You're fine, you're fine—go and trust me, man."

Wearing only Wellington boots, my underwear, and my mask and snorkel, I should've been at an amphibious Radical Faerie gathering. I slid from the canoe into the water.

I could stand up. The water was up to my chest.

"Eek!" I cried out. "Something nipped my leg!"

"It's little fishes. Curious about you."

I put my head under. Sardines were schooling about. The visibility was at best a foot, like diluted coffee.

What was that splashing in the distance? I'd seen the trailer to *Anaconda*.

I looked back at Manuel, who was dozing off. I was scared, but I snorkeled anyway toward the giant lupuna until I was right underneath it holding onto the submerged buttress roots. Recalling Drew's story about the golden statue, I stood on the muddy bottom and looked up the trunk toward the massive crown. My lower back pain was gone. My boots were firmly planted. Humbled by the lupuna's power, I was standing in my own.

When Manuel wasn't looking, I lifted my hands like the exultant underwater statue in the Florida Keys and the branches of dying elkhorn coral near it. Though I felt as tall and rooted as the lupuna, I also felt small. Even so, it wasn't the smallness of C-PTSD. It was awe-induced insignificance. I was no one's puppet, no one's whore.

I didn't realize it at the time, but snorkeling in a flooded rainforest, I was swallowing minute amounts of the river's microbiome in my snorkel, just as the microbiome of Raja Ampat's astoundingly biodiverse reefs had found its way into my body.

Bacteria and repressed memories are invisible. So was the methane, king of greenhouse gases, rising in the Amazon from the plant matter rotting underwater.

What I couldn't see was as important as what I could.

CHAPTER 22

Alanna

Hours after returning to the Shenandoah Valley, I was back on Grindr, sure that Madre Ayahuasca would manifest my soulmate for me within a three-mile radius. I updated my profile to say I was looking for something long-term. Few took it seriously.

"Up for anything," tweakers and closeted Mennonite farmers typed. "Looking for fun?"

"For enduring love," I wrote, not caring what they thought, erasing their dick pics as quickly as they appeared. "I won't settle for less."

I chatted with a strawberry-blond triathlete who grew up here and left for good after high school. He seemed wholesome. Grindr with him was like eHarmony.

On a whim, that day we met up for lunch. He showed up in his sweaty gym clothes while I was wearing a girl's avocado-print T-shirt. Downing a couple of cocktails, he was nice enough as we awkwardly talked about the high rents and unfulfilling scene in his part of California.

Suddenly, an impossibly svelte acquaintance I'll call Maggie approached our table. I told her I'd just gotten back from Peru.

"I don't know what you're doing in a couple weekends," she said, trying to sound casual, "but there's going to be a gathering."

"What kind?" I asked.

"For plant enthusiasts. Look for a message on Facebook," she said as she left. The dude was too tipsy to register any of this.

Soon my conversation with him died down, and he asked if he could see my apartment. Once inside, he took a shot of my whiskey, and I smoked weed, which reactivated some of the ayahuasca. In the ensuing hookup, our hearts fluttered red and synchronized. There were times when we throbbed like an underwater homing beacon, like a horse galloping toward the sunrise. Then he left. We never spoke again.

At first, I felt bad about myself, as if my trials at Dreamglade had been for nothing. *The more you give in to your cravings*, I could almost hear Dr. Doronn telling me, *the harder it will be to stop*. As I unpacked my duffel bag from my trip, though, I became more self-accepting. The hookup wasn't meaningless. Hadn't our souls soared together? That's lovemaking, isn't it?

The next day Maggie messaged me: "I am going up north for aya on June 8. There is still space if you are interested...let me know. The medicine woman is a former psych nurse."

Maggie and I weren't close. Only a handful of close friends, sworn to secrecy, knew I'd gone to Peru for "aya." I took it as an auspicious sign that a day after getting back to small-town Virginia, I was being invited to another ayahuasca ceremony. What were the chances? Humbled by my slip with the triathlete, I decided to go. Even if I wasn't as depressed, my work was far from done.

I should also say that while it can take Big Pharma antidepressants six to eight weeks to kick in, if they ever do, ayahuasca takes at most a day, and the uplifting effects can last at least a month. In addition, 80 percent of first-time ayahuasca users like me have been found to retain improvements in mental health even after six months. That doesn't mean they were blissful forevermore, their lives suddenly manageable and easy, their addictions vaporized. Ingesting ayahuasca probably can't do that.

I GOT TO THE QUIET residential neighborhood in the late afternoon. Thirteen of us crammed into an upstairs den without air conditioning as the medicine woman met with us individually outside. That took three hours; we'd all been fasting since noon. As sunset approached, we were still sweating. It had been the sort of hot, dusty day that makes climate change real even to skeptics. The open windows didn't help much. *What if the neighbors hear us and call the police?* I thought. *We're in an uptight DC suburb, and isn't that Keebler Elf still attorney general?*

Lavender and patchouli filled the room as two college-age girls anxiously dabbed on essential oils and read one another's tarot cards. Maggie was beside the main altar in downward-facing dog, and I was to her far left squashed in the corner, too close to an elderly man. We were going to be there all night, well into the morning.

When it was my turn, I walked downstairs to the front patio. At first, I thought she introduced herself as "Adara."

"Hi, Greg, I'm Alanna," she said graciously, as if she were at once a Sunday school teacher, real estate agent, and therapist. She was poised and radiant, in her late twenties, wearing a handwoven Mexican smock and a huge rainbow-bead pendant.

After giving a brief overview of how she ran her ceremonies, she read through my intake form, confirming I hadn't been taking hard drugs, opiates, or antidepressants.

"*Releasing of childhood abuse trauma,*" she said, reading my response softly, "*forgiveness of self and family, releasing of shame, inviting love and abundance and creative inspiration into my life as never before. Releasing of held tension in lower back and jaw.* Ayahuasca can help with all of this,

Greg. I'm so glad you're here to build on your hard work in Peru. Do you have any questions for me?"

In general terms I told her about my last ceremony at Dreamglade, the breakdowns and breakthroughs. "If I'm freaking out, is there someone I can talk to?"

"Yes, raise your hand and let us know. Ayahuasca heals on so many levels. Physical, emotional, mental, spiritual. Trust what's coming up for you. And if Madre Ayahuasca is being too hard on you, you can ask her to ease off."

At that point in her life, she told me, she had apprenticed with medicine teachers in South America for over five years, far longer than most in the West. She was a trained, licensed psych nurse. Every other word wasn't *like*; her favorite word was *discipline*, as in committing to practices no matter how you feel. She didn't brag about her attainments, though there were many. More than anything, she didn't sexualize me, not even once, always respecting my boundaries. She seemed trustworthy, and I needed her to be.

I should say that all too often in spiritual circles, the truth of our oneness can be an excuse for bad behavior. Too many lost, middle-class souls have taken a weekend spiritual workshop only to advertise themselves as shamanic healers Monday morning. You can make quick money, find "sacred" sex, and avoid dealing with your trauma, but one day life will checkmate you, and there won't be another quick fix.

FINALLY, THE CANDLELIT ceremony began.

After a period of silent meditation, she shook her seed-filled rattle and sang Santo Daime songs in Portuguese. She chanted Sanskrit mantras her female guru had taught her in India, and performed original songs about bliss, forgiveness, and the rainforest. Meanwhile, a man across from me was wailing and pounding his fists against his yoga mat. As with Raul at times at Dreamglade, my mind was racing with irrational thoughts about him—the music sounded foreboding.

When Alanna called me over for my second dose, I told her the screaming man made me not want to drink more. "I know it's father stuff I'm projecting, but I don't want to melt down."

"Then maybe this is the perfect time for you to look at this fear more closely," she said. Inwardly, I groaned. How many times had a therapist said that to me to make sure I booked another appointment?

On the medicine, Alanna was warmer. As her high-intensity Spotify playlist blared, we chatted as if we'd known each other for years. I ended up telling her about my father.

"If you have those feelings, it happened," she said. "Don't second-guess yourself."

When I told her about my mother, her eyes squeezed shut and she shuddered. "Whaaat? Are you serious? Of course that's abuse," she said. "Those are unbelievable wounds for a man, for anyone, really." I held my breath, dreading she'd say I was gay because of my mom, which is the horseshit of the ex-gay movement and Freud.

She poured me another dose. Somehow getting it down, I went back to my corner, at once skeptical, scared, and hopeful.

ALANNA HAD BEEN DISTURBED by what I shared with her, which in turn stirred me up further. Getting into the fetal position, I saw a few fractals, then utter blackness filled my mind. It was as if I were the nothingness before the Big Bang. Mindfulness felt like repression. I wasn't only feeling annihilation panic. I *was* annihilation panic.

I cried out for Alanna.

"I'm dying," I kept saying as she squatted down to coach me.

"If only you were so lucky," she said matter-of-factly, smiling serenely like the Green Face. "Awakening is dying." I know how that sounds, but you can't fake the kind of conviction that was in her voice. I believed it.

"What if I go psycho?" I asked, my mind going supernova, then shriveling back up.

"That's a story in the mind," she said, having me take more deep breaths. I knew my ego needed to tell fear-based stories to perpetuate itself, but I was still on red alert. "You're already free."

After I calmed down a bit, she returned to the altar. The panic rushed back.

In my head, I was one or two years old, but this was different from the regression at Dreamglade. This time, Alanna was my new mother. In emotional flashbacks from when I was very little, I was remembering desperately needing my mother—but she didn't come. She must have been too busy cleaning.

Alanna gulped coconut water and slowly tuned her guitar. She began a new song, this one to Saraswati, the Hindu goddess of artistic inspiration.

"Help me!" I called out. A few people sat up. Everyone else was lying down, eyes closed, deep in their journeys. She had me come sit next to her.

She kept singing, and my terror grew, even though I was holding on to her knee. *I need to talk*, I mouthed. Fingering her guitar, she breathed deeply in an exaggerated way to encourage me to do the same.

That didn't work. My anxiety grew, and her assistant opened his arms to me. I crawled over. He hugged me and kissed my forehead. I was petrified. I worried what he thought of our embrace, but he reminded me that he had initiated it. He asked me to hold my breath until the count of eight. I couldn't do it.

"Let go, let go, it's okay," he said.

But, as they can be, those were empty, impossible words. "There's a huge sea monster passing over me," I said, "and it won't stop."

As he kept holding me, it started to feel creepy, though he wasn't doing anything wrong—it was me. I crawled back beside Alanna, who was still singing. I was inconsolable, overwhelmed by I-need-Mommy-right-now panic.

Dipshit, I thought, *you're the one who stopped talking to your bedridden mother!*

Quit hounding me, I heard my mother say as she would when I needed something important. *The more you bug me, the longer I'll take.*

All I wanted was for Alanna to stop singing and set me right. Like Dr. Doronn, though, she wanted me to realize my fear couldn't kill me. I'd be about to get up to go hide in the corner again, but then she'd grin and sing encouragement my way, indicating I should stay next to her. I looked over at her. Part of me felt guilty for upstaging her, but the rest of me was pure infantile neediness. Critical periods of development had been reopened, all right.

I don't know what I said to interrupt her singing, but my meltdown began. She brought me back to my spot and asked me to lean back against the wall. "Less talking, more feeling," she said, crouching down in front of me, her hand on the center of my chest.

"Breathe, Greg, breathe," she said, seemingly unflappable, but that didn't help much. So she turned to a traditional fail-safe: spitting agua de Florida, a kind of South American shamanic cologne, on me three times, spraying me as if she were putting out a fire—because, in a sense, she was. Then she blew mapacho over my pelvis and down my back. In the jungle, if that doesn't calm you down, they might tie you to a tree.

Alanna paused the ceremony. Holding on to her assistant as if I were my mother walking with a physical therapist, we made our way outside to the fire. Maggie and I held hands.

I couldn't look at the flames for very long. Alanna passed around scraps of cedar bark, which we took turns throwing into the fire as symbols of things we were letting go of. "This is my shame," I whispered, tossing the bark into the flames, "this is my yabadabadoo divahood."

Resting my cheek on the ground, I looked over at Alanna sitting on a log, staring at the fire. Though composed, she looked drained, almost dejected. I realized I had committed an unspoken taboo: interrupting an icaro and an entire ceremony in the process.

Eventually, Maggie and I lay on our backs away from the fire. We looked up. The moon was a nightlight made from a sea biscuit.

We WENT BACK INSIDE, and the ceremony continued until midmorning. In the sharing circle at the end, I don't remember exactly what I said, but I know I apologized to Alanna and the group and thanked her profusely. I felt mortified, but the love in the room was strong.

There's a better word from Santo Daime for the steadfastness I admired, even envied in Alanna that night: *firmeza*. "Firmness" is not the right translation. It's more the ability to stand in oneself, to sit with whatever comes up in ceremony, and not sucking anyone else into your psychodrama as I had with her. Firmeza is safely piloting the ship through treacherous waters. It's equanimity. Witness consciousness. Rootedness. Commitment, the scariest word of all. The antidote, it seemed to me, to impulsiveness and addiction.

"The point of drinking medicine isn't to drink more," she told us after our shares. "The real work begins after a ceremony. Forming new habits based on what the medicine shows you requires discipline. Or you can go back to your old way of living." In other words, like love and forgiveness, cultivating firmeza is work.

I wanted what she had. I wanted firmeza.

CHAPTER 23

Brazil

After we broke our nearly twenty-four-hour fast, Alanna mentioned to everyone at the table that in a few weeks she was visiting her teacher in Brazil. "It's during the *feitio*, the making of the ayahuasca sacrament for the Santo Daime church. We'll actually help them harvest the vine, pick the leaves. If you'd like to join, let me know."

A week or so later, sitting in a nursing chair in the Target baby department, I phoned Alanna about the trip. She was going to Flor de Jurema, a Santo Daime community in the far west of Brazil, in the state of Acre along the Croa River. The leader was Davi Nunes de Paula, who had been her teacher for several years. She encouraged me to come.

If I stayed in Virginia for the rest of the summer, my downward spiral, I figured, would resume. I was filling my time with life-affirming enough things—hiking, teaching an online poetry course, boogying at an eighties dance party in Richmond with friends, attending a bluegrass festival in the countryside—but still, with all the unstructured time, I worried I'd backslide.

Even if it meant charging it to my Visa, I would join Alanna in the Amazon. I wanted to prove to myself—and to her—that I could hold my own on ayahuasca, that I could steer and land the psychedelic spaceship.

I reassured concerned friends that multiple studies of long-term ayahuasca use have shown that it isn't addictive. Neuroimaging has revealed that the reward centers of the brain associated with addictive drugs—the same regions associated with porn and presumably hookup apps—are not activated in healthy volunteers on ayahuasca. You might think my digital addiction was being replaced by an ayahuasca addiction, but that's neurochemically impossible.

THE FIRST CEREMONY IN BRAZIL, like all the others there, took place in an open-air temple in the rainforest. Plastic chairs were arranged around a hexagram-shaped altar, men on one side, women on the other. The jungle roared with cicadas as men tuned their guitars.

Soon a line formed to Davi serving the ayahuasca, which the church considers a sacrament and calls *daime*, which translates "Give me"—"Oh my Mother of Rivers," one hymn reads, "Give me faith and courage / Give me your protection / Give me your comfort." Davi was a bit older than me, tall, with steel glasses and poofy silver hair. Like the other Brazilian men, he was dressed in the Santo Daime uniform for initiated members: black slacks and a white button-up shirt with a black tie. Standing in line, I watched his hands as he elegantly poured the doses.

When it was my turn, I took the cup and imagined my father receiving communion in Chattanooga in the fifties, when anti-Catholic sentiment still ran deep in the South. Back then, neighborhood kids relentlessly taunted him, calling him "Fish," the only animal the Church allowed to be eaten on Fridays. When the priest learned my father would be transferring from the Catholic school to the local prep school to play football, he got in his face and told him if he left he was going to hell. My dad believed it. He was in fifth grade.

When he'd tell me this, his throat tightened and his eyes filled with tears: he couldn't suppress how traumatic it was for the priest to threaten him with eternal damnation. Reliving the memory, Dad couldn't seem to weave it into a larger understanding of himself. I still wonder what he left out of the story. Why, for instance, was the priest so possessive of him? Why was it that important for him to stick around? Those silences have always gnawed at me.

I swallowed the ayahuasca for both my father and me, looking at the dark circles around Davi's eyes. He winked. His body language said, *It's okay, I'm a safe person.*

We all stood for opening prayers, the same ones Alanna used but in Portuguese. Then we began singing. Following along in the Santo Daime hymnal was hard, but the Portuguese words for *stars, baptism,* and *forest* were obvious enough.

The brew came on strong, especially potent, I'd later find out, because this was a *cura* ceremony, meant to heal the community and the planet. The musicians on ayahuasca were singing and playing instruments just fine, but I couldn't follow the lyrics. In my mind, I was about a year old, scared in my crib. The Door shook.

Then from the top of my head, a pair of glass antlers started poking through—or was it a city of crystal skyscrapers? Whatever it was glinted as it prairie-dogged out of my skull for hours. Although I was determined to stay put and not cause a scene, the things emerging from my head were freaking me out. Meanwhile, the guitar-playing was ear-splitting. My nerves were being picked and strummed. The *tch-tch* of the tin maracas beating out quarter notes sounded like an emergency.

Andrew, the ginger hippie who also came here with Alanna, scampered outside to sit by the firepit. My teeth chattering, I staggered out to join him, proud that I slipped out of the temple without asking for help.

Though being by the fire next to Andrew calmed me down a bit, sirens were still going off in my body.

"You feeling it, brother?" Andrew asked.

"Oh, I'm feeling it alright," I said. "Like a moose at mating time. How about you?"

"Not even a little bit. I wonder if it's because I'm Jewish and all this churchy Jesusy talk kinda weirds me out."

"Yeah, I have to translate the Christian stuff into my own language," I said. "I never went to church growing up, but I knew not to call my Baptist crushes on Wednesday nights or at all on Sundays."

I stopped myself from unloading my trauma onto him—my new social reward learning was kicking in. I was sick of declaring myself a victim: psychedelics and coral reefs had made it clear that there was more to me than my parents' mistakes. There was a neurological basis for this realignment over the last month. In quieting down my brain's default mode network—considered by some researchers to be the ego—ayahuasca was allowing me to observe rather than believe the garbage in my head, and to tell myself new stories.

Just then, a shrieking woman stormed out of the temple into the jungle. Maybe her own Door opened. The music was still racing.

Andrew and I walked back. One of the Brazilian men, a designated "guardian" of the ceremony, ran after us and tried to get us to come back. We were polite, but we weren't having it.

At breakfast the next morning, though no one exactly scolded us, Andrew and I learned we had committed a big no-no: leaving a ceremony early. As a religion, Santo Daime doesn't care what you believe as long as you're following its strict ritualistic protocols, which help foster a safe container. Out of respect to our host, I needed to call still more bullshit on my panic and stay put during the next ceremony.

THE NEXT AFTERNOON after a small dose, we went to the temple to help make the medicine. With dull knives we scraped the bark off the vine pieces to be pounded and cooked with the chacruna leaves. Six steel vats of ayahuasca were cooking in front of us, clouds of steam often obscuring the looming double-beamed cross. To my right was the Huni Kwin chief whom Davi had befriended years ago—they banded together to better protect themselves from illegal logging and land grabs, all too common in the Amazon. To my left was a mural of Mestre Irineu, the Afro-Brazilian rubber tapper who founded Santo Daime a century ago after having ayahuasca visions of the Queen of the Forest, an entity synonymous with the Virgin Mary. She had him undergo a difficult initiation and then gave him one wish.

With each scrape of the harvested vine, I became less self-involved. In my mind, I saw a woman I'll call Ann, one of my best friends in high school; we helped one another survive Jacksonville, even if it meant sneaking into parks at night to smash Publix pies into each other's faces to de-stress. Sitting there breathing in the bark dust and dirt, I vividly felt her unhappiness and burnout, twinges of her chronic pain. A year before, she told me she didn't have real friends in her fast-paced city. She was too busy working and being a mom. *Who in my life*, she seemed to ask, *can I be myself around and not be judged? Who is here to take care of me?*

For a time, there was only the scraping away of suffering, no one's in particular, onto the temple floor. The forest went silent. Then there was only the sound of Ann's voice. She was reciting the Marcus Aurelius quote she had engraved on a framed photo of us: "Love only that which is part of your destiny."

"I'm glad I know you," I whispered as I finished scraping. "Whatever it takes, be well, my friend."

A LITTLE LATER in the afternoon, Alanna and one of Davi's men led us into the jungle. "The whole forest is always singing," he said, Alanna translating, "not only the birds."

As we unwittingly forest-bathed, we came to an enormous lupuna, known in Brazil as *samaúma*. The same species of kapok in the Tahuayo Reserve I meditated under, snorkeled around, and for a moment joined with. But this one wasn't partially submerged in a flooded river. White tuffs of lupuna seed hairs were strewn across the ground.

"The samaúma is a very sacred tree to the native people," he told us. "Sacred because the man who brought ayahuasca to humanity was buried underneath one. Once upon a time he was captured by a boa-constrictor woman. In a city under the river, she taught him about healing with ayahuasca. But he was her prisoner. A wise crab rescued him, and he returned to his village to share his knowledge of the medicine."

Under the lupuna, the man served us *hapeh*, which is snuff made from jungle tobacco, a sacred medicine revered by some even more than ayahuasca. Grandfather medicine, some call it. As we sat on one of the lupuna's gigantic roots, the man used a hollow bone like a blow gun to blast the powder into our nostrils.

Afterwards, reeling, I plopped down between two buttress roots and sat cross-legged, spitting out the brown goop that had found its way into my throat. Sitting in meditation like Alanna nearby, I wept as Andrew barfed.

Fire shot out of my head. Then I was the fire. What was being incinerated in the kiln of consciousness? The prospect of suicide, the comfort of victimhood.

And what was going up in flames to the east of us in Brazil? The rainforest, already too dry, slashed and burned for our hamburgers and tofu.

I coughed, blowing my nose and hocking loogies and apocalyptic thoughts. Thick and brown like river mud. Bullet ants be damned, I got on my back like a starfish, getting filthy with the forest's microbiome, listening to the forest singing.

THE FOLLOWING NIGHT there was a concentration ceremony, a long period of silent meditation while we were on the medicine. I vowed to remain in the temple, having spent the day in my hammock getting psyched up. To remind myself I was clean no matter what, I clawed at the ground to get dirt in my nails.

I looked at Alanna across the temple. It gave me strength to look at a woman I could call my teacher and coach, instead of my replacement mommy-boss. Neither she nor Davi was ever going to do for me what I could do for myself. They reminded me, a grown man, of my autonomy.

As we sat in the temple watching our breath, things were rising from my head again. Crystal shafts. A cable for a space elevator. An ayahuasca vine. A sword. This time, though, I understood all the antler-stalk-cable things as umbilical cords connecting me with a transcendental reality. A place, if you can call it that, where ideals like honor and decency—like husband, father, mother, and son—exist in their nonphysical perfection, akin to Plato's Realm of the Forms. Connected so with timeless values and archetypes, I had a felt sense of them. They were absorbable, real.

In this way, the medicine again reparented me, this time by a father as well as mother. I couldn't see these new parents, but they made themselves known as they instilled themselves in me. I got to experience myself as if I'd been raised by parents with integrity. I was welcomed into a cosmic family. It wasn't cheesy—I didn't become the fourth son on *The Brady Bunch* or anything. I was watched over and nurtured, co-regulating with my new parents. As we bonded, I didn't panic. I received the safe touch of a cuddling father whom I could look in the eye and say, "I want to be you when I grow up."

"Physiologically, we see activation of the same emotional brain centers with ayahuasca administration as we do in attachment relationships": this electrifying sentence in a pioneering paper by Jessica Nielson and Julie Megler was highlighted, starred, and circled in my research binder. In other words, ayahuasca stimulates the same brain regions that being deeply bonded to someone does, such as a therapist, parent, or partner. The C-PTSD medicine Davi poured activated my brain's left amygdala and parahippocampal gyrus, and over minutes that were years in an alternate timeline, I had the parents I needed. They asked me to pause in the ever-changing multiverse. Listen. Feel the sensations and learn. Let my character be reconstituted like a caterpillar in a cocoon.

I opened my eyes to look at the back of Davi's head.

OUTSIDE AFTER THE CEREMONY, I looked straight up at the constellation Sagittarius, my teapot-shaped Zodiac sign. There between Jupiter and Saturn was the center of the galaxy, where a supermassive black hole—or hefty bale of dark matter—might live. No one knows for sure.

I started to say something grandiloquent to the sky like, "I vow that I will evolve—," but a presence shushed me, the way a reading teacher stops you when you stumble and tells you to start over.

You're loved no matter what, it said.

Standing with my dirty fingernails by the temple outhouse, I was surrounded by unconditional love. It was different from what I felt outside Indexia's hut or in the river at the European trailer park. For a second or two, I knew overriding, universal care. Every wayward hair in my beard was accepted. My grandma donkey-laugh. My shit-talking about Kirstie Alley and my love for Joan Rivers. My making a project out of evolving, of personal growth—baked into most self-improvement, after all, is self-hatred.

"I'm loved no matter what," I repeated back.

Flor de Jurema was a bootcamp for neuroplasticity. A dojo for firmeza in the Anthropocene, the Age of Roundup and TikTok. Every ceremony, all eight of them in ten days, was a masterclass in grace.

CHAPTER 24

Davi in America

"Once when I drank ayahuasca, she very gently explained
to me... 'Look, I give to you, but I take away... I take away
defects and I give you responsibilities.'"

—DON JOSÉ CAMPOS, *The Shaman & Ayahuasca*

When I came back from Brazil, I downloaded Grindr—but then deleted it right away. Between the buttress roots of Davi's lupuna, I had vowed to stay celibate for at least a month. Unlike past therapy, my sessions with James after Brazil were consistently useful, a supplement to my medicine work that for a time reopened important critical periods. Focusing more on my strengths, I kvetched less about the past as I turned my ayahuasca insights into new habits of thought, word, and action.

That fall, Kathryn and I hung out a lot, eating apple slices with coconut peanut butter on her porch near campus—because she was familiar with altered states, she was the only friend who might understand what I went through in Brazil. I had cozy times with Rob and Chip at a local brewery but drank kombucha and LaCroix instead of strong

IPAs. I hid the Ritalin, threw out my poppers, and put more effective blockers on my devices, so that the news and certain hookup apps weren't as accessible. I went on a few dates, but no one seemed right.

When I wasn't hiking with Chip to identify plants, I went out alone into the wilderness to hang my hammock and just be rocked— my mind, as usual, would tell me why I should feel shortchanged and betrayed, but I didn't believe it as much. I dropped the storyline and felt the sensations, relaxing my shoulders on the exhale, visualizing the junk thoughts being released from my heart. If I needed to, I called on the protection of my new internalized parents. Otherwise, I chilled, receiving the forest, trying to cultivate joy and remember Davi.

In the weeks after Brazil, I went to bed early and slept ten or twelve hours a night. In Santo Daime, the ceremonies are referred to as *trabalho*, Portuguese for "work." That's an understatement. Even today when I think of Flor de Jurema, I feel utterly grateful and downright exhausted.

APPALACHIA. AYAHUASCA. They almost rhyme.

It's still hard for me to believe, but a month after I left Brazil, Davi randomly came to a farm in my isolated pocket of Virginia, the ancestral land of the Manahoac and Monacan tribes. Davi traveled over five thousand miles to serve the medicine and raise awareness about the headline-making fires in the Amazon. Thanks to deforestation and climate change, the rainforest was for the first time on record releasing more greenhouse gases than it stored. "Our house is burning. Literally," French President Emmanuel Macron had tweeted a month earlier. We soon learned a new name for the Amazon, even though the oceans in fact absorb much more carbon: the Lungs of the Planet. By 2064, one study recently predicted, the Amazon rainforest will be replaced by dry scrubland if we don't rapidly reduce our CO_2 emissions.

"We will protect the forest as long as we have the strength to do so," Davi wrote in a group email to us. "You are invited to participate in the movement for the preservation of Pacha Mama," the Quechua term for Mother Earth. "We are the gardeners of this natural garden."

Gardener strikes me as the right word. The Amazon, which had complex societies with five million inhabitants when Europeans first arrived, has been cultivated for thousands of years. Its biodiversity, scientists theorize, may be partly the result of Indigenous forest management. Like Raja Ampat, the Amazon and I can't rightly be called *virgin*. We aren't ruined either, not yet.

THE ROLLING PASTURES WENT DARK. Shenandoah Mountain, the long sandstone ridge along the border with West Virginia, faded. And thirty of us found our spots in a 1990s-style living room with high ceilings for the first of two back-to-back ceremonies.

From Alanna's introduction, I finally found out more about Davi. He had been working with rainforest medicines since age nine, when he received kambô, the venom of the monkey tree frog applied to little burns on the skin. The medicine, which briefly causes unbelievable nausea and purging, cured him of a life-threatening illness. An Indigenous healer in the Juruá Valley of Brazil introduced Davi to ayahuasca when he was eighteen, and his life dramatically shifted. He was called to activism, healing work, and Santo Daime, and then church leadership, marriage, and fatherhood.

Alanna went on to explain that we wouldn't be sitting very much these two nights. "This is Umbandaime," she said. "An offshoot of Santo Daime. There are forest spirits called *caboclos* that enter the drummer and sing through him. The songs heal the room as we dance."

No, no, Alanna, I thought to myself, *no one ever said anything about dancing and possession!*

"Yes," she said, smiling at me, as if this were news to her too, "we're going to be dancing."

AFTER WE CHANTED the usual Santo Daime prayers, we lined up in front of the fireplace to receive our dose and then meditated.

Suddenly, Davi started playing his atabaque, a tall calfskin hand drum. Alanna called out into the candlelit room, "Everyone, please stand."

When we weren't standing in place clapping hands, we danced freeform, at first half-heartedly, with his drumming. This was no hoedown. It wasn't at all like getting down to Britney at bars after three rum and Diet Cokes. In the utterly platonic company of others, I was claiming—and sharing—my space. In moments I was a Pangea made of amphibian spawn in a fathomless vernal pool, but I was also utterly myself. What others were seeing was not an old, cropped pic of me after a crash diet, taken in the golden hour with just the right filter. This was my actual skinny-fat body—huge and klutzy, wide-hipped, asymmetrical, sex-weary, traumatized—moving through four dimensions.

Yet as I often am in groups, I was at times hypervigilant, especially when certain folks got too close. Alanna had advised us to turn inward and not focus on anyone in particular. At times while triggered, I could see I was projecting my issues onto others to make them either my saviors or my perpetrators. But this old pattern had to die—it had kept me single and scared. Firmeza was my North Star. Even as I felt like I was writhing in the ballroom of a sinking ship, over and over I brought my focus back to my breathing, my feet, and Davi's drumming. I trusted this ayahuasca—I helped make it, after all.

In the Shenandoah Valley with Davi, the medicine did not spare the rod. It was one thing for me to silently meditate with my eyes closed— it was quite another to dance open-eyed with strangers to unfamiliar, high-tempo rhythms as the medicine reprimanded me like a strict, caring father. I saw where I was headed if I kept up my ways—the emptiness of lifelong bachelorhood, blackmail, jail time, professional ruin, the fulfillment of my father's death wish. It showed me the very real possibility of a catfishing psychopath leaving me for dead by the railroad tracks in Bumblefuck, Virginia. It showed me what a meth addiction would be like on top of other addictions. Like a hot stovetop, fear and remorse can be instructive.

Dancing while scared shitless, I was practicing showing up vulnerable with my brothers and sisters, feeling triggered without fighting, fleeing, or freezing.

As you know, for me the simple act of bonding could be panic-inducing. Moving together to the beats of Davi's drum, the other participants and I couldn't help but tune into one another deeply. To sense our collective goodwill and learn to trust again. Silent and rarely making eye contact, we were co-regulating through body language, at times synchronizing our moves, creating strong bonds between us. By respecting the ground rules and maintaining good boundaries, we were assuring one another that the container was sound, that it was now safe to feel our true feelings and risk connection. This very special training ground in his ceremonies kept me coming back.

Today, I can appreciate Umbandaime as a treatment for C-PTSD. It's genius: dancing on ayahuasca allows the surfacing panic to be physically shaken off the way gazelles do after close calls with cheetahs. It's like pee shivers that go on for minutes instead of seconds. Peer-reviewed research on this topic is virtually nonexistent. But anecdotal evidence from dance therapists, Umbandaime practitioners, and others abounds. As Davi played his drum into the early morning, we twirled and jumped, and I flung my fear off into space. My body, I learned, can help me let go when my mind by itself can't.

THE NEXT TWO WEEKENDS, I left Virginia before dawn on Friday to drive all the way to New York, first to a house in the Catskills, then to a Brooklyn loft, for more Umbandaime ceremonies with Davi. Though I wanted to accept him as a father figure of sorts, I needed to know I wasn't joining a cult and that he was as upstanding as I thought.

As I sashayed and swayed on the medicine, I sometimes gathered the courage to look right at him. He almost seemed like a different person from the man I met in Brazil. Instead of his conservative Santo Daime uniform, he wore white karate pants and a white smock with Hindu gods printed on it. We sang no hymns about Jesus and Mary. As he drummed, he was wilder than I'd seen him yet still controlled. The reparenting energy I spoke about earlier radiated off him—Siggy must have been activated big-time inside me, stimulating brain regions involved in bonding. I knew little about Davi's personal life, but I knew he had been a committed father and husband. By osmosis, whatever his human mistakes might have been, he transmitted things to me my dad never did. How to be in a marriage. How to stay true and loving as a husband. Firmeza.

In one ceremony, after Davi blew jungle tobacco into both my nostrils with his bird bone, I was transported back to Brazil, to the mural of Saint Sebastian outside next to my hammock. The saint was in the usual pose, in only a loincloth, his arms tied to a fig tree behind him, his bare chest porcupined with arrows. *This*, I thought, *is the suffering of life—in the end we're all ambushed by death.* Then I zoomed to a purplish fig hanging above him. I orbited it hopefully, as if it were a potential Planet B. It was sweetness. The sweetness that suffering always contains if you look for it, even if it strikes others as insensitive.

Davi would later tell us that if we felt healing from Umbandaime, it wasn't because of him. He was only a medium, he'd say, for the medicine. Don't put anyone on a pedestal, yet we all need role models.

MOTHERSHIP

AT ONE OF THE FINAL CEREMONIES, Davi spoke briefly about how the medicine brings us the maternal love of the Yoruba ocean goddess Yemanja. Bathed in that love, he said, it's okay to live like an unnoticed forest creature. "Humility," he said, "is necessary for nobility." Then I took a second dose. My heart filled with memories of my mother—the way she'd laugh and make me laugh, the baked ziti she'd cook for Christmas dinner. I missed her. I went into the other room and balled up on the couch.

Davi eventually found me. "Get up" was all he said.

I did what the man said.

Get up: what Saint Anthony says to the murdered man, what E.T. says with his humming to the pot of wilted flowers, what springtime says to thaw a frozen snake in Walden Pond. My biological father felt dead to me. Something, or someone, was rising in his place.

IN ONE VISION I HAD at the ceremony in New York, I stood by my sleeping mother's bed. One of her tuxedo cats was curled up at her feet. On her nightstand was a Danielle Steel novel and a box of latex gloves for her caregivers. Her gray hair was matted, streaked with white. Her right side was paralyzed from the stroke.

Then thin shafts of light began to fall on her right side. Cathedral light like in the coral-encrusted mangroves. Sparkly rainbows poured from my belly toward her. It was like a Care Bear stare blasting love at Professor Coldheart, who in the TV special enslaved a kid and sought to lock the world in ice.

On the other side of the bed were Mamo in her nurse's uniform and her father, Orlando, in his World War I surgical gown. They were performing some kind of soul surgery.

Forgive, I heard, *forgive*. My breathing slowed and so did my mother's. Our right hands and feet wiggled in sync, powered by choirs of icaro-singing insects and frogs and monkeys. Her body was being restored. Her critical periods had been reopened for new learning. The neurons killed by her brain bleed came back to life. Her muscles regrew; her coordination and vitality returned. She chanted the loving-kindness prayer the Buddha taught his students to recite when they were scared meditating alone in the jungle:

May you be safe and protected
May you be happy
May you be healthy
May you be at ease

Suddenly my mother turned into millions of bioluminescent plankton. She became a star field, then a swarm of fireflies rushing into my brain. She and I were healing one another. *We're the same*, I heard. It was the voice of the rainforest.

THE AFTERNOON BEFORE the last ceremony in Brooklyn, Davi's final stop in America, I sat on a bench in Prospect Park and felt the wind on my face. I recalled the Grindr profile I saw before I went to Dreamglade that read "THE PLANET IS DYING FUCK WHOEVER YOU WANT." But then I thought, *Why tap at a screen for hours like a cocaine lever when you could be doing anything else?*

Eventually, I walked inside the Brooklyn Museum. At one entrance was a wall-sized stone relief from Assyria almost three thousand years ago. A muscular, bearded genie was fertilizing a sacred plant with a pinecone dipped in pollen. In the Akkadian language, the little sign said, the words for *pinecone* and *purifier* are almost identical.

Kneeling in the Egyptian collection was a falcon-headed god. His left hand was at his chest, his right arm raised, the same shape, I learned, as the hieroglyphic for *rejoicing*. I thought of another man making his body a prayer—the bronze statue underwater in the Florida

Keys—and how ayahuasca, like coral, had me exulting with the same intensity.

A century and a half ago, inspired by this very same Egyptian statue, Whitman wrote that Egyptian spirituality "respected the principle of life in all things—even in animals. It respected truth and justice above all other attributes of men. It recognized immortality." Maybe it was the medicine from the night before—but walking past mummies and sculptures of long-dead pharaohs and their children and pets, I felt the swift passage of thirty-one dynasties and one hundred seventy rulers over three millennia in ancient Egypt. Their lives were as special as ours, as deserving of eternal bliss, yet now they're gone. They are dead leaves that have long since been carried down a creek on Shenandoah Mountain. My quarrels, my trauma—they're nothing.

I looked down at my phone:

THAT WAA

*WAS

THE

BEST THING

TO EVER HAPPEN TO ME

It was Kathryn. The night before in Virginia, she drank ayahuasca for the first time, ostensibly for a psychology research paper. "The universe is loving & eating itself," she typed. "It's just...easy, aligned love. Everything else is a lie."

Elated for her, I reread her texts in the American Art Galleries, where I spent a while with a painting by Black artist John Biggers called *Web of Life*. It's a sketch for a mural that used to hang in the science building at Texas Southern University, a historically Black university in Houston.

It's winter on the left side of the canvas. The animals of my Florida childhood—racoons, squirrels, possums—are curled up sleeping inside dead oaks; woodpeckers and kingfishers are perched on the branches. A marsh of sorts holds motionless fish in clear water. Above, women in Africa are proudly carrying harvest baskets on their heads.

On the right side of the canvas, it's summer; African American men are sowing seeds in a field; plants are sprouting, no, exploding green; a waterfall empties into a lagoon with starfish, pufferfish, angelfish, and an octopus. There are paddles of coral and seashells found in Florida.

In the center, a naked Black woman and man have joined hands, a variation on God creating Adam.

And below them underground in a womb-burrow of sorts is Mother Earth. She is cradling her breastfeeding child. With easy, aligned love, she looks down at her baby, concentrating on her endless, thankless task: sustaining life.

THAT NIGHT IN THE CEREMONY, The Door opened.

While we were meditating on our backs, I relived what my father did to me. Actual picture memories of what he did. As if to protect me from the worst of them, at times my field of vision filled with plastic push buttons. Orange and blue-black buttons on some long-forgotten Fisher Price toy. They formed a squinched-up face looking back at me like a robotic owl, defeated and triumphant at the same time. It made me retch.

After a time, we were asked to stand up and begin dancing again. At first, I couldn't—I didn't want to offend Davi, but I was reeling.

Once I was finally standing, I felt the wooden floor of the loft beneath my feet. It confirmed I hadn't died. *This happened*, I stomped my feet to say, *these visual flashbacks are as real as this wood*. As the memories came up for hours on end, I better understood why trusting men had been so hard, why my father seemed to feel so guilty when I came out of the closet. My best guess: according to his twisted homophobic logic, he turned me gay. And does his childhood priest somehow figure into all of this?

MOTHERSHIP

I stomped the floor again. "*Viva la floresta!*" we all cried out. "Viva! Long live the forest! Viva!" Davi's drumming quickened.

I told myself new stories: My mother discovered for herself what he was doing. She spent the rest of my childhood and adolescence trying to clean me of his traces.

What's done is done, I thought.

SINCE THE LAST CEREMONY with Davi in October 2019, I've walked through The Door many times. Drinking ayahuasca, I've been facing these flashbacks (a.k.a. hyperactivating my amygdala) so they could be liberated (a.k.a. to achieve fear extinction) and no longer control my life. As survivor and ayahuasca user John Pasquina is quoted as saying in Nielson and Megler's paper, "I had a very powerful experience where I was forced to relive a traumatic memory repeatedly until I no longer held any negative energy toward it. It resulted in my ability to view the memory without the negative reaction"—after most ceremonies, I could have written the same thing. Though the panic has lessened, the picture memories that surfaced still appear. They don't immobilize me, though, or have me reaching for Grindr. Instead, they're like fading nightmares incorporated into a more empowering life story.

At the same time, though, a different kind of fear is growing in me, and in many others. Annihilation panic is giving way to extinction panic. Which is to say the medicine had also shown me possible glimpses of the future. The Amazon as a dry savanna instead of a lush rainforest. Dayan in fifty years, after its reefs are dead. Once Adara herself came to me in ceremony—she was holding a Ganesha crucifix made of elephant ivory from her twenty-third century religion. She looked too thin.

"HOW ARE WE GOING to take care of the earth," a farmer-friend asked me later that fall, "if we can't take care of each other?"

210

Reality, I was still realizing, isn't a set of 200 Grindr squares or 195 countries. It's a single seamless organism we call the universe. I've come to trust that's not a metaphor. This time-space reality is alive. It's conscious. I have faith now that, like our indescribable essence, the mycelial mat of the cosmos is curious, caring, utterly available. Devoid of neuroticism. Love knowing itself as love.

After my ceremonies with Davi, I often thought of E.T., who embodies almost supernatural compassion and shows us another way to be an "intelligent" being. Elliot, telepathically merged with the so-called alien, comes to see that the self isn't fixed. He knows his intergalactic, interspecies neighbor as himself; indeed, E and T are the first and last letters of Elliot's name. "You must be dead because I don't know how to feel," he says to E.T. lying in a government-issued tomb. The boy experiences the truth of non-separation—that we are one with nature, with one another, and no, not in some fucked-up, codependent way.

Someday when physicists prove all that and overhaul our definition of life, it won't sound like animistic hooey to the mainstream. "Our toddlers speak of plants and animals as if they were people," Potawatomi biologist and writer Robin Wall Kimmerer writes in *Braiding Sweetgrass*, "extending to them self and intention and compassion—until we teach them not to. We quickly retrain them and make them forget."

Or as Whitman declares, "I am the mate and companion of people, all just as immortal and fathomless as myself"—but let's substitute "creatures" for people. "Who need be afraid of the merge?" he asks, and I ask it again and again, my mental snow globe shaking.

Homing

Homing (v.): an animal instinctually returning
to its territory after leaving

At the end of my sabbatical that spring, I was on lockdown in the Andes without Grindr. I wrote, cooked, and slept too much. Several mornings a week, double masked, I was allowed to leave my mud-brick cottage to go to the market for eggs and purple potatoes. And I began FaceTiming with a man named Anthony. Not the saint in Goya's fresco, silly. I mean the butch dreamboat who conducted endangered-species surveys for a living.

Several months earlier, Tony and I had matched on Tinder while I was visiting friends in Jacksonville. When we met for coffee on New Year's Eve, he reminded me of the surfers I drooled over in high school. He was four years older than I was, a mix of a red panda and Hugh Jackman as the Wolverine, with the salt-and-pepper bearing of a ship's captain you make excuses to go see on the bridge.

In the coffee shop, Tony told me he had grown up in a staunchly evangelical household that was so conservative he wasn't allowed to watch *The Golden Girls*. He had been terrified his family would disown him if they found out he wasn't straight.

After being married for ten years, his wife divorced him. They didn't have any children. "I thought we were soulmates," he said. "Then one day I came home, and she was gone." He was shattered. In time, he stopped binge drinking to cope, slowly came to terms with his complicated sexuality, and eventually, at age forty-two, came out to his friends and family.

"You're bodacious," I murmured, feeling his bravery.

As I sipped my dirty chai and listened, I felt weirdly safe. Was it because I was leaving the country the next day for the semester-long sabbatical? Because I didn't live in Florida any longer and he did? In any case, Tony and I weren't frantically typing messages to one another's faceless torsos at 3:00 a.m. We were connecting in person, as humans, sitting across the street from my old middle school that had gone condo.

"Can I kiss you?" I asked before he dropped me off at my car.

"Uh, yeah," he said, fluttering his eyes, "yes, you can!" It was Tony's first kiss from a man. For a moment, it felt like mine too.

After our date, he texted me exuberantly. It took me a while to respond—I kept thinking, *Ugh, I mean, he lives in Florida and if he likes me so much, what's the matter with him?* I worried he was breadcrumbing me along only to ghost me when someone closer and less weird materialized. At the same time, I was attracted to him. On Valentine's Day, I called him from Lima to say hello. He wasn't playing games, I realized after our soulful conversation. Like me, he was slowly learning he was capable of committed love with another man. After that, I stayed in better touch, still wary.

Our daily FaceTime conversations while I was holed up in Peru went on for hours. One morning he texted me an experience he had after meditating the night before:

I hopped in bed, closed my eyes and I was launched into a speedy slideshow of images and thought, zooming around unwillingly on a search for the source of your pain, or what I perceive you might be working to heal on your medicine journeys...u have told me you're estranged from family, so I guess I'm picking up those vibes? I also felt some anger that you had been suffering, or someone in particular brought this suffering to you.... I landed on a woman, maybe your mother? Sister? I don't even know if you have siblings.... it was heavy, BUT there was some love energy mixed in there too, like support of some kind, and of course flashes of your smiling handsome face. So it was wild.

Here was someone who could read me, risking rejection to show me how deeply he already accepted me. In general terms I had told him how Grindr had affected my life, but like you, he didn't want a lot of details and never will. Dad jokes were told. Trust blossomed. Resonance between us grew, like two boys at summer camp effortlessly becoming friends. We kept our pants on—and I kept my trauma history to myself. When the supposedly last emergency flight to the US popped up, I took it.

On Earth Day 2020, as I pulled into Tony's driveway in Jacksonville for our second date, he knocked his knees together, dancing like a turkey. Laughing, I stepped out of Lambcake and into the salt air: the ocean was only a five-minute bike ride away. I thought I was in familiar territory, taking yet another doomed chance with a guy in Florida, my estranged parents and childhood home only a short drive away.

We smoked a joint. Collapsing into his bed from exhaustion, I spent the night. The next day he built a bookshelf for all the books I had unboxed and gave me a house key. Apparently, I was moving in.

He had asked that we take it slow, but we didn't. On nights we got physical, he couldn't fall asleep. When he told me not to be so handsy and said we should sleep separately, I began packing up my things.

"If you don't want me, why am I here?"

"Repeat after me," he said, "it's been six days since Tony had his first sexual experience with a man." I said it back, cracking a smile. "I don't want you to leave. But I've lived alone for ten years since the divorce, so I need some breathing room. We're winging this, and we knew it'd be risky."

Two WEEKS LATER, we were sharing the same bed again—I knew not to spoon him like an anxious baby lemur. We shopped for patio pillows at T.J. Maxx, and I unboxed my things again.

Around the same time, we went to a nearby island where years before he had been a park ranger. On holiday breaks during college, I had gone there to walk through the fallen oaks exposed to the tides. This time around, though, the boneyards of twisted, bleached branches weren't reflections of my wish to die.

As we clambered over black tide pools of lava-like hardpan, I was in a waking dream, back with my family as we searched for sea biscuits. But as Raul, Drew, Alanna, and Davi reminded me, I was a man. Tony was with me, even if he didn't want to hold my hand there. Living in Florida after cutting ties with my parents, I returned to the stage sets of my youth like this shoreline but stood taller, without a director, breaking character as often as I could. In his own way, Tony was doing the same. We improvised.

We came to a makeshift shelter made of driftwood. I sat down while Tony, like an osprey fortifying his nest for his mate, patched it up with more sticks. Soon, a boat beached itself nearby, spitting out sunburned, dad-bod dudes and their girlfriends onto the sand, their Confederate flag waving.

"Let's get going," Tony said.

"People think we're brothers anyhow," I said, gathering our things. "We're fine."

Walking back to the car, he was far ahead of me, as if he were on the beach by himself, a "straight" ranger once again. We drove home in silence, on the edge of another argument. Part of him wanted me to leave, but much more of him knew I needed to stay.

LIVING TOGETHER DURING the pandemic before vaccines was 24/7 DIY therapy: we took turns playing shrink and freaking out. As Tony puts it, we were like two feral racoons thrown into the same cage—bonding with one another brought up anguish we'd spent decades trying to self-medicate. Sometimes as he wept, I'd rock him like a baby, and he'd do the same for me. Our old negative associations with home were giving way to more coziness, mutual respect, and honesty.

As Tony worked through the trauma of being closeted for forty-two years, there were times when my just holding him filled him with panic. Like so many men, he associated same-sex tenderness with ostracism and damnation. But he was determined to deprogram himself. As if we were Kermit and Miss Piggy, he drove us around on our moped as I held on to his waist, getting waves and funny faces along the way, never knowing what was next. In our living room, I led a mushroom ceremony for him, leading to a breakthrough in trust: he heard his deceased mother say my name and tell him that she was happy for us, that she could be my mom too. We were never the same.

Our workouts also helped us chill out. To this day, every morning, we're up by 5:30 to meditate and go to the gym for difficult workouts I would never ever do on my own. Long before he met me, high-intensity weight training kept Tony from killing himself and, over time, grew his firmeza, easing his panic as we built a life together. Exercise increases levels of BDNF, the same neuroplasticity-promoting protein released by yoga, meditation, intermittent fasting—and psychedelics.

Now, after over three years of intense exercise and medicine work, I've come to believe that psychedelics reopen critical periods for physical development, too. In Gül Dölen's latest, as-yet-unpublished research study, stroke victims are administered MDMA to see if the critical recovery period for motor skills is reopened. Though no data has been released yet, I can tell you that after over thirty ayahuasca ceremonies, I no longer have the C-PTSD body I did in high school or even when I first tried psychedelics. For the first six months with Tony, my body was so stiff I got in and out of the car like an elderly man.

Now my neck is unfrozen. My spine is straighter, my shoulders wider and not caving forward. My lower back no longer hurts, and below my waist I have more feeling. I've shed most of the fat I kept around my hips for protection—I'm not on the couch for weekends at a time on Grindr, or ever, for that matter. I'm muscular, with abs, and if I need to, I can physically defend myself. My body is mine, and no one else's.

"You ever hear you look like a cross between a mop bucket and a moose?" I sometimes ask to lighten the mood.

"Naw," he replies like a tipsy preschooler, "but you remind me of Dick Trickle's cousin Dick Pickle. Come here, Porkchop, and give me a hug!"

EVEN AS I WAS FALLING in love in Jacksonville, it didn't feel like home. As I crossed over a bridge, cleaned a flounder, or watched mocking-birds fight, I thought about the good parts of my childhood. I also imagined my mother growing older, crying in bed, wondering if I'd change my mind and send a card. I pictured my father swinging his golf club and pouring milk onto his shredded wheat. Still, I prayed for the man and woman who gave me life.

"We're hardwired for connection with our parents," James told me one day on Zoom when I worried I'd made a mistake in severing ties. "In the wild, leaving your family behind as a child would mean certain death. So the feelings you've having are leftover evolutionary defenses meant to protect you. But not now, not here. Don't take the alarm bells to mean you're doing the wrong thing or that you're a bad person. In some ways, what you're feeling now is worse than grieving your parents' actual deaths."

By trial and error, Tony and I are learning how to be good husbands in a monogamous marriage. To manifest the honor and loyalty that I wasn't raised with, that Tony's boyhood church relentlessly valued between man and wife. We're getting better at cultivating joy and breathing through the fear that bonding can stir up. "The best indices of resolution," Judith Herman observes at the end of *Trauma and Recovery*, "are the survivor's restored capacity to take pleasure in her life and to engage fully in relationships with others." We both survived, and, if you can excuse the word, grace found us.

ANOTHER REASON JACKSONVILLE no longer felt like home was climate change. As I sat on Tony's plant-filled deck, the days and nights felt hotter than when I was a boy. Because they were: as I've said, compared to 1970, there are now twelve more days with a heat index of ninety degrees or more in Jacksonville. As a result, Cuban treefrogs moving north are pushing out native frog species, and it's only a matter of time until invasive Burmese pythons migrate here from the Everglades. At nearby Guana River State Park, we noticed that mangroves were slowly replacing marsh grasses because of fewer freezes. During thunderstorms, the rain fell harder than I ever recalled; the wind seemed stronger as it rattled the sabal palms and sugarberry tree. Developers had razed huge tracts of carbon-sequestering piney woods in northeast Florida for malls that will be abandoned in fifteen years and for cheaply made, overpriced homes. South of us at Vilano Beach, houses were already falling into the ocean—sea levels in Jacksonville had risen four and a half inches since I was born, ten inches since 1930.

It was uncanny. I remembered what the land and sea were like when I was younger. I felt the personal and ecological differences between then and now. And the personal and the ecological got so jumbled I couldn't tell them apart. In my mind, literal death—from the Sixth Mass Extinction but also from COVID-19 and the murder of people of color like George Floyd by police—got tangled with the absence of my parents. I was feeling a muted version of what Australian philosopher Glenn Albrecht calls *solastalgia*. This is homesickness you feel at home. The pain (*-algia*) experienced after the solace (*solas-*) of nature is gone. In its most intense forms, it's traumatic.

As when you and your people walk through the charred rainforest where you've harvested medicines for centuries, especially needed after 1492.

As when the mountain behind your church in Big Stone Gap, Virginia, has been destroyed by mountaintop removal mining—and the coal, once burned, will add to global warming.

As when the reefs that protected and fed your village have died.

Pondering for too long that we're stuck on a warming, overpopulated planet with at least thirteen thousand nuclear warheads during a mass extinction event—that could be traumatic too. As in the movie *Interstellar*, we are feeling increasingly trapped on Earth, but most of us aren't conscious of it yet. Matthew McConaughey and Anne Hathaway aren't going to travel through a wormhole to save us.

What we're facing amounts to global C-PTSD. Remember Herman's definition of the disorder: "prolonged, repeated" interpersonal trauma we can't flee from. In this case, it's interpersonal because it's Mother Earth who is "turning" on us with floods, droughts, wildfires, heat waves, hurricanes, and new pandemics turbocharged by warmer temperatures. Interpersonal, too, because we're turning on each other.

Epilogue

It was September 2021, early in the fall semester. After a year of Zoom teaching from Florida, I was required to come back to my university in person. There was an indoor mask mandate, so my students and I sat outside on the grass. To co-regulate and build trust, we needed to see each other's faces.

My students and I were discussing a chapter in Robin Wall Kimmerer's *Gathering Moss*, "Learning to See," a title that could be our three-word syllabus. Nature itself, not my words so much, did a lot of the teaching that semester. I asked them to look up at the maple next to us and tell us what they saw.

"Pointy leaves," said one, still shy.

"Rough, whitish bark," said another softly.

I asked them to look again, as if this maple were the last tree on Earth. "What do you see," I asked, "that no one else does?"

"The one leaf at the edge of that branch," Jacob said, pointing and squinting, "is lighter than the others and has a torn edge." Next thing I knew, he was under the maple feeling the bark with his hands, and Pierre joined him. They said it didn't smell like much. After laughter and some awkward silences, Becky was up and ready to lick the bark.

In a lull in our discussion, I looked out at my thirteen students. Most of them had done the reading; they didn't vape in class—they actually wanted to be here. I saw talented, humane Chloe, who would go on to write about body dysmorphia and a slug. Soulful, concerned Dan, who in his first essay will see cultural chaos writ wet in the roiling of a mountain stream. Quiet, fierce Carmen, who after looking at a hen-of-the-woods mushroom, will memorialize her Bolivian *abuelita* who fed her chicken *salteñas* with raisins and olives. Students like them gave me hope. I also ached for them.

As I taught this exceptional class, I was reminded that not all young people need to be taught to care about books or the earth. "It's not enough to name the problem," I told them later in the semester as they worked on their dynamite eco-manifestos. "What are we going to do about it?" I was reminded that in the coming years, community will be as important as any seawall or solar farm. It also got me thinking that while I'm childless, I will have a legacy: as an educator, I'm passing on knowledge, skills, and perhaps even the courage to rise up and defend our planet. My best teachers had done that for me. They had enlarged my circle of compassion.

I was different than before my sabbatical. As a professor and human, I had more self-respect, more of a desire to serve, to mentor my students—but I was still learning how to love. How to love Tony, yes, but also how to let myself be embraced by creeks and forested mountains. To choose for myself the misty bath of Hone Quarry's waterfall in the national forest, as if it were belonging itself that was soaking me: *shower me as you wish—it's what I want.*

A nine-year-old named Adara in the twenty-third century couldn't be more important than these students—they were my children, right then, right there, on leaves of grass. Someday I hope to hike with my students to that waterfall.

IN LATE JANUARY, I rushed down to Florida to say goodbye to my mother. Unable to breathe on her own because of a reaction to anti-seizure meds she had taken for a UTI, she had been on a ventilator in the ICU for over two weeks. The doctor said she wouldn't last much longer. She was waiting for me, he said.

"I'm not going anywhere," I told her first thing, as much for myself as for her. "You're not going to be alone ever again—I'm staying with you." I read her Wordsworth and the twenty-third Psalm. I kissed her and reminded her of the reefs we snorkeled, especially the clown trig-gerfish she adored with yellow lips and electric-white blotches on black.

Remembering Drew's advice about reconciliation, the whole night and morning I wept and told her I was sorry and I forgave her, asking her to forgive me. "We're good, the slate is clean," I said over and over as if it were a spell that I believed in. "I'm not proud of the man who left four years ago, but I'm proud of who I am today." She heard me, wiggling her toes and opening her bleary eyes a smidge. They opened the widest for Tony. "Don't worry," he sobbed to her while I spoke to a nurse outside, "we're going to get married someday soon. I'll take care of him."

She wouldn't have wanted to die with massive tubes coming out of her, so at the doctor's suggestion, I okayed what's called a "compassionate withdrawal" of the ventilator and IVs. In the precious minutes afterward, Tony and I held her. I sang to her. Rodgers and Hammerstein, "Silent Night," Alanna's dearest chants in Sanskrit. I hummed Raul and Lidia's icaros. I sang and sang.

She took her last breaths. We slowed down, softened, savored. Lasting fifteen minutes, she died with dignity. We laid three tulips, her favorite, on her body.

THERE WASN'T A FUNERAL. She didn't want one. But before her casket was hoisted into the mausoleum crypt, I looked inside. Seeing her embalmed corpse frightened me. It also offered wisdom I could get no other way in a culture terrified of death, inconvenienced by grief.

I rushed back to work, teaching my classes indoors with all of us in masks, holding Zoom office hours, staring at my laptop for hours, going through the motions of what Tony and I call "the robot life." It had been a year since my last ayahuasca ceremony. It was time.

On my spring break, I flew to Peru to work with a gentle curandero named Chichi, who had forty years of experience with jungle medicines. In a ceremony one night, I felt something new: I wanted the ayahuasca out of my system. It was a hyperspatial Code Red. But there is no off button.

I screamed beyond the top of my lungs. And kept screaming. Monkeys froze in the trees outside. The other participants remained calm. Thinking I might start hitting myself, I asked Chichi's assistant Alex to tie me up, but he refused.

"Get off me!" I yelled, feeling a familiar presence. "I'm an adult now, and you better get away from me!" Careful to keep his distance, Chichi sang an icaro invoking a flamingo-red river flower called bobinsana. He knew what was up.

My mother was here in the Amazon, exactly two months after dying. She and I weren't done yet. Still stuck on Earth, her soul was breaking into my body.

"Yuck, yuck, YUUUCK!" she kept saying through me as she settled into my being, as if she'd found dead toads again. "How could your father do that to you?" With full access to my mind and cells, she finally understood firsthand what it was like to be me.

A couple spaces over was my Mexican friend Devana, who sang a song in praise of Shiva, the Hindu god of death and transformation. The mantras kickstarted my decades of training: *Unclench the fist behind your eyes. Let go, let go.* I connected with my breath. My mother never could snuff me out completely.

"I'm feeling it!" I yelled as Devana sang of the surrender at the core of all religions, trying to activate my prefrontal cortex so I could direct the process a bit more. "I'm letting it go!"

"Say his name," Alex said. "Tell the forest what he did to you."

I proclaimed the seven syllables of my father's name. I prosecuted my parents aloud for the billionth time.

Then my mother took over. "Look at all the people you've been with!" She could feel all the hookups I'd had in my life, and together she and I shrieked their life force out into the night, emptying me of their traces.

Epilogue

A portal opened above like the eye of a galactic hurricane. The screaming got louder, scarier, as if knives were involved. In a way, they were. She must have sounded the same way during my birth—the doctor stupidly refused to perform a C-section and pulled too hard to get me out. Her pain was unbearable. I was huge. "Ahh! Oh my goodness, help me, help me!"

She had given excruciating birth to me, and forty-two years later, I was doing the same for her. Crazy as it sounds, counting on my yogic training, she was using me to slingshot herself into her next life.

Getting more centered, I shamelessly held court, saying trite things that still feel momentous: "This is *my* body. A gift from the earth. Sacred. I didn't take care of it, no, but I didn't kill myself either. I don't want to be this person anymore."

Energy was rising from the top of my head. It wasn't kundalini or whatever. It was my mother's tortured soul. I breathed in deeply like an ice geyser about to blow.

"Love is the answer. It's always been the answer."

As she ascended, I shook. I quieted down, and the ceremony continued. Chichi, brushing my body with piñon colorado leaves, channeled a song from a pink river dolphin. Later Alex stood me clothed in the shower.

At dawn I saw it. My mother was gone. I never understood her. I remember her as a storm, or as a deer stepping into a meadow. They appear and pass on. But how? Why?

In the middle of absolute nowhere, my mother held an impromptu funeral for herself on her volcanic, melodramatic terms: possession, exorcism, ascension. But as the bereaved do in any funeral, I was also affirming a new self.

A YEAR LATER, Tony and I got married in our succulent-filled sunroom. Long before the tungsten rings from Amazon Marketplace were slipped on our fingers, though, it felt like we were already husbands.

When were we wed in spirit? I think it was two summers before, right after we moved to Virginia together, when I brought him to the Hone Quarry waterfall. We had it to ourselves. The crayfish and old maples, the light shimmering across the sandstone boulders. Around our necks, we each wore a pearl from the island next to Konstan's.

After we horsed around in the natural pool, he sat still on a flat rock. "I listen to my breath," he said, "and hear the tides." He remembered his mom shutting her eyes in the nursing home and, for minutes at a time, being utterly at peace. What he wouldn't give to eat one last Miracle Whip and bacon sandwich with her.

In just my undies, I stepped onto the ledge underneath the waterfall. The water breaking over me was cold. Relentless. It was a curse, it was destiny, it had integrity and was utterly free. Throwing my hands up, I rejoiced. Tony hollered back, soon taking my place under the water. For an hour, we forgot our shame and felt jubilation: we weren't calling hogs—Tony and I were declaring ourselves worthy of love.

I slipped back into the creek. I watched it meander down the mountain, listening to it as mindfully as I did my mother's last breath—and I heard her singing her off-key icaro to me:

Row, row, row your boat
Gently down the stream
Merrily, merrily, merrily, merrily
Life is but a dream

All I ever needed to know was in her song: Stay soft-hearted ("Gently"), cultivate joy ("Merrily"), and work hard ("Row"). In this, our sacred, maddening dream, you can relax. Stop paddling. The water will carry you to the sea. The mothership will bring you home.

Notes

Epigraphs

"*Do we need forests?*" Jeff Orlowski, *Chasing Coral*, Netflix documentary, 2017, https://www.netflix.com/title/80168188.

"Nothing on earth is more gladdening" Annie Dillard, *The Writing Life* (New York: Harper Perennial, 1989), 98.

Prologue

3   *Over 90 percent of coral has died in Florida* Paul Voosen, "Scientists Track Florida's Vanishing Barrier Reef," *Science*, April 24, 2019, https://www.science.org/content/article/scientists-track-florida-s-vanishing-barrier-reef.

3   *Then I showed them the graph* Using Antarctic ice core records (https://www.ncdc.noaa.gov/data-access/paleoclimatology-data/datasets/ice-core) as well as data from NOAA (https://gml.noaa.gov/ccgg/trends/) and NASA (http://data.giss.nasa.gov/gistemp/), Brian Magi, Associate Professor of Atmospheric Sciences in the Department of Geography and Earth Sciences at UNC Charlotte, created the graph. To view a more detailed version of it, visit: https://pages.charlotte.edu/mesas/2015/01/15/climate-change-and-debate/.

3   *"410 parts per million of CO_2"* Rebecca Lindsay, "Climate Change: Atmospheric Carbon Dioxide," NOAA, May 12, 2023, https://www.climate.gov/news-features/understanding-climate/climate-change-atmospheric-carbon-dioxide. This webpage provides an excellent overview of how rising CO_2 levels impact ocean chemistry and the climate.

3   *"James Madison breathed in 280 ppm"* Rob Monroe, "What Does This Number Mean?" *The Keeling Curve Blog*, Scripps Institution of Oceanography, UC San Diego, May 12, 2015, https://keelingcurve.ucsd.edu/2015/05/12/what-does-this-number-mean/. Check out the paragraph at the bottom that begins "Prior to the Industrial Revolution."

3   *"Temperatures right now are playing catch up"* Rebecca Lindsay, "If Carbon Dioxide Hits a New High Every Year, Why Isn't Every Year Hotter Than the Last?" NOAA, May 12, 2023, https://www.climate.gov/news-features/climate-qa/if-carbon-dioxide-hits-new-high-every-year-why-isn't-every-year-hotter-last.

3   *"And coral is one of the most sensitive"* "How Can Corals Teach Us about Climate?," NOAA/National Centers for Environmental Education, June 8, 2016, https://www.ncei.noaa.gov/news/how-can-corals-teach-us-about-climate.

4   *"One way to open your eyes"* Rachel Carson, *The Sense of Wonder: A Celebration of Nature for Parents and Children* (New York: Harper Perennial, 2017), 67.

4   *Remembering that much of the Amazon* Adam Voiland, "Reflecting on a Tumultuous Amazon Fire Season," NASA Earth Observatory, https://earthobservatory.nasa.gov/images/146355/reflecting-on-a-tumultuous-amazon-fire-season.

4   *"'I am with you now'"* James Cameron, *Avatar*, Twentieth Century Fox, 2009.

5   *Ask the endangered Shenandoah salamander* Jeb Wofford, "2022 Weather in Review: Shenandoah National Park," National Park Service, January 26, 2023, https://www.nps.gov/articles/000/2022-weather-in-review-shenandoah-national-park.htm.

5   *When they were in second grade* "When Words Become Endangered: Oxford Junior Dictionary Removes Nature Words," *National Wildlife Federation Blog*, October 1, 2009, updated January 20, 2014, https://blog.nwf.org/2009/10/when-words-become-endangered-oxford-junior-dictionary-removes-nature-words/.

6   *I clicked ahead to the dictionary definition* New Oxford American Dictionary, s.v. "wonder," accessed August 20, 2019, Apple OS Dictionary app.

7   *The Buddha asked his monks* Samyutta Nikaya 56.48, tr. Thanissaro Bhikkhu, 1998, https://www.accesstoinsight.org/tipitaka/sn/sn56/sn56.048.than.html.

8   *"Despite the hysterics"* James Walcott, "Rush to Judgment," *Vanity Fair,* April 10, 2007, https://www.vanityfair.com/news/2007/05/wolcott200705.

8   *"The most beautiful thing about a tree"* David Finkel, "Dialing for Dittos," *Washington Post,* June 12, 1994, https://www.washingtonpost.com/lifestyle/style/dialing-for-dittos/2012/10/02/bc11e83e-0cac-11e2-bb5e-492c0d30bff6_story.html.

9   *channeling the Double Rainbow Guy* Paul "Bear" Vasquez, "Yosemitebear Mountain Double Rainbow 1-8-10," YouTube, January 8, 2010, https://youtu.be/OQSNhk5ICTI.

9   *Robin Williams* Peter Weir, *Dead Poets Society,* Touchstone Pictures, 1989.

9   *"prolonged, repeated trauma"* Judith Herman, *Trauma and Recovery* (New York: Basic Books, 1992), 119.

9   *"In most homes, even the most oppressive"* Ibid., 74.

9   *C-PTSD, also known as* For a concise yet comprehensive overview of C-PTSD, including diagnostic criteria, see the frequently cited paper by Alexandra Cook et al., "Complex Trauma in Children and Adolescents," *Psychiatric Annals* 35, no. 5 (May 2005), https://bpb-us-e1.wpmucdn.com/sites.northwestern.edu/dist/f/1961/files/2022/08/Complex-trauma-in-children.pdf. See also part 3 of Bessel Van der Kolk, *The Body Keeps the Score* (New York: Penguin Books, 2014), particularly chapter 10 ("Developmental Trauma: The Hidden Epidemic").

1 / What Would E.T. Do?

13   *"Maybe what we can do"* Aimee Nezhukumatathil, *World of Wonders* (Minneapolis, MN: Milkweed Editions, 2020), 159.

14   *maybe because soil contains bacteria* Pagan Kennedy, *The Atlantic,* "How to Get High on Soil," January 31, 2012, https://www.theatlantic.com/health/archive/2012/01/how-to-get-high-on-soil/251935/.

15   *"The capacity for induced trance or dissociative states"* Herman, *Trauma and Recovery,* 102.

16   *"a sapling—a miniature redwood"* Melissa Mathison, "A Boy's Life"/*E.T. The Extraterrestrial* (shooting script), Script Slug, September 8, 1981, https://www.scriptslug.com/script/e-t-the-extra-terrestrial-1982.

16   *Now climate change in the form of more wildfires* Becki Robins, "To Save the Redwoods, Scientists Debate Burning and Logging," *Scientific American*, December 20, 2019, https://www.scientificamerican.com/article/to-save-the-redwoods-scientists-debate-burning-and-logging/.

16   *"He needs to go home"* Steven Spielberg, *E.T. The Extraterrestrial*, Universal Pictures, 1982.

17   *"You may not come near me!"* "Erica Kane and the Bear" (clip from *All My Children*, September 4, 1985), YouTube, https://youtu.be/h17XM_KoXcM.

19   *All it takes researcher Jaak Panksepp found* Jaak Panksepp, *Affective Neuroscience: The Foundations of Human and Animal Emotions* (New York: Oxford University Press, 1998), 18–19.

2 / Row

25   *I needed the dopamine* For more on this key neurotransmitter and its role in addiction, see Daniel Lieberman and Michael Long, *The Molecule of More: How a Single Chemical in Your Brain Drives Love, Sex, and Creativity—and Will Determine the Fate of the Human Race* (Dallas: BenBella Books, 2018).

3 / The Lantern

35   *"Clap your hands"* and *"Ouuuuch"* Steven Spielberg, *E.T. The Extraterrestrial*, Universal Pictures, 1982.

35   *"The wound is healed"* Mathison, "A Boy's Life"/*E.T. The Extraterrestrial* (shooting script), Script Slug, September 8, 1981, https://www.scriptslug.com/script/e-t-the-extra-terrestrial-1982.

36   "warm little pond" Dirk Schulze-Makuch, "Back to Darwin's Warm Little Pond," Smithsonian Magazine, October 30, 2017, https://www.smithsonianmag.com/air-space-magazine/back-darwins-warm-little-pond-180967008/

36   *Sea biscuits!* Leslie Bruce, "Sand Dollars and Sea Biscuits," *The Water Column* 4, no. 2 (October 1989), https://nsgl.gso.uri.edu/masgc/masgcn89008/The%20Water%20Column%20v4n2.pdf.

4 / Exultation

38   *The year before, in 1987* Derek P. Manzello, "Rapid Recent Warming of Coral Reefs in the Florida Keys," *Scientific Reports* 5 (2015), https://doi.org/10.1038/srep16762.

38   *I couldn't fathom that the ocean* "OHC Reaches Its Highest Level in Recorded History," NOAA/National Centers for Environmental Information, January 22, 2020, https://www.ncei.noaa.gov/news/ocean-heat-content-rises.

39   *For thousands of years* Check out J. B. C. Jackson, "Reefs since Columbus," *Coral Reefs* 16, suppl. 1, S23–S32 (1997), https://doi.org/10.1007/s003380050238; and Andrew Bruckner, *Proceedings of the Caribbean Acropora Workshop: Potential Application of the U.S. Endangered Species Act as a Conservation Strategy*, NOAA Technical Memorandum NMFS-OPR-24, January 2003, 3 and 11.

39   *But since 1975, the Florida Keys have lost* Michon Scott, "With 'Mission: Iconic Reefs,' NOAA Aims to Restore Florida Keys with Climate-Resilient Corals," March 6, 2023, NOAA, https://www.climate.gov/news-features/features/mission-iconic-reefs-noaa-aims-restore-florida-keys-climate-resilient-corals.

39   *At Dry Rocks today* To see dramatic before-and-after photos of reefs in the Florida Keys and hear oral histories from divers and scientists, check out "Voices from Florida's Changing Coral Reefs," NOAA National Centers for Environmental Information, March 31, 2021, https://storymaps.arcgis.com/stories/2f188242d0a44af48d990ff351397553. For more heartbreaking photographic documentation and insightful reflection, visit Philip Dustan, "Caribbean Coral Reefs Through Time: 1972–2013," https://biospherefoundation.org/project/coral-reef-change/.

39   *in my lifetime, coral coverage in the Keys* "Restoring Seven Iconic Reefs: A Mission to Recover the Coral Reefs of the Florida Keys," NOAA Fisheries, https://www.fisheries.noaa.gov/southeast/habitat-conservation/restoring-seven-iconic-reefs-mission-recover-coral-reefs-florida-keys. Historical coral coverage on reefs in the Keys, as the restoration timeline graphic states, is estimated to have been 30–40 percent. Special thanks to Erica Towle, PhD, for explaining this statistic to me.

39   *the keystone species of elkhorn and staghorn coral* "Elkhorn Coral," NOAA Fisheries Species Directory, https://www.fisheries.noaa.gov/species/elkhorn-coral; and "Staghorn Coral," NOAA Fisheries Species Directory, https://www.fisheries.noaa.gov/species/staghorn-coral.

39   *These two coral species* Valérie F. Chamberland et al., "Restoration of Critically Endangered Elkhorn Coral (*Acropora palmata*) Populations Using Larvae Reared from Wild-Caught Gametes," *Global Ecology and Conservation* 4 (July 2015), https://doi.org/10.1016/j.gecco.2015.10.005.

40   *On top of that, seawater increasingly acidic* Brian Kahn, "Florida Reefs Begin to Dissolve Much Sooner Than Expected," *Scientific American*, May 4, 2016, https://www.scientificamerican.com/article/florida-reefs-begin-to-dissolve-much-sooner-than-expected/.

40   *Until the bulb was replaced* Tim Gilmore, "First Baptist Church Lighthouse Replica," *JaxPsychoGeo*, July 2, 2017, https://jaxpsychogeo.com/the-center-of-the-city/first-baptist-church-lighthouse-replica/.

40   *"a demon-possessed pedophile"* Susan Sachs, "Baptist Pastor Attacks Islam, Inciting Cries of Intolerance," *New York Times*, June 15, 2002, https://www.nytimes.com/2002/06/15/us/baptist-pastor-attacks-islam-inciting-cries-of-intolerance.html.

40   *Council members who voted no* Thanks to Jimmy Midyette, the footage from this service can be viewed on YouTube: "First Baptist Jax Honors Councilmembers Who Voted Against LGBT Rights—August 2012," https://www.youtube.com/watch?v=CtBaxVT5etQ. The quote from Pastor Brunson appears one minute in.

41   *I pointed out that it's been documented* For an overview of relevant research, check out Volker Sommer and Paul L. Vasey, eds., *Homosexual Behaviour in Animals: An Evolutionary Perspective* (Cambridge, UK: Cambridge University Press, 2011).

41   *What I didn't know at eight or seventeen* As Judith Herman writes in *Trauma and Recovery* on p. 203, "Gaining possession of oneself often requires repudiating those aspects of the self that were imposed by the trauma. As the survivor sheds her victim identity, she may also choose to renounce parts of herself that have felt almost intrinsic to her being. Once again, this process challenges the survivor's capacities for both *fantasy and discipline.*" (italics mine)

43   *asking the brain regions involved in PTSD* J. Douglas Bremner, "Traumatic Stress: Effects on the Brain," *Dialogues in Clinical Neuroscience* 8, no. 4 (2006), https://doi.org/10.31887/DCNS.2006.8.4/jbremner.

43   *one that covers less than 1 percent* Florida Keys "The Variety of Species Living on a Coral Reef," National Marine Sanctuary, https://floridakeys.noaa.gov/corals/biodiversity.html#:~:text=Covering%20less%20than%20one,anywhere%20else%20in%20the%20world.

5 / Dieback

44 *"To stand at the ruins"* Sofia Samatar, "Standing at the Ruins," *The White Review*, November 2021, https://www.thewhitereview.org/feature/standing-at-the-ruins/.

44 *We couldn't conceive that because humanity* Simon L. Lewis and Mark A. Maslin, "Defining the Anthropocene," *Nature* 519 (2015), https://doi.org/10.1038/nature14258.

45 *CO_2 levels have risen by over 25 percent* Jule G. Charney et al., *Carbon Dioxide and Climate: A Scientific Assessment*, Report of an Ad Hoc Study Group on Carbon Dioxide and Climate, National Academy of Sciences, Washington, DC, 1979, 4. According to the report, CO_2 levels were 334 ppm in 1979. CO_2 levels in July 2023 were 422 ppm. That's an increase of 26.3 percent.

45 *and now in Jacksonville, there are twelve more days* Danielle Uliano, "Florida Summer Heat: Here's How Our Temperatures Have Changed over the Years," News4Jax, June 6, 2022, https://www.news4jax.com/weather/2022/06/06/florida-summer-heat-heres-how-our-temperatures-have-changed-over-the-years/.

45 *with historically redlined, minority neighborhoods* Steve Patterson, "Years after Redlining, Jacksonville's Have-Not Neighborhoods Suffer More in Heat, Study Says," Jacksonville.com, February 17, 2020, https://www.jacksonville.com/story/news/local/2020/02/17/years-after-redlining-jacksonvilles-have-not--neighborhoods-suffer-more-in-heat-study-says/112231794/.

45 *"That was unheard of twenty years ago"* Kevin Bouffard, "Study Offers Warning for Florida Farmers from Global Warming," AP News, July 23, 2017, https://apnews.com/article/3c5d892109164e0eb0703d85482529f0.

45 *It's digital* Betul Keles et al., "A Systematic Review: The Influence of Social Media on Depression, Anxiety and Psychological Distress in Adolescents," *International Journal of Adolescence and Youth* 25, no. 1 (2019), https://doi.org/10.1080/02673843.2019.1590851.

45 *They're hooked* Conghui Su et al., "Viewing Personalized Video Clips Recommended by TikTok Activates Default Mode Network and Ventral Tegmental Area," *NeuroImage* 237 (2021), https://doi.org/10.1016/j.neuroimage.2021.118136.

45 *Every semester when we discuss the EPA statistic* "Indoor Air Quality," Environmental Protection Agency, https://www.epa.gov/report-environment/indoor-air-quality#note1.

47   *As Glacier National Park continued melting* Nadja Popovich, "Mapping 50 Years of Melting Ice in Glacier National Park," *New York Times*, May 24, 2017, https://www.nytimes.com/interactive/2017/05/24/climate/mapping-50-years-of-ice-loss-in-glacier-national-park.html.

47   *Mass shootings became more commonplace* "Counting America's Mass Shootings," *The Economist*, June 13, 2016, https://www.economist.com/graphic-detail/2016/06/13/counting-americas-mass-shootings.

47   *Social inequality continued to soar* John Cassidy, "Piketty's Inequality Story in Six Charts," *The New Yorker*, March 26, 2014, https://www.newyorker.com/news/john-cassidy/pikettys-inequality-story-in-six-charts.

47   *Mobile phones proliferated* Vini Khurana et al., "Cell Phones and Brain Tumors: A Review Including the Long-Term Epidemiologic Data," *Surgical Neurology* 72, no. 3 (2009), https://doi.org/10.1016/j.surneu.2009.01.019. See Figure 2.

47   *Walmart became the largest private employer* "Timeline, An Overview of Wal-Mart," *PBS NewsHour*, August 20, 2004, https://www.pbs.org/newshour/economy/business-july-dec04-timeline_08-20.

47   *"In the effort to placate her abusers"* Herman, *Trauma and Recovery*, 105.

6 / Stone Foundation

51   *"prayed over by witches"* Kimberly Daniels, "Why Celebrating Halloween Is Dangerous," *Charisma*, October 27, 2009, https://charismamag.com/spiritled-living/spiritual-warfare/why-celebrating-halloween-is-dangerous/.

51   *"If it wasn't for slavery"* Dan MacGuill, "Did Florida State Rep. Kimberly Daniels Once Say, 'I Thank God for Slavery'?" Snopes, January 2, 2019, https://www.snopes.com/fact-check/kimberly-daniels-thank-god-slavery/. A recording was removed from YouTube for violating its hate speech guidelines, but as of July 2023, one was available on Facebook: https://www.facebook.com/pulsenigeria247/videos/if-it-wasnt-for-slavery-id-be-in-africa-worshipping-a-tree-kimberly-daniels/1817064225053664/.

51   *she also offers her services as an exorcist* Kim Daniels, *Clean House, Strong House* (Lake Mary, FL: Charisma House, 2003), 151–152.

52   *"The Dream of a Common Language" Strayed writes* Cheryl Strayed, *Wild* (New York: Vintage, 2012), 60.

52 *"She died a famous woman denying"* Adrienne Rich, *The Collected Poems of Adrienne Rich* (New York: W. W. Norton, 2016), 443.

53 *That was my C-PTSD body* For more information on the physical consequences of childhood trauma, see Alexander C. McFarlane, "The Long-Term Costs of Traumatic Stress: Intertwined Physical and Psychological Consequences," *World Psychiatry* 9, no. 1 (February 2010), https://doi.org/10.1002/j.2051-5545.2010.tb00254.x; and Luisa Lo Iacono et al., "Psychobiological Consequences of Childhood Sexual Abuse: Current Knowledge and Clinical Implications," *Frontiers in Neuroscience* 15 (2021), https://doi.org/10.3389/fnins.2021.771511.

54 *"Transcendental Etude"* All quotes from this poem in the rest of the chapter are from Rich, *The Collected Poems of Adrienne Rich*, 510-515.

56 *"the unquestionable ability of man"* Henry David Thoreau, *Walden* (Project Gutenberg eBook, 1995), https://www.gutenberg.org/files/205/205-h/205-h.htm.

7 / Adrienne

59 *dead elm raising bleached arms* These three italicized phrases are from Rich, *The Collected Poems of Adrienne Rich*, 510-515.

59 *"What is the count of the scores"* Walt Whitman, "Crossing Brooklyn Ferry," Poetry Foundation, https://www.poetryfoundation.org/poems/45470/crossing-brooklyn-ferry.

8 / Crazing Lake

65 *"Who would have suspected so large"* Thoreau, *Walden*, https://www.gutenberg.org/files/205/205-h/205-h.htm.

68 *as well as the Coral Triangle* For an overview of this ecologically rich area, see J. E. N. Veron et al., "Delineating the Coral Triangle," *Galaxea, Journal of Coral Reef Studies* 11 (2009), https://doi.org/10.3755/galaxea.11.91.

68 *Reefs in the Western Hemisphere* Katie L. Cramer et al., "The Transformation of Caribbean Coral Communities Since Humans," *Ecology and Evolution* 11, no. 15 (August 2021), https://doi.org/10.1002/ece3.7808. As these authors state, "Living cover of reef-building corals has declined on Caribbean reefs by 50% to 80% since systematic monitoring began in the late 1970s," though I suspect this is an overly conservative estimate.

9 / Lag Time

71   *"Recognition is famously"* Amitav Ghosh, *The Great Derangement: Climate Change and the Unthinkable* (Chicago: The University of Chicago Press, 2016), 4.

71   *on May 9, 2013, the daily average concentration of* CO_2 Jessica Blunden, "2013 State of the Climate: Carbon Dioxide Tops 400 ppm," NOAA, July 13, 2014, https://www.climate.gov/news-features/understanding-climate/ 2013-state-climate-carbon-dioxide-tops-400-ppm.

71   *By comparison, there was about a third less* CO_2 Rob Monroe, "What Does This Number Mean?" *The Keeling Curve Blog*, Scripps Institution of Oceanography, UC San Diego, May 12, 2015, https://keelingcurve.ucsd. edu/2015/05/12/what-does-this-number-mean/. Check out the paragraph at the bottom that begins "Prior to the Industrial Revolution." (280 is two-thirds of 420 ppm.)

71   *Sidenote: more tigers are in captivity* Jamie Landers, "5 Things to Know about Owning Tigers in Texas," *Dallas Morning News*, August 18, 2022, https://www.dallasnews.com/news/texas/2022/08/18/5-things-to-know-about-owning-tigers-in-texas/.

71   *The last time it was at 400 ppm* Julie Brigham-Grette and Steve Petsch, "The Arctic Hasn't Been This Warm for 3 Million Years—and That Foreshadows Big Changes for the Rest of the Planet," *Discover Magazine*, September 30, 2020, https://www.discovermagazine.com/environment/the-arctic-hasnt-been-this-warm-for-3-million-years-and-that-foreshadows-big.

71   *Over the past sixty years, in fact,* CO_2 *levels* Rebecca Lindsey, "Climate Change: Atmospheric Carbon Dioxide," May 12, 2023, https://www. climate.gov/news-features/understanding-climate/climate-change-atmospheric-carbon-dioxide.

72   *In other words, the warming effect* To learn more, check out Kirsten Zickfeld and Tyler Herrington, "The Time Lag between a Carbon Dioxide Emission and Maximum Warming Increases with the Size of the Emission," *Environmental Research Letters* 10, no. 3 (March 10, 2015), http:// doi.org/10.1088/1748-9326/10/3/031001; and Rebecca Lindsey, "If Carbon Dioxide Hits a New High Every Year, Why Isn't Every Year Hotter Than the Last?" NOAA, May 12, 2023, https://www.climate.gov/news-features/ climate-qa/if-carbon-dioxide-hits-new-high-every-year-why-isn't-every-year-hotter-last.

73 *In fact, with the largest brain* Csilla Ari and Dominic P. D'Agostino, "Contingency Checking and Self-Directed Behaviors in Giant Manta Rays: Do Elasmobranchs Have Self-Awareness?" *Journal of Ethology* 34 (2016), https://doi.org/10.1007/s10164-016-0462-z.

73 *Some months later, I found a video online* To view the video "Endangered Sharks, Whales and Rays Butchered at Indonesian Market," filmed on September 6, 2013, visit: https://www.newsflare.com/video/310563/charity-causes/endangered-sharks-whales-and-rays-butchered-at-indonesian-market.

74 *Sulfuric acid from the nearby Ramu Nico Basamuk chemical plant* Personal communication with unnamed locals in Madang, August 2013. Since 2013, the plant has committed additional serious violations of PNG environmental laws: http://www.sulphuric-acid.com/sulphuric-acid-on-the-web/acid%20plants/Ramu-Nickel.htm.

75 *There is no hope of reefs surviving* David Adam, "How Global Warming Sealed the Fate of the World's Coral Reefs," *The Guardian*, September 2, 2009, https://www.theguardian.com/environment/2009/sep/02/coral-catastrophic-future.

75 *which annually lets out about seven concert grand pianos' worth of* CO_2 Check out EPA data on the 2010 Honda Insight: https://www.fueleconomy.gov/feg/Find.do?action=sbs&id=26365&#tab2. Click on "Energy and Environment." Based on fifteen thousand annual driving miles, Lambcake releases 3.6 tons (7,200 pounds) of CO_2, which translates into about seven concert grand pianos (at 1,000 pounds each).

76 *With every mile driven, nearly a half pound* According to the same EPA website as above, a 2010 Honda Insight releases 217 grams of CO_2 per mile, which is about a half pound.

76 "If the stars should appear one night" Ralph Waldo Emerson, "Nature" (Project Gutenberg eBook, 2009), https://www.gutenberg.org/cache/epub/29433/pg29433-images.html.

78 *Beauty's mother is Death* Wallace Stevens, "Sunday Morning," Poetry Foundation, https://www.poetryfoundation.org/poetrymagazine/poems/13261/sunday-morning.

78 *"God is Change"* Octavia Butler, *Parable of the Sower* (New York: Grand Central, 1993), 3.

78 *a dead zone the size of New Jersey* Casey Smith, "New Jersey-Size 'Dead Zone' Is Largest Ever in Gulf of Mexico," *National Geographic*, August 2, 2017, https://www.nationalgeographic.com/science/article/gulf-mexico-hypoxia-water-quality-dead-zone.

78 *Since 1950, we've destroyed* Corryn Wetzel, "The Planet Has Lost Half of Its Coral Reefs Since 1950," *Smithsonian Magazine*, September 17, 2021, https://www.smithsonianmag.com/science-nature/the-planet-has-lost-half-of-coral-reefs-since-1950-180978701/.

79 *We've pulled 90 percent of large fish* John Nielsen, "Report: Commercial Fleets Killing Off Giant Fish," *All Things Considered*/NPR, May 14, 2003, https://www.npr.org/2003/05/14/1263623/report-commercial-fleets-killing-off-giant-fish.

79 *half the coral on the Great Barrier Reef* Robinson Meyer, "Since 2016, Half of All Coral in the Great Barrier Reef Has Died," *The Atlantic*, April 18, 2018, https://www.theatlantic.com/science/archive/2018/04/since-2016-half-the-coral-in-the-great-barrier-reef-has-perished/558302/.

79 *The chairman of the GBR Marine Park Authority* Rod McGuirk, "Australia Lowers Great Barrier Reef Outlook to 'Very Poor'," AP News, August 30, 2019, https://apnews.com/article/d2cb4e79356a4068a8c3d31163ed3ac8#.

79 *As Craig Foster says* Pippa Ehrlich and James Reed, *My Octopus Teacher*, Netflix documentary, 2020, https://www.netflix.com/title/81045007?source=35.

10 / Otter

85 *Sea otters have the densest fur* Josh Cassidy, "The Fantastic Fur of Sea Otters," KQED, January 6, 2015, https://www.kqed.org/science/25908/the-fantastic-fur-of-sea-otters.

85 *An entire human head* "12 Facts about Otters for Sea Otter Awareness Week," US Department of the Interior, September 14, 2021, https://www.doi.gov/blog/12-facts-about-otters-sea-otter-awareness-week.

86 *Horrified, my mind churned* Michael James Werner, "Sea Otters v. Climate Change," KQED QUEST, January 14, 2014, https://www.youtube.com/watch?v=XHOmbAMkCJs.

86 *Research by Chris Wilmers and colleagues* Chris Wilmers et al., "Do Trophic Cascades Affect the Storage and Flux of Atmospheric Carbon? An Analysis of Sea Otters and Kelp Forests," *Frontiers in Ecology and the Environment* 10, no. 8 (October 2012), https://doi.org/10.1890/110176.

86   *"the innate tendency to focus on life"* E. O. Wilson, *Biophilia* (Cambridge, MA: Harvard University Press, 1984), 1.

87   *Looming over the estuary were the tall, twin stacks* Kera Abraham, "Moss Landing Inventor Makes a Tool against Global Warming," *Monterey County Weekly*, September 11, 2008, updated May 17, 2013, https://www.monterey countyweekly.com/news/local_news/moss-landing-iventor-makes-cement-a-tool-against-global-warming/article_c88d8b7f-41c0-5a50-a3f7-b3631a1ccac5.html.

87   *But in in a kelp ecosystem roughly the size of West Virginia* Michon Scott, "Caring for Sea Otters Offers Climate Bonus," NOAA/Climate.gov, February 6, 2015, https://www.climate.gov/news-features/featured-images/caring-sea-otters-offers-climate-bonus.

88   *"I will make inseparable cities"* Walt Whitman, "For You O Democracy," Poetry Foundation, https://www.poetryfoundation.org/poems/51567/for-you-o-democracy.

88   *After I came back home, I found a research paper* Heather S. Harris et al., "Lesions and Behavior Associated with Forced Copulation of Juvenile Pacific Harbor Seals (*Phoca vitulina richardsi*) by Southern Sea Otters (*Enhydra lutris nereis*)," *Aquatic Mammals* 36, no. 4 (2010), https://doi.org/10.1578/AM.36.4.2010.331.

89   *"The survivor's overriding fear is a repetition"* Herman, *Trauma and Recovery*, 206.

89   *"cannot be terminated by ordinary means"* and *"major jolt to the body"* Ibid., 109.

90   *"I do it to prove I exist"* Ibid.

11 / Ice

92   *Bursts of that salty sea* Frank Postberg et al., "Detection of Phosphates Originating from Enceladus's Ocean," *Nature* 618 (2023), https://doi.org/10.1038/s41586-023-05987-9.

92   *"Love does not consist of gazing at one another"* Antoine de Saint-Exupéry, *Airman's Odyssey* (New York: Houghton Mifflin Harcourt, 2012), 195.

94   *"Maybe some women aren't meant to be tamed"* Michael Patrick King, "Ex and the City," *Sex and the City*, October 3, 1999.

95   *Home one night from a bar* Michael J. Pepin, "John/Cindee," *Obsessed*, season 2, episode 1, A&E, June 21, 2010. All quoted dialogue from the episode comes from this source.

97   *keeping the water a liquid with the gigawatts* "Enceladus the Powerhouse," NASA, March 7, 2011, https://solarsystem.nasa.gov/resources/15249/enceladus-the-powerhouse/.

12 / Trees

98   *This was the state's worst year for drought* Angela Fritz, "Study: California Drought Is the Most Severe in at Least 1,200 Years," *Washington Post*, December 4, 2014, https://www.washingtonpost.com/news/capital-weather-gang/wp/2014/12/04/study-california-drought-is-the-most-severe-in-at-least-1200-years/.

98   *some rural counties almost running out of water* Kurtis Alexander, "California Drought: Communities at Risk of Running Dry," SF Gate, January 29, 2014, https://www.sfgate.com/news/article/California-drought-communities-at-risk-of-5184906.php.

99   *H.E.A.L. stands for* Rick Hanson, PhD, *"It's Possible to Heal Yourself,"* *https://www.rickhanson.net/possible-heal/*. Hanson's website is an excellent resource for additional relevant peer-reviewed research on experience-dependent neuroplasticity.

99   *In Patañjali's Yoga Sutras* Patañjali, The *Yoga Sūtra of Patañjali*, tr. Chip Hartranft, *The Arlington Center*, https://www.arlingtoncenter.org/Sanskrit-English.pdf. The relevant verse (II.33) is *vitarka-bâdhane pratipakœa-bhâvanam*, which Hartranft translates as "Unwholesome thoughts can be neutralized by cultivating wholesome ones."

99   *but they must also be installed* Jonathan L. C. Lee, "Memory Reconsolidation Mediates the Strengthening of Memories by Additional Learning," *Nature Neuroscience* 11 (2008), https://doi.org/10.1038/nn.2205. For an overview of the neuroscience behind H.E.A.L. and research into its efficacy, check out Rick Hanson et al., "Learning to Learn from Positive Experiences," *The Journal of Positive Psychology* 18, no. 1 (2021), https://doi.org/10.1080/17439760.2021.2006759.

99   *"Imagine or feel that the experience"* Rick Hanson, *Buddha's Brain* (Oakland, CA: New Harbinger Publications, 2009), 70.

99   *"the perfection underlying life"* and *"the untroubled mind"* Agnes Martin, *Writings*, ed. Dieter Schwarz (Berlin: Hatje Cantz Publishers, 2005), 31, 35.

100 *"Velcro for the bad"* Rick Hanson, "The Brain: Velcro for the Bad, Teflon for the Good," YouTube, January 31, 2020, https://youtu.be/BwPvynau2o Y?si=ZR-VXgpePxRHVeGS.

100 *I knew the social media apps* Paul Lewis, "'Our Minds Can Be Hijacked': The Tech Insiders Who Fear a Smartphone Dystopia," *The Guardian*, October 6, 2017, https://www.theguardian.com/technology/2017/oct/05/smartphone-addiction-silicon-valley-dystopia.

100 *That porn, and presumably Grindr* Valerie Voon et al., "Neural Correlates of Sexual Cue Reactivity in Individuals with and without Compulsive Sexual Behaviours," *PLOS ONE* 9, no. 7 (2014), https://doi.org/10.1371/journal.pone.0102419.

101 *More than anything else, the many leaves* Nadia Drake, "What Is the Multiverse—and Is There Any Evidence It Really Exists?" *National Geographic*, March 13, 2023, https://www.nationalgeographic.com/science/article/what-is-the-multiverse.

102 *"If every second of our lives"* Milan Kundera, *The Unbearable Lightness of Being*, tr. Michael Henry Heim (New York: Harper and Row, 1984), 5.

103 *"the balmy winds breathed"* William Bartram, *Travels* (UNC Chapel Hill/Documenting the American South electronic edition, 2001), https://docsouth.unc.edu/nc/bartram/bartram.html.

104 *"lulled asleep by the mixed sounds"* Ibid.

13 / Return

106 *which had bankrolled climate change deniers* "Exxon's Climate Denial History: A Timeline," Greenpeace, https://www.greenpeace.org/usa/fighting-climate-chaos/exxon-and-the-oil-industry-knew-about-climate-crisis/exxons-climate-denial-history-a-timeline/.

108 *"possess it all"* Edward Abbey, *Desert Solitaire* (New York: McGraw-Hill, 1968), 5.

109 *having just created an ocean sanctuary* Cynthia Barnett, "Hawaii Is Now Home to an Ocean Reserve Twice the Size of Texas," *National Geographic*, August 26, 2016, https://www.nationalgeographic.com/science/article/obama-creates-world-s-largest-park-off-hawaii.

109 *that have more species of fish and coral* Johnny Langenheim, "Indonesia Winning Battle to Save World's Richest Reef System," *The Guardian*, February 12, 2015, https://www.theguardian.com/environment/the-coral-triangle/2015/feb/12/indonesia-winning-battle-to-save-worlds-richest-reef-system.

109 *and contain an astounding 75 percent of all known hard coral* Yuanike Yuanike et al., "A Biodiversity Assessment of Hard Corals in Dive Spots within Dampier Straits Marine Protected Area in Raja Ampat, West Papua, Indonesia," *Biodiversitas Journal of Biological Diversity* 20, no. 4 (April 2019), https://doi.org/10.13057/biodiv/d200436.

113 *And if it knew Europeans needed only twenty-seven years* Jacob Mikanowski, "The Giant Sea Mammal That Went Extinct in Less Than Three Decades," *The Atlantic*, April 19, 2017, https://www.theatlantic.com/science/ archive/2017/04/pleistoseacow/522831/.

113 *"maps of the world in its becoming"* Cormac McCarthy, *The Road* (New York: Vintage, 2006), 287.

114 *"Soulmates only exist"* Michael Patrick King, "The Agony and the Ex-Tacy," *Sex and the City*, June 3, 2001.

114 *I marveled at how these forests are* Matt Jenkins, "Carbon Capture," *Nature Conservancy*, September 1, 2018, https://www.nature.org/en-us/ magazine/magazine-articles/carbon-capture/#photoCaption-hero -banner_article_hero.

114 *"I cherished shallow areas like this one"* Mark Erdmann, PhD, Skype interview, February 25, 2017.

114 *which has an ambient sound of ninety decibels* Richard C. Niemtzow, "Loud Noise and Pregnancy," *Military Medicine* 158, no. 1 (January 1993), https:// doi.org/10.1093/milmed/158.1.10.

115 *"Trauma doesn't like to be touched"* Esther Perel, "Trauma Doesn't Like to Be Touched," *Where Should We Begin?* podcast, season 1, episode 10 (2017), https://books.apple.com/us/audiobook/ep-9-trauma-doesnt-like-to- be-touched/id1255215686.

117 *the suicide rate for girls aged fifteen* Jeff Orlowski, *The Social Dilemma*, Netflix documentary, 2020, https://www.netflix.com/title/81254224.

14 / Adara

120 *"What about the seventh generation?"* Oren Lyons, "An Iroquois Perspective," *American Indian Environments: Ecological Issues in Native American History* (New York: Syracuse University Press, 1980), 173–174.

120 *Patrol boats shoot dynamite fishermen on sight* Erdmann, Skype interview, February 25, 2017. This paragraph's information about efforts to protect Raja Ampat is from the interview.

120 *will melt Arctic sea ice about the size of my office on campus* I used the International Civil Aviation Organization's Carbon Emissions Calculator (https://applications.icao.int/icec/Home/Index) to calculate the carbon emissions per passenger on my San Francisco–Sorong roundtrip flights, with connections in Singapore and Jakarta, which was about 4,000 pounds (1.8 metric tons). For every metric ton of CO_2, three square meters of Arctic ice is melted, so I caused 5.4 m^2 to melt, which is about 60 square meters. For the research connecting CO_2 emissions with Arctic sea ice loss, see Brady Dennis, "Here's How Much of the Arctic You're Personally Responsible for Melting," *Washington Post*, November 3, 2016, https://www.washingtonpost.com/news/energy-environment/wp/2016/11/03/heres-how-much-of-the-arctic-youre-personally-responsible-for-melting/. As Dennis writes, "The average American, for instance, emits more than 16 metric tons of carbon each year, according to the World Bank. That would amount to the melting of about 48 square meters of ice in the Arctic, or about enough to cover the floor plan of a 500-square-foot apartment."

121 *three days later in Central Park* Check out "New York City Has Its Warmest Christmas Ever," WABC-TV, December 25, 2015, https://abc7ny.com/christmas-warm-weather-bryant-park-ice-skating/1134498/; and Paul Grondahl, "Record-Wrecking Heat on Christmas Eve in Albany," *Times-Union* (Capital Region of New York), https://www.timesunion.com/local/article/At-6-30-a-m-record-breaking-Christmas-Eve-6719249.php.

123 *Mark told me that in his experience* Erdmann, Skype interview, February 25, 2017.

123 *during a global mass bleaching of corals* S. Sully et al., "A Global Analysis of Coral Bleaching over the Past Two Decades," *Nature Communications* 10, no. 1264 (2019), https://doi.org/10.1038/s41467-019-09238-2.

124 *Coral and macroalgae are in a delicate balance* Forest Rohwer and Merry Youle, *Coral Reefs in the Microbial Seas* (Plaid Press, 2010), 128.

124 *Overfishing of those grazers* Kat Kerlin, "Reef Fish That Conquer Fear of Sharks May Help Control Excess Algae," UC Davis News, January 12, 2017, https://www.ucdavis.edu/news/reef-fish-conquer-fear-sharks-may-help-control-excess-algae. Rohwer and Youle also discuss these linkages.

124 *Overall, Mark told me, fish stocks* Erdmann, Skype interview, February 25, 2017.

124 *Raja Ampat's population has increased* For the details, view "Raja Ampat, Indonesia," City-Facts, https://www.city-facts.com/raja-ampat/population.

124 *and now thousands of tourists come here* "'Instagram Tourism,' Are There Too Many Tourists in Raja Ampat?" *Bird's Head Seascape Blog*, https://birdsheadseascape.com/regional/instagram-tourism-are-there-too-many-tourists-in-raja-ampat/.

15 / Purple

127 *"I think it pisses off God"* Alice Walker, *The Color Purple* (New York: Harcourt Brace Jovanovich, 1982), 167.

129 *as if my wetsuit were a peacock mantis shrimp's retina* Ed Yong, "Nature's Most Amazing Eyes Just Got a Bit Weirder," *National Geographic*, June 3, 2014, https://www.nationalgeographic.com/science/article/natures-most-amazing-eyes-just-got-a-bit-weirder.

129 *one of the 108 billion who have ever lived* Mona Chalabi, "What Are the Demographics of Heaven?" FiveThirtyEight, October 14, 2015, https://fivethirtyeight.com/features/what-are-the-demographics-of-heaven/.

130 *after it melts, nine feet of water* Juan Siliezar, "Antarctic Ice Sheet Melting to Lift Sea Level Higher Than Thought, Study Says," *Harvard Gazette*, April 30, 2021, https://news.harvard.edu/gazette/story/2021/04/study-says-antarctic-ice-sheet-melt-to-lift-sea-level-higher-than-thought/.

130 *30 trillion human cells and about as many bacteria* Ron Sender, Shai Fuchs, and Ron Milo, "Revised Estimates for the Number of Human and Bacteria Cells in the Body," *PLOS Biology* 14, no. 8 (August 19, 2016), https://doi.org/10.1371/journal.pbio.1002533.

130 *as it does to fish when algae begin to smother it* Hannah Waters, "When Attacked, Corals Send Out Chemical Signals to Recruit Bodyguard Fish," *Smithsonian Magazine*, November 8, 2012, https://www.smithsonianmag.com/science-nature/when-attacked-corals-send-out-chemical-signals-to-recruit-bodyguard-fish-115253278/.

130 *95 percent of the universe* "Dark Energy, Dark Matter," NASA Science, https://science.nasa.gov/astrophysics/focus-areas/what-is-dark-energy.

130 *"People think pleasing God"* Walker, *The Color Purple*, 167.

130 *Dendrodoris tuberculosa* Check out its entry in the Sea Slug Forum: http://www.seaslugforum.net/find/dendtube.

16 / Rehab

137 *I quickly learned that UTIs in the elderly* Chandrani Dutta et al., "Urinary Tract Infection Induced Delirium in Elderly Patients: A Systematic Review," *Cureus* 14, no. 12 (December 8, 2022), https://doi.org/10.7759/cureus.32321.

17 / Dayan

138 *"I'm an activist so my grandchildren"* Konstan Saleo, in-person interview, Dayan Homestay, May 2018.

139 *"If you look the right way"* Frances Hodgson Burnett, *The Secret Garden* (Project Gutenberg eBook, 2005), https://www.gutenberg.org/files/17396/17396-h/17396-h.htm.

139 *In my lifetime, we will probably lose coral reefs* Laura Parker and Craig Welch, "Coral Reefs Could Be Gone in 30 Years," *National Geographic*, June 23, 2017, https://www.nationalgeographic.com/science/article/coral-reef-bleaching-global-warming-unesco-sites.

139 *"If you can't love yourself"* RuPaul Andre Charles, *RuPaul's Drag Race*, World of Wonder, 2009–present.

141 *His father, Leo, Konstan told me* Saleo, in-person and WhatsApp interviews, Dayan Homestay, May 2018 and July 22, 2019, respectively.

141 *West Papua, one of the poorest provinces* Check out the data: "Poverty in Indonesia," Indonesia Investments, https://www.indonesia-investments.com/finance/macroeconomic-indicators/poverty/item301.

141 *Joy, the manager of the nearby pearl farm* Joy [last name not given], in-person interview, unnamed pearl farm next to Dayan Island, May 2018.

142 *I was responsible for two tons* See the Ch. 14 note about airplane CO_2 and Arctic sea ice.

142 *Over three quadrillion pounds of carbon* Hannah Ritchie, "Who Has Contributed Most to Global CO_2 Emissions?" *Our World in Data*, October 1, 2019, https://ourworldindata.org/contributed-most-global-co2. Note: 1.5 trillion tonnes are equal to approximately 3.3 quadrillion pounds.

142 *By the end of this century or even sooner* Henry Fountain, "Global Warming's Deadly Combination: Heat and Humidity," *New York Times*, March 8, 2021, https://www.nytimes.com/2021/03/08/climate/climate-change-heat-tropics.html.

18 / A Joy Forever

146   "*A thing of beauty*" John Keats, *Endymion* (Project Gutenberg eBook, 2008), https://www.gutenberg.org/files/24280/24280-h/24280-h.htm.

147   "*I am enamoured of growing outdoors*" Walt Whitman, *Song of Myself* (1855), Walt Whitman Archive, https://whitmanarchive.org/published/LG/1855/poems/1.

147   "*We saw that there was a long belt*" Dorothy Wordsworth, *Journals of Dorothy Wordsworth, Vol. I* (of 2), ed. William Knight (Project Gutenberg eBook, 2013), https://www.gutenberg.org/files/42856/42856-h/42856-h.htm.

148   "*Whatever the vexations*" Carson, *The Sense of Wonder*, 100.

150   "*I am here not only to evade*" Abbey, *Desert Solitaire*, 6.

19 / Change Your Mind

153   "*Normal waking consciousness feels*" Michael Pollan, *How to Change Your Mind: What the New Science of Psychedelics Teaches Us about Consciousness, Dying, Addiction, Depression, and Transcendence* (New York: Penguin Press, 2018), 308.

154   *which he explained we already produce in our bodies* Steven A. Barker, "N, N-Dimethyltryptamine (DMT), an Endogenous Hallucinogen: Past, Present, and Future Research to Determine Its Role and Function," *Frontiers in Neuroscience* 12, no. 536 (August 6, 2018), https://doi.org/10.3389/fnins.2018.00536.

154   *A substance possibly released* Rick Strassman, *DMT: The Spirit Molecule* (Rochester, VT: Park Street Press, 2001), 221.

155   "*Life is this simple*" Larry Culliford, "Thomas Merton at 100," *Psychology Today*, February 2, 2015, https://www.psychologytoday.com/us/blog/spiritual-wisdom-secular-times/201502/thomas-merton-100.

156   *60–70 percent of patients on SSRIs* Silvia Alboni et al., "Fluoxetine Treatment Affects the Inflammatory Response and Microglial Function According to the Quality of the Living Environment," *Brain, Behavior, and Immunity* 58 (November 2016), https://doi.org/10.1016/j.bbi.2016.07.155.

156   *whether SSRIs offer more relief than a placebo* Tim Newman, "Do Antidepressants Work Better Than Placebo?" *Medical News Today*, July 18, 2019, https://www.medicalnewstoday.com/articles/325767. This article offers a good overview of the ongoing debate.

157 *A 2020 study published* Alan K. Davis et al., "Survey of Entity Encounter Experiences Occasioned by Inhaled *N,N*-dimethyltryptamine: Phenomenology, Interpretation, and Enduring Effects," *Journal of Psychopharmacology* 34, no. 9 (2020), https://doi.org/10.1177/0269881120916143.

157 *In the first clinical trials in 2021* "Small Pharma Reports Positive Top-Line Results from Phase IIa Trial of SPL026 in Major Depressive Disorder," *BioSpace*, January 25, 2023, https://www.biospace.com/article/releases/small-pharma-reports-positive-top-line-results-from-phase-iia-trial-of-spl026-in-major-depressive-disorder/.

157 *DMT causes the number of spines* Calvin Ly et al., "Psychedelics Promote Structural and Functional Neural Plasticity," *Cell Reports* 23 no. 11 (2018), https://doi.org/10.1016/j.celrep.2018.05.022.

158 *A 2009 smoking-cessation study* Matthew W. Johnson et al., "Pilot Study of the 5-HT2AR Agonist Psilocybin in the Treatment of Tobacco Addiction," *Journal of Psychopharmacology* 28, no. 11 (2009), https://doi.org/10.1177/0269881114548296.

158 *By comparison, a 2021 study published* Timothy B. Baker et al., "Effects of Combined Varenicline with Nicotine Patch and of Extended Treatment Duration on Smoking Cessation: A Randomized Clinical Trial," *JAMA* 326, no. 15 (2021), https://doi.org/doi:10.1001/jama.2021.15333.

158 *"a reboot of the system"* Pollan, *How to Change Your Mind*, 266.

158 *"Ayahuasca could come to represent the only"* Antonio Inserra, "Hypothesis: The Psychedelic Ayahuasca Heals Traumatic Memories via a Sigma 1 Receptor-Mediated Epigenetic-Mnemonic Process," *Frontiers in Pharmacology* 9, no. 330 (2018), https://doi.org/10.3389/fphar.2018.00330.

159 *though strong anecdotal evidence* Jessica L. Nielson and Julie D. Megler, "Ayahuasca as a Candidate Therapy for PTSD," *The Therapeutic Use of Ayahuasca*, ed. Beatriz Labate and Clancy Cavnar (Berlin: Springer, 2014), https://doi.org/10.1007/978-3-642-40426-9_3.

161 *Papers like the one by Rafael Faria Sanches* Rafael Faria Sanches et al., "Antidepressant Effects of a Single Dose of Ayahuasca in Patients with Recurrent Depression: A SPECT Study," *Journal of Clinical Psychopharmacology* 36, no.1 (2016), https://doi.org/10.1097/JCP.0000000000000436. See also: Cecile Giovannetti et al., "Pilot Evaluation of a Residential Drug Addiction Treatment Combining Traditional Amazonian Medicine, Ayahuasca and Psychotherapy on Depression and Anxiety," *Journal of Psychoactive Drugs* 52, no. 5 (August 4, 2020), https://doi.org/10.1080/02791072.2020.1789247.

161 *Study after study showed that ayahuasca* Check out José Carlos Bouso and Jordi Riba, "Ayahuasca and the Treatment of Drug Addiction," in *The Therapeutic Use of Ayahuasca*, Beatriz Labate and Clancy Cavnar (Berlin: Springer, 2014), https://doi.org/10.1007/978-3-642-40426-9_6; Gerald Thomas et al., "Ayahuasca-Assisted Therapy for Addiction: Results from a Preliminary Observational Study in Canada," *Current Drug Abuse Reviews* 6, no. 1 (2013), https://doi.org/10.2174/15733998113099990003; and Amanda A. Nunes et al, "Effects of Ayahuasca and Its Alkaloids on Drug Dependence: A Systematic Literature Review of Quantitative Studies in Animals and Humans," *Journal of Psychoactive Drugs* 48, no. 3 (2016), https://doi.org/10.1080/02791072.2016.1188225.

161 *non-addictive and well-tolerated* Rafael Guimarães dos Santos, "Safety and Side Effects of Ayahuasca in Humans—An Overview Focusing on Developmental Toxicology," *Journal of Psychoactive Drugs* 45, no. 1 (2013), https://doi.org/10.1080/02791072.2013.763564.

161 *led to increased mindfulness* A. Murphy Beiner and K. Soar, "Ayahuasca's 'Afterglow': Improved Mindfulness and Cognitive Flexibility in Ayahuasca Drinkers," *Psychopharmacology* 237, no. 4 (January 2020), https://doi.org/10.1007/s00213-019-05445-3.

161 *its capacity to spark "divergent creative thinking"* K. P. C. Kuypers et al., "Ayahuasca Enhances Creative Divergent Thinking While Decreasing Conventional Convergent Thinking," *Psychopharmacology* 233 (2016), https://doi.org/10.1007/s00213-016-4377-8.

161 *enhance overall mental health and well-being* M. V. Uthaug et al., "Sub-Acute and Long-Term Effects of Ayahuasca on Affect and Cognitive Thinking Style and Their Association with Ego Dissolution," *Psychopharmacology* 235 (2018), https://doi.org/10.1007/s00213-018-4988-3.

20 / Dreamglade

164 *"hemlock and stars"* Jay Griffiths, *Wild: An Elemental Journey* (New York: Penguin, 2008), 12.

165 *Days later I asked Raul in Spanish* Raul Buenapico Ramirez, in-person interview, Dreamglade Shamanic Healing Center, Iquitos, Peru, May 3, 2019.

166 *since DMT molecules had attached to some of my Siggies* This is my simplified paraphrase of what Dr. Antonio Inserra conveyed to me in our warm, eye-opening Zoom interview on May 17, 2021.

166 *Research by Robin Carhart-Harris* "Your Brain on LSD Looks a Lot Like a Baby's," NPR, April 17, 2016, https://www.npr.org/2016/04/17/474569125/ your-brain-on-lsd-looks-a-lot-like-a-babys.

167 *"Babies and children are basically tripping"* Pollan, *How to Change Your Mind*, 328.

167 *"A feeling as if something limitless, unbounded"* and *"a source of vital renewal"* Ayon Maharaj, "The Challenge of the Oceanic Feeling: Romain Rolland's Mystical Critique of Psychoanalysis and His Call for a 'New Science of the Mind,'" *History of European Ideas* 43, no. 5 (2017), https://doi.org/10.1080/0 1916599.2017.1356741.

172 *This is called co-regulation* K. D. Rosanbalm and D. W. Murray, "Co-Regulation from Birth through Young Adulthood: A Practice Brief," OPRE Brief #2017-80, US. Department of Health and Human Services, 2017, https:// fpg.unc.edu/sites/fpg.unc.edu/files/resources/reports-and-policy-briefs/ Co-RegulationFromBirthThroughYoungAdulthood.pdf. Aspects of the imagined mother-baby interactions were also inspired by a 1983 brilliant self-published article by Robert Lewis, MD, "Cephalic Shock as a Somatic Link to the False Self Personality," Body-Mind Central, https://bodymind-central.com/publications.

172 *Using what's called neuroception* Stephen W. Porges, "Neuroception: A Subconscious System for Detecting Threats and Safety," *Zero to Three* 24, no. 5 (May 2004), 19–24.

173 *a mother only needs to be "good enough"* Marilyn Wedge, "What Is a 'Good Enough Mother'?" *Psychology Today*, May 3, 2016, https://www.psychology today.com/us/blog/suffer-the-children/201605/what-is-good-enough-mother.

173 *"the experience of feeling loved by her"* Rachel Harris, *Listening to Ayahuasca: New Hope for Depression, Addiction, PTSD, and Anxiety* (Novato, CA: New World Library, 2017), 211.

174 *"Over and over, the answer is"* Stephanie Foo, *What My Bones Know: A Memoir of Healing from Complex Trauma* (New York: Ballantine, 2022), 288.

21 / Tahuayo

175 *it's one of the most biodiverse sections* Pablo Puertas and Richard E. Bodmer, "Conservation of a High Diversity Primate Assemblage," *Biodiversity & Conservation* 2 (1993), https://doi.org/10.1007/BF00051959. See also "Tamshiyacu Tahuayo Region," Amazonia Expeditions, https://perujungle. com/tamshiyacu-tahuayo/.

176   too many foreign "medicine men" Mitra Taj, "Canadian Accused of Killing Peruvian Medicine Woman Lynched in Amazon," Reuters, April 22, 2018, https://www.reuters.com/article/us-peru-crime/canadian-accused-of-killing-peruvian-medicine-woman-lynched-in-amazon-idUSKBN1HT0TR.

176   Given how malleable the brain is Frederick S. Barrett et al., "Emotions and Brain Function Are Altered up to One Month after a Single High Dose of Psilocybin," Scientific Reports 10, no. 2214 (2020), https://doi.org/10.1038/s41598-020-59282-y.

176   Giving MDMA ("molly") to octopuses See Eric Edsinger and Gül Dölen, "A Conserved Role for Serotonergic Neurotransmission in Mediating Social Behavior in Octopus," Current Biology 28, no. 19 (October 8, 2018), https://doi.org/10.1016/j.cub.2018.07.061; and Romain Nardou et al., "Oxytocin-Dependent Reopening of a Social Reward Learning Critical Period with MDMA," Nature 569 (2019), https://doi.org/10.1038/s41586-019-1075-9.

176   Marked by heightened neuroplasticity, a critical period J. Miguel Cisneros-Franco et al., "Chapter 8—Critical Periods of Brain Development," Handbook of Clinical Neurology 173 (2020), https://doi.org/10.1016/B978-0-444-64150-2.00009-5.

177   A psychedelic experience, Dölen theorizes Nick Jikomes, "Gul Dolen: Social Cognition, MDMA, Oxytocin, Metaplasticity, Critical Periods, Autism & Octopuses," Mind & Matter Podcast, March 16, 2022, YouTube, https://youtu.be/9W87eY9adR0.

177   And mindfulness diminishes addictive cravings Eric L. Garland et al., "Mindfulness Training Targets Neurocognitive Mechanisms of Addiction at the Attention-Appraisal-Emotion Interface," Frontiers in Psychiatry 4, no. 173 (2014), https://doi.org/10.3389/fpsyt.2013.00173.

177   Neurogenesis Jose A. Morales-Garcia et al., "N,N-dimethyltryptamine Compound Found in the Hallucinogenic Tea Ayahuasca, Regulates Adult Neurogenesis in Vitro and in Vivo," Translational Psychiatry 10, no. 331 (2020), https://doi.org/10.1038/s41398-020-01011-0.

178   "the tree with the lights in it" and "It was less like seeing" Annie Dillard, Pilgrim at Tinker Creek (New York: HarperCollins, 2007), 31 and 33.

178   In a wide variety of studies, forest bathing Bum Jin Park et al., "The Physiological Effects of Shinrin-yoku (Taking in the Forest Atmosphere or Forest Bathing): Evidence from Field Experiments in 24 Forests across Japan," Environmental Health and Preventive Medicine 15, no. 1 (May 2, 2009), https://doi.org/10.1007/s12199-009-0086-9.

179   *One famous study found that* Roger S. Ulrich, "View through a Window May Influence Recovery from Surgery," *Science* 224, no. 4647 (1984), https://doi.org/10.1126/science.6143402.

179   *But there were other medicines of sorts* Jeffrey Craig and Susan L. Prescott, "Here's Why a Walk in the Woods or a Dip in the Ocean Is So Great for Your Health," *Science Alert*, February 1, 2016, https://www.sciencealert.com/here-s-why-a-walk-in-the-woods-or-a-dip-in-the-ocean-is-so-great-for-your-health.

180   *In Amazonian wetland forests like this one* Bruno Garcia Luize et al., "The Tree Species Pool of Amazonian Wetland Forests: Which Species Can Assemble in Periodically Waterlogged Habitats?" *PLOS ONE* 13, no. 5 (2018), https://doi.org/10.1371/journal.pone.0198130.

180   *In the entire Amazon, there are* "Amazon Rainforest Is Home to 16,000 Tree Species, Estimate Suggests," *The Guardian*, October 18, 2013, https://www.theguardian.com/environment/2013/oct/18/amazon-rainforest-tree-species-estimate.

180   *in Shenandoah National Park* "Full Species List of Trees, Shrubs & Vines," National Park Service, March 10, 2015, https://www.nps.gov/shen/learn/nature/upload/SHEN_Plants_Trees-shrubs-vines-508-_web.pdf.

180   *some of it bypassing the blood brain barrier* Monika Jankowska-Kieltyka et al., "The Air We Breathe: Air Pollution as a Prevalent Proinflammatory Stimulus Contributing to Neurodegeneration," *Frontiers in Cellular Neuroscience* 15 (2021), https://doi.org/10.3389/fncel.2021.647643.

180   *gut bacteria, which produce 95 percent* Natalie Terry and Kara Gross Margolis, "Serotonergic Mechanisms Regulating the GI Tract: Experimental Evidence and Therapeutic Relevance," *Handbook of Experimental Pharmacology* 239 (2016), https://doi.org/10.1007/164_2016_103.

180   *A 2015 study* Jose C. Clemente et al., "The Microbiome of Uncontacted Amerindians," *Science Advances* 1, no. 3 (2015), https://doi.org/10.1126/sciadv.1500183.

181   *according to what's known as the hygiene hypothesis* Petra I. Pfefferle et al., "The Hygiene Hypothesis—Learning from but Not Living in the Past," *Frontiers in Immunology* 12 (2021), https://doi.org/10.3389/fimmu.2021.635935.

22 / Alanna

184 *it can take Big Pharma antidepressants* Rodrigo Machado-Vieira et al., "The Timing of Antidepressant Effects: A Comparison of Diverse Pharmacological and Somatic Treatments," *Pharmaceuticals (Basel, Switzerland)* 3, no. 1 (2010), https://doi.org/10.3390/ph3010019.

184 *ayahuasca takes at most a day* Fernanda Palhano-Fontes et al., "Rapid Antidepressant Effects of the Psychedelic Ayahuasca in Treatment-Resistant Depression: A Randomized Placebo-Controlled Trial," *Psychological Medicine* 49, no. 4 (2018), https://doi.org/10.1017/S0033291718001356.

184 *In addition, 80 percent of first-time ayahuasca users* Daniel F. Jiménez-Garrido et al., "Effects of Ayahuasca on Mental Health and Quality of Life in Naïve Users: A Longitudinal and Cross-Sectional Study Combination," *Scientific Reports* 10, no. 4075 (2020), https://doi.org/10.1038/s41598-020-61169-x.

190 *It's more the ability to stand in oneself* Ido Hartogsohn, "Set and Setting in the Santo Daime," *Frontiers in Pharmacology* 12 (2021), https://doi.org/10.3389/fphar.2021.651037.

23 / Brazil

192 *Neuroimaging studies have shown that the reward system* Jonathan Hamill et al., "Ayahuasca: Psychological and Physiologic Effects, Pharmacology and Potential Uses in Addiction and Mental Illness," *Current Neuropharmacology* 17, no. 2 (2019), https://doi.org/10.2174/1570159X16666180125095902.

194 *In quieting down my brain's default mode network* Fernanda Palhano-Fontes et al., "The Psychedelic State Induced by Ayahuasca Modulates the Activity and Connectivity of the Default Mode Network," *PLOS ONE* 10, no. 2 (2015), https://doi.org/10.1371/journal.pone.0118143.

196 *And what was going up in flames* Kiley Price, "2019 in Review: The Amazon Burned. What Happened—and What Happens Now?" *Conservation International Blog*, December 19, 2019, https://www.conservation.org/blog/2019-in-review-the-amazon-burned-what-happened-and-what-happens-now.

198 *"Physiologically, we see activation"* Nielson and Megler, "Ayahuasca as a Candidate Therapy for PTSD," *The Therapeutic Use of Ayahuasca*.

198 *The C-PTSD medicine Davi poured* Jordi Riba et al., "Increased Frontal and Paralimbic Activation Following *Ayahuasca*, the Pan-Amazonian Inebriant," *Psychopharmacology* 186, no. 1 (2006), https://doi.org/10.1007/s00213-006-0358-7.

24 / Davi in America

200 *"Once when I drank ayahuasca"* Don José Campos, *The Shaman & Ayahuasca* (Studio City, CA: Divine Arts Media, 2011), 83.

201 *Thanks to deforestation and climate change* Luciana V. Gatti et al., "Amazonia as a Carbon Source Linked to Deforestation and Climate Change," *Nature* 595 (2021), https://doi.org/10.1038/s41586-021-03629-6.

201 *"Our house is burning"* Scott Neuman, "Macron Urges G-7 Members to Put Amazon Fires at Top of Agenda," NPR, August 23, 2019, https://www.npr.org/2019/08/23/753639869/macron-urges-g7-members-to-put-amazon-fires-at-top-of-agenda.

201 *even though the oceans in fact absorb* Bella Isaacs-Thomas, "When It Comes to Sucking Up Carbon Emissions, 'the Ocean Has Been Forgiving.' That Might Not Last," *PBS Newshour*, March 25, 2022, https://www.pbs.org/newshour/science/the-ocean-helps-absorb-our-carbon-emissions-we-may-be-pushing-it-too-far.

201 *By 2064, one study recently predicted* Robert Toovey Walker, "Collision Course: Development Pushes Amazonia toward Its Tipping Point," *Environment: Science and Policy for Sustainable Development* 63, no. 1 (2020), https://doi.org/10.1080/00139157.2021.1842711.

202 *The Amazon, which had five million inhabitants* Linda A. Newson, "The Population of the Amazon Basin in 1492: A View from the Ecuadorian Headwaters," *Institute of British Geographers, Transactions* (*Institute of British Geographers:* 1965) 21, no. 1, 5–26, https://www.jstor.org/stable/622921.

202 *Its biodiversity, scientists theorize* Robinson Meyer, "The Amazon Rainforest Was Profoundly Changed by Ancient Humans," *The Atlantic*, March 2, 2017, https://www.theatlantic.com/science/archive/2017/03/its-now-clear-that-ancient-humans-helped-enrich-the-amazon/518439/.

202 *Umbandaime* For more information about this syncretic religion, check out Juno Sisoian, "Umbandaime—Ayahuasca Meets Afro-Brazilian Mediumship," *EntheoNation Blog*, n.d., https://entheonation.com/blog/umbandaime/.

204 *But anecdotal evidence from dance therapists* Check out Cat Sandoval, "People Are Using Unusual Exercise to Shake Off Trauma," Scripps News, February 15, 2023, https://scrippsnews.com/stories/people-are-using-unusual-exercise-to-shake-off-trauma/; and Heather Jo Flores, "Daily Somatic Healing Dance for C-PTSD Recovery," YouTube, https://youtu.be/yyjgYV74n6U.

208 *Whitman wrote that Egyptian spirituality* Deirdre Lawrence, "Walt Whitman and the Arts in Brooklyn," Brooklyn Museum/Google Arts & Culture, https://artsandculture.google.com/story/walt-whitman-and-the-arts-in-brooklyn-brooklyn-museum/zAWRQ1no_hcA8A?hl=en.

208 *was spent with a painting by Black artist John Biggers* "Web of Life: John Biggers," Brooklyn Museum, https://www.brooklynmuseum.org/opencollection/objects/200283.

210 *"I had a very powerful experience"* Nielson and Megler, "Ayahuasca as a Candidate Therapy for PTSD."

211 *"You must be dead"* Steven Spielberg, *E.T. The Extraterrestrial*, Universal Pictures, 1982.

211 *"Our toddlers speak of plants"* Robin Wall Kimmerer, *Braiding Sweetgrass* (Minneapolis, MN: Milkweed, 2013), 57.

211 *"I am the mate and companion of people"* Whitman, *Song of Myself* (1855), https://whitmanarchive.org/published/LG/1855/poems/1.

Epilogue

217 *high-intensity weight training* James W. Whitworth et al., "Feasibility of Resistance Exercise for Posttraumatic Stress and Anxiety Symptoms: A Randomized Controlled Pilot Study," *Journal of Traumatic Stress* 32, no. 6 (2019), https://doi.org/10.1002/jts.22464.

217 *Exercise increases levels of BDNF* Gretchen Reynolds, "How Exercise Leads to Sharper Thinking and a Healthier Brain," *Washington Post*, April 5, 2023, https://www.washingtonpost.com/wellness/2023/04/05/exercise-brain-thinking-bdnf/.

218 *In Gül Dölen's latest, as-yet-unpublished research study* Rachel Nuwer, "The Psychedelic Scientist Who Sends Brains Back to Childhood," *Wired*, June 15, 2023, https://www.wired.com/story/the-psychedelic-scientist-who-sends-brains-back-to-childhood/.

219 *"The best indices of resolution"* Herman, *Trauma and Recovery*, 212.

219 *there are now twelve more days* Danielle Uliano, "Florida Summer Heat: Here's How Our Temperatures Have Changed over the Years," News4Jax, June 6, 2022, https://www.news4jax.com/weather/2022/06/06/florida-summer-heat-heres-how-our-temperatures-have-changed-over-the-years/.

219 *As a result, Cuban treefrogs have moved north* Connie Timpson, "Cuban Tree Frogs Are Wiping Out Florida Natives," *Florida Times-Union*, July 5, 2019, https://www.jacksonville.com/story/special/special-sections/2019/07/05/garden-qampa-cuban-tree-frogs-are-wiping-out-florida-natives/4700927007/.

219 *At nearby Guana River State Park* Ayurella Horn-Muller, "'Protectors of the Coast': What Mangroves' Northward March Means for Northeast Florida," WJCT News, March 22, 2019, https://news.wjct.org/first-coast/2019-03-22/protectors-of-the-coast-what-mangroves-northward-march-means-for-northeast-florida.

219 *sea levels in Jacksonville had risen* "Sea Level Rise," National Park Service, last updated February 17, 2022, https://www.nps.gov/timu/learn/nature/sea-level-rise.htm.

220 *what Australian philosopher Glenn Albrecht calls* Glenn Albrecht et al., "Solastalgia: The Distress Caused by Environmental Change," *Australasian Psychiatry* 15, suppl. 1, S95–S98 (2007), https://doi.org/10.1080/10398560701701288.

220 *with at least thirteen thousand nuclear warheads* Joe Phelan, "How Many Nuclear Weapons Exist, and Who Has Them?" *Scientific American*, March 22, 2022, https://www.scientificamerican.com/article/how-many-nuclear-weapons-exist-and-who-has-them/.

Acknowledgments

My deepest intergalactic gratitude to my incredible agent, Wendy Levinson, and my visionary editor at Regalo Press, Gretchen Young. Their faith in *Mothership: A Memoir of Wonder and Crisis* has meant more to me than I can possibly express. Thanks also to Maddie Sturgeon, Caitlyn Limbaugh, Donna DuVall, and everyone else at the press who helped *Mothership* get off the ground and into the air. I bow to Sarah Russo, Laura Di Giovine, Laci Durham, and Peter Dyer at Page One Media.

Thank you (∞!) to the courageous scientists, journalists, physicians, therapists, and explorers whose work forms the bedrock of my book: Gül Dölen, PhD (Johns Hopkins), Mark Erdmann, PhD (Conservation International), Rick Hanson, PhD (Greater Good Science Center/UC Berkeley), Judith Herman, MD (Harvard Medical School), Antonio Inserra, PhD (McGill University), Brian Magi, PhD (UNC Charlotte), and Michael Pollan (Harvard University). Thanks also to Laure Katz, PhD, Erica Towle, PhD, Gene Shinn, PhD, Walter Jaap, PhD, and Erin Lipp, PhD, for rich correspondence and helpful interviews.

For generous support that made this book possible, I also want to record my deep appreciation to the Bread Loaf Writers' Conference, the Hermitage Artist Retreat, the James Merrill House, and the Virginia Center for the Creative Arts. The English Department at

Acknowledgments

James Madison University and the Stanford Creative Writing Program also provided much-needed funding, inspiration, and moral support—much gratitude to them and my colleagues. Special thanks to Christina Ablaza at Stanford and Morgan Aderton, Angela Carter, Rose Gray, Kat Mauser, and Becky Childs at JMU.

Thank you to the editors of the following publications in which parts of this book first appeared, often in radically different forms: *AGNI Online, Al Jazeera, The American Poetry Review, The American Scholar, Essay Daily, The Georgia Review, The Iowa Review, Kenyon Review (KR Online), Mudlark, Poetry Daily, Prairie Schooner, The Rumpus, The Southeast Review,* and *The Southern Review*.

For their endless support and incisive criticism, thank you to my nonfiction writing teachers Amy Ettinger and Laura Pritchett. Thanks to Erica Cavanagh, Amy Holman, Maria Hummel, and Laurie Kutchins for their encouragement early on. Deep gratitude also to my writing teachers Eavan Boland, Henri Cole, Ken Fields, Jorie Graham, Carl Phillips, D. A. Powell, Peter Sacks, and Natasha Trethewey. To my English teachers Janet Hall, Kathy Mackey, Carol Matchett, Elizabeth Renfroe, and Marion Williamson. And to my science teachers Tess Durant, Mike Lincoln, Lydia Welsh, and Paul Wieseke.

Without question, *Mothership* wouldn't have been possible without Madre Ayahuasca and the curanderos who serve this life-saving medicine. Special thanks to Alanna Collins, ChiChi, Davi Nunes de Paula, Nadine Purdy, Lidia Huayta Ramirez, Raul Buenapico Ramirez, Alonso del Rio, Devana Sternblume, and Alejandro Werika. The debt I owe you and the rainforest cannot be repaid. Thank you for defending the Amazon and protecting the medicine.

Thanks also to Konstan Saleo and the people of Raja Ampat who over the years have fed me, sheltered me, and given me permission to dive their ancestral reefs—I stand in solidarity with you to guard your culture, your land, and your waters. I'm grateful, too, for the guidance that Doug Meikle has offered me and his tireless promotion of Indigenous conservation tourism in West Papua.

To my JMU students in Environmental Literature of Wonder and Crisis, The Environmental Imagination, and my poetry workshops, thank you for teaching me how to care. Much appreciation to my fabulous grading faculty members Dan Levine and Courtney Swartzentruber. And muchas gracias to my hardworking, brilliant JMU English research assistants Keagan Bragg, Jules Perez, and Ardyn Tennyson.

Thank you to my champion and dear friend Garrard Conley, whose trailblazing memoir *Boy Erased* has been medicine for many aching souls. Gratitude also to my friends Bethanne Patrick, Kirstin Valdez Quade, and Sofia Samatar for setting a sustaining example of grace, grit, and literary comradeship. Thank you for believing in me.

For friendship and support at critical junctures, thanks to Zac Addison, Rob Alexander, Amber Barnes, Chip Brown, Matt Colaciello, Erin Gahan Clark, Jess Daddio, Paige DePrete, Nicholas Eliopulos, Taylor Evans, Scott Farris, Jay Gordon, Mo Jones, Kathryn, David Kornhaber, Linda, Nico Medina, Billy Merrell, the Pooley family, Caroline Prendergast, Puma, Stacy Rae Reed, Adrian Rivas, Adam Ritter, Marcela Santamarina, Linden Shearer, Elizabeth Tallent, Eva Valencia, Drew Whelpley, and Alex and Sarah Jane Yeats.

And to my husband, Tony Pooley: without you, *Mothership* would still be in drydock. My heart would be too. I love you galaxies and galaxies.

About the Author

Photo credit: Matt Mendelsohn

A former Stegner Fellow and Jones Lecturer at Stanford University, Greg Wrenn is the author of *Centaur* (University of Wisconsin Press, 2013), which National Book Award–winning poet Terrance Hayes awarded the Brittingham Prize in Poetry.

Greg's work has appeared in *The New Republic, Al Jazeera, The Rumpus, Kenyon Review, New England Review, The Iowa Review*, and elsewhere. He has received awards and fellowships from the James Merrill House, the Bread Loaf Writers' Conference, and the Poetry Society of America.

As an associate English professor, Greg teaches environmental literature and creative writing at James Madison University, where he weaves climate change science into literary studies. He was educated at Harvard University and Washington University in St. Louis.

Greg is a trained yoga teacher and a PADI Advanced Open Water Diver, exploring coral reefs around the world for over twenty-five years. He lives in the mountains of Virginia with his husband and their growing family of trees.